W9-BIG-567

Gone Home

NEW MAP OF KENTUCKY

FROM AUTHENTIC REPORTS OF COUNTY SURVEYORS

THROUGHOUT THE STATES OF KENTUCKY

PUBLISHED BY
MIDDLETON STROBRIDGE & Co.
94. West Fourth St. Cin.O.

1861
with
HARLAN COUNTY
highlighted

SCALE OF MILES.

Gone Home

Race and Roots through Appalachia

· ·

KARIDA L. BROWN

The University of North Carolina Press Chapel Hill

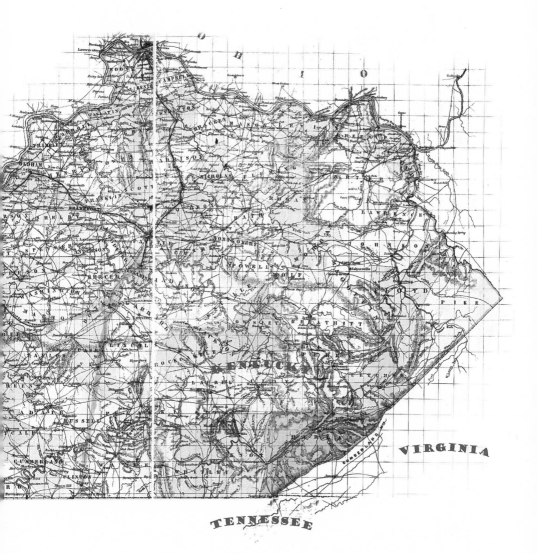

This book was published with the assistance of the Authors Fund of the University of North Carolina Press.

The University of North Carolina Press has been a member of the Green Press Initiative since 2003.

Library of Congress Cataloging-in-Publication Data
Names: Brown, Karida, 1982– author.
Title: Gone home : race and roots through Appalachia / Karida L. Brown.
Description: Chapel Hill : University of North Carolina Press, [2018] |
    Includes bibliographical references and index.
Identifiers: LCCN 2018010259 | ISBN 9781469647036 (cloth : alk. paper) |
    ISBN 9781469647043 (ebook)
Subjects: LCSH: African Americans—Kentucky—History. | African
    Americans—Kentucky—Social conditions. | Kentucky—Race relations. |
    African Americans—Appalachian Region, Southern—History. |
    African Americans—Appalachian Region, Southern—Social conditions. |
    Appalachian Region, Southern—Race relations. | Migration,
    Internal—United States—History—20th century. | Coal mines and
    mining—Kentucky—History. | Appalachian Region, Southern—Social
    conditions—History.
Classification: LCC E185.92.K4 B76 2018 | DDC 305.896/0730769—dc23
    LC record available at https://lccn.loc.gov/2018010259

Cover illustration by Charly Palmer.
Title page illustration: *New Map of Kentucky*, 1861. Southern Historical Collection, Louis Round Wilson Special Collections Library, University of North Carolina at Chapel Hill.

Portions of this book were previously published in a different form and are used here with permission. Chapter 6 includes material from "The 'Hidden Injuries' of School Desegregation: Cultural Trauma and Transforming African American Identities," *American Journal of Cultural Sociology* 4, no. 2 (June 2016): 196–220. The research appendix includes material from "On the Participatory Archive: The Formation of the Eastern Kentucky African American Migration Project," *Southern Cultures* 22, no. 1 (Spring 2016): 113–27.

MIX
Paper from responsible sources
FSC
www.fsc.org   FSC® C013483

For the generation of African Americans who so proudly say
"My daddy was a coal miner."

Contents

Figures and Tables

Gone Home

Introduction

· ·

Mass migration always conditions subjectivities. Whether a result of religious persecution, famine, labor shortage, or the prospect of greater prosperity, every mass movement of a people can be traced through the particular conditions under which the migrant Self is formed and transformed. The shared struggles and strivings, and the peaks and valleys of the myriad of hopes, disappointments, tragedies, and joys that accompany the migration experience, shape a people. The black experience with migration in the United States has been framed by what is commonly referred to as "the African American Great Migration": a period between 1910 and 1970 during which approximately six million blacks migrated from the rural South to the urban centers of the Midwest, the Northeast, and, much later, the West. It is true that this period marked an epoch transformation in American history, as it completely redistributed the racial composition of the American city. Yet we still know very little about what this decades-long journey meant to the millions of American black folk who experienced it.

This is a book about the emergence and transformation of African American subjectivity. By this I mean the interior and subjective understandings of Self, and in this case, of a people: birthed into freedom out of the battered womb of the Civil War, striving in a dogged pursuit to reach their ideals of freedom and citizenship—those of life, liberty, equality, and the pursuit of happiness; a claim to the land that generations ago had been forced on them in bondage; and a sense of belonging in the national life of the United States of America. Through this pursuit, collectively, black Americans continually confront a somewhat peculiar version of the fundamental questions of the human condition: Who am I? What am I? and, as they look to their fellow Americans, Who are "we" as a people? These questions are the primary matter of concern for this book.

Up until the mid-twentieth century, the question of *what* black people were to the United States of America remained undetermined. Were they citizens or subjects? What were their rights and duties to the nation? If citizens, should they forever be subjugated into a separate and second class?

The answers to these questions were largely resolved juridically through the passage of a series of federal laws adopted between the mid-nineteenth and twentieth centuries. In the 1800s, it was the ratification of the Thirteenth, Fourteenth, and Fifteenth Amendments to the Constitution. Through these laws, it was settled: black people were free, they were citizens, and they could vote. However, the law of the land was quickly undermined by race prejudice, materializing through various state and local level de jure and de facto segregationist laws and practices, as well as through the majority white public in the form of social segregation, racial violence, and everyday discrimination and disdain for their fellow black Americans. In essence, Negros were given freedom but found themselves without liberty.[1] In the twentieth century, African American citizenship was rearticulated through a series of federal civil rights legislation passed in the 1950s and 1960s, including *Brown v. Board of Education* in 1954, the Voting Rights Act of 1965, and the Fair Housing Act of 1968.

Through all these legal transformations, black peoples' relationship to the American body politic was transformed; and under this legal rubric of fits and starts, the African American citizen was made. However, these were issues not only of *what* black people in America were as citizens but of *whom* they were as a people. As the pendulum of humanity swung from slavery to freedom, from subject to citizen, they too, as a people, were *transformed*. African American subjectivity, what W. E. B. Du Bois called the "souls of black folk," emerged out of a continual tug-of-war between struggle and striving.

· · · · · ·

Focusing on the first three-quarters of the twentieth century, I present the contours of the emergence and transformation of the African American self through a community biography of a single population—a group of unusual suspects: the black Appalachians who hail from the coalfields of eastern Kentucky. Over the course of two generations, between 1910 and 1970, tens of thousands of African Americans migrated into and out of this region of the country. The first generation migrated out of the bowels of the Deep South to the mountains of eastern Kentucky in search of liberty and citizenship. The second generation, their children, grew up in Appalachia but moved once they came into young adulthood. This generation migrated in the midst of rapid industrial decline and in the wake of the American civil rights movement. They too left home in search of that same liberty and citizenship for which their parents and parents' parents strove.

It is through the collective memories of the latter generation that I tell this story. In one lifetime, this group of black folks lived through the pre– and post–civil rights era, experiencing firsthand the transition from second-class to full citizens. As the last generation born into the oppressive structures of legal Jim Crow segregation, they were central actors in dismantling it. In speaking of this embodied experience, with its massive political, legal, and civil transformation, one of my research participants, Albert Harris, put it best: "We went through a transformation as to who we were. We went from Colored, to Negroes, to African-Americans . . . and Black. We went through all of those." Their transformation took place not only on a legal-political terrain but also on a geographical one. Theirs is one of the many journeys taken by six million African Americans in the mass migration out of the Deep South into every nook and cranny of the country in search of the dignity, humanity, and rights that were promised to them by the U.S. Constitution yet denied in everyday life. These mass movements of the progeny of America's formally enslaved emerged into what is now known as the African American Great Migration.

The African American Great Migration, 1910 to 1970

The grumblings of the African American Great Migration began during the period leading up to World War I, sometime in the early 1900s. Demand for unskilled labor in urban centers in the North and Midwest was urgent at this time of industrial boom—the steel in Pittsburgh needed milling, meat in Chicago needed packing, and railroad tracks all throughout the country needed laying—and labor was scarce. World War I had brought the influx of able-bodied migrants from southern and eastern Europe nearly to a halt, even after the war had come and gone. As the United States was poised to take its place as the manufacturing powerhouse of the world, nearly 90 percent of America's black population still resided in the South—and they were primed for a revolution of a different sort.

The African American Great Migration is a term used to refer to the sixty-year period, between 1910 and 1970, during which an estimated six million African Americans voted with their feet and left the South.[2] It started off as a trickle, but the outpouring of black migrants from the South to the North increased with rapid intensity each census year for the next six decades. There exists today a library of books, memoirs, newspaper clippings, and speeches describing life in the Deep South during that era, which gives context to the racial terror that black people endured: a tale told many times—and worth retelling. There is a vast literature on the social and economic forces that conditioned this dramatic outpouring of black migrants, and its effects on city and community and on the lives of the many social groups affected by this macrostructural transformation.[3] Inspired by W. E. B. Du Bois's canonical *The Souls of Black Folk*, this book is concerned with how this phenomenal mass movement of a people transformed, rearticulated, and solidified "the strange meaning of being black" in America through the arc of the twentieth century. What did the Great Migration mean to the six million black folks who left the South and migrated into the urban landscapes of the Midwest, the North, and the West? For the early wave of migrants—the first million or so who left between 1910 and 1930—how did they manage to get to their destinations? What did it take? And more so, what were they hoping to find?

The African American Great Migration is a massive and heterogeneous event. It was the largest U.S. demographic transition of the twentieth century, and it forever transformed the racial composition of the American city. This was the era in which the country's "Chocolate Cities" were born,[4] when black folks migrated largely from rural and urban communities in Alabama, Mississippi, Louisiana, Florida, Georgia, the Carolinas, and Virginia. They were agriculturalists, miners, artisans, mechanics, caterers, and domestic laborers. And the vast majority of them were the children of people who only got to whet their parched lips with the taste of liberty, but who would never have the chance to quench their thirst. The amalgam of migration stories out of these places culminated into one of the greatest events in American history. For this book, however, I chose to focus on one specific migration story—the journey in and through central Appalachia—to attend to the sweet yet too often overlooked fact that African Americans are a heterogeneous group and that, as such, they embody a variety of origin stories, cultural repertoires, and—harking back to W. E. B. Du Bois—a panoply of *souls*.[5]

I also chose this particular micromigration because it is a story that needs to be told. African Americans for too long have been made invisible to the regional history of Appalachia.[6] In scholarly works and the popular media alike, Appalachia is represented as poor, backward, and almost always white. However, thousands of African American families migrated during the early 1900s to the coalfields of West Virginia, eastern Kentucky, and eastern Tennessee—many still call Appalachia home. Lastly, I chose this migration story because it represents an intergenerational stepwise migration, a concept essential to understanding how mass migrations unfold.

While big cities in the North, Midwest, and West were a final destination for the majority of participants in the Great Migration, there were many popular "layover" stops along the way.[7] Although some migrants traversed straight from the Deep South to New York City, Chicago, or Detroit, more often they moved from rural towns—such as Boligee, Alabama, or Saluda, North Carolina—to semi-industrial cities, such as Birmingham or Charlotte. Once settled, they would gain additional skills and social capital and then, after a few years, migrate to another city that was larger and farther away from the South. Some families made their way out of the Deep South in one lifetime, whereas others took multiple generations. This is the more nuanced and sloppier version of the story of the African American Great Migration. It was a mass migration of fits and starts, of great hopes and disappointments, of struggle and striving.

The coalfields of eastern Kentucky were one layover stop in this decades-long mass movement. It was a place where many early movers in the Great Migration stopped for one generation and transformed from "peasants to proletariats" by becoming skilled laborers.[8] As coal miners, they were able to secure a steady wage labor, a company-owned home to offer shelter and security to their families, and consistent yearlong education for their children. This next generation, the coal miners' daughters and sons, grew up in the hollows of Harlan County, Kentucky. For them, Appalachia was both home and a launching pad from which they would join the other five million African Americans in the second wave of the Great Migration.

Gone Home

gone

[gawn, gon]

verb

1. past participle of *go*.

adjective

2. departed; left.

3. lost or hopeless.

Because this is a story about migration, it is also a story about home. What I illustrate through this one intergenerational stepwise migration through Harlan County, Kentucky, is what an elusive concept "home" is to black people. The historic catastrophe of slavery made us homeless. Our genealogies do not trace back to a specific African ancestral lineage in terms of nation or ethnicity, although they often do so phylogenetically in soul and affinity. In the United States, black people's relationship to home has been one of continual dislocation and displacement. From the era of racial terror in the South (1880s–1920s), characterized by ethnic cleansing in the form of banishment[9] and public torture in the form of lynchings;[10] to the period of mass dislocation in northern and midwestern cities, caused by eminent domain in the 1940s, 1950s, and 1960s;[11] to the present-day predicament of urban gentrification,[12] African Americans have been systematically uprooted and relegated to the margins of place in societal order.

The protagonists of this book embody these dispensations of mass displacement along the color line. From one generation to the next, this group of African American migrants found themselves uprooted from their home, once again facing the challenge to make themselves anew. For them, migration was not a conscious decision; it was a taken-for-granted way of life. However, through their collective experience with dislocation, displacement, and homelessness, they reveal much about the practice of homemaking, communal memory, and reinscribing oneself back into place.

The home that they experienced in Appalachia no longer exists. Physically, the coal towns that were once thriving economically and bursting at the seams with people are now in ruins. As you will read in the chapters to come, while there are many white families that still remain in the region, black people and their communities were systematically disappeared through the process of industrial decline and ruination.[13] African Americans have also been displaced from Appalachia in the popular imagination, in that their experiences and contributions to the region and to the coal economy have been largely erased from representations of the place. In response to this double erasure, this group of black people, who now live in diaspora throughout the United States, have adopted a set of practices, repertoires, and rituals to relocate and re-place themselves back in those mountains.[14]

Through the chapters of this book, I invite you to come home with them. Experience the coalfields of central Appalachia in a way that largely exists only in communal memory and commemoration. Experience what it was like to grow up as a black person in a company-owned town in Appalachia in the era of Jim Crow segregation, and then to *transform* into an entirely new type of citizen by coming of age at the height of the civil rights movement and the African American Great Migration. I invite you to come to know these things from the standpoint of lived experience—from *within* the veil of the color line.[15]

On Reflexivity, Form, and Voice

I am a third-generation descendant of this population. My mother and father were both born and reared in Lynch, Kentucky, and they subsequently migrated to Long Island, New York, where they raised my brother and me. My earliest childhood memories include pilgrimages "back home" to the mountains during Memorial Day weekend as well as what seemed at the time to be exotic voyages to the Eastern Kentucky Social Club (EKSC) reunions. Both of my grandfathers, Major Brown and Thornton Davis, migrated from rural towns in Alabama to Lynch, Kentucky, where for a combined six decades they "worked the mines" for the United States Steel Corporation (U.S. Steel). My grandmothers, Leona Myrick (maiden name) and Mamie Davis (maiden name), were among the legion of unsung heroes of their era—the women who toiled at home while their husbands worked the mines to make ends meet. My grandmothers raised sixteen and eleven children, respectively, and bore the sole responsibility for running the household. The story of this generation of women, wives, and mothers is its own independent work. Although my family connections were not my primary motivation for selecting this case, they definitely produced an overflowing well of energy, stamina, and joy in continuing on with the research—even when times got hard and the project seemed insurmountable.

The works that gave me the courage to write this book in the form and voice that I present to you are Isabel Wilkerson's *The Warmth of Other Suns*, Zora Neale Hurston's *Their Eyes Were Watching God*, and W. E. B. Du Bois's *The Souls of Black Folk*.[16] I feel it necessary to out myself in terms of the writerly tradition with which I identify in this text because I am a sociologist, and we sociologists are supposed to conform to certain academic writing conventions—especially in our first book—which are not necessarily adhered to in this book. However, I made intentioned decisions about form, voice, and the presentation of oral history data based on the fact that this is a book about the inner workings of the self: of the spirit, soul, and stock from which a people come.

Over the course of three years, between 2013 and 2016, I traveled the country conducting oral history interviews with the men and women who embody this migration story. They have dispersed throughout the United States and settled in cities and towns in every region of the country. When I met with them, they ranged in age from their late sixties to their mid-nineties, and they were ready to tell their stories. Fourteen states, thirty-one cities, and one hundred fifty-three interviews later, I am honored to have the invitation to share their journey with you.

My decisions as a writer are also a result of the fact that the making of this book was wholly a community-driven effort. My research participants, whom you will meet up close and personal throughout the chapters of this book, generously shared intimate stories of their lives in support of the book's production—so much so that this research project developed into an ongoing community-driven archive: the Eastern Kentucky African American Migration Project (EKAAMP), housed at the Southern Historical Collection at UNC Chapel Hill.[17] This research required a collective digging up of our pasts,[18] and through that process we all caught "archive fever."[19] To that end, all the oral history interview recordings and transcripts used in this study, as well as thousands of photographs, documents, manuscripts, and objects, are housed in the EKAAMP archive for public use.[20] The only way that I could even attempt to convey the struggle, striving, hope, joy, sorrow, and love that they shared in their oral history interviews and through their archival donations was to spill it onto the text and offer this story to you in the spirit in which it was given.

The voices you will encounter in these chapters will be a combination of the official company archives of the coal mining companies that owned the towns in Harlan County, Kentucky, and of the African American people who shared their stories through oral history interviews. For my fellow academics—faculty and graduate and undergraduate students—the "academese" appears at the back of the text in the Research Appendix, in which I delve into a discussion about the research design, data, sampling, theoretical framework, and community-driven archive that emerged out of this project. But for now, I will let you get to the story.

Let's go to Appalachia.

When the construction gangs laid down their tools at these points on the eve of the First World War, the vast backward Cumberland Plateau was tied inseparably to the colossal industrial complex centering in Pittsburgh, and a dynamic new phase in the region's history had begun.

—Harry M. Caudill, *Night Comes to the Cumberlands*

1 The Coming of the Coal Industry

. . . .

Nestled in the mountainous southeastern corner of the state, Harlan County is located in the Appalachian region of eastern Kentucky, otherwise known as the Cumberland Plateau. The natural topography consists of rugged, verdant mountains that lead up to the highest point of elevation in the commonwealth—reaching some 4,100 feet high. Once populated by Native tribes, dating back to a time unrecorded, and by white settlers of Scotch-Irish origin, as early as the 1670s,[1] this region's history is replete with stories of racial violence toward Native and African peoples, frontiersmanship, slavery, poverty, and some of the most notorious family feuds in American history.[2] However, it was not until the turn of the twentieth century, with the coming of the coal mining industry, that the region transformed from a sparsely populated unadulterated wonder of the American landscape into a hotbed of industry, contestation, and international mass migration.

Classified by the U.S. Census as the South, Kentucky was an always already contested place. A border state laden with the historical legacies of the tug-of-war between the Union and the Confederacy, with a third of its area consumed by the ever-contested "other" region of central Appalachia, the Commonwealth of Kentucky is best described as a state with multiple personality syndrome. Embedded in this matryoshka doll of geographic ironies lies Harlan County. Known for its coal, timber, and apple pie moonshine, it not only is the most mineral-rich county in Kentucky but also directly borders Virginia and is a whisper away from Tennessee. And as history has revealed time and again, borders are political. Please believe that its nickname, Bloody Harlan, is hard earned and apt.

By the 1880s, speculative investors from the North, both large and small, entered the region and convinced the Scotch-Irish mountaineers to sell the mineral rights to their land. It was not that the mountaineers did not have a sense of their rights or attachment to the place. Rather, it was that they understood their relationship to the land through the notion of autochthony,[3] as opposed to capitalist logics of property ownership. It was this ideological mismatch that created the conditions for the northern oligarch to come in and purchase, for pennies on the dollar, nearly all the land in what is now known as central Appalachia.[4] What the mountaineers had done in such brutal fashion to the indigenous peoples who had lived on the land before their arrival was now being exacted upon them. However, these new pioneers employed more graceful tactics of displacement, including sleights of hand, contracts, and slick talk. Physically absent and emotionally unattached to the place, these northern industrialists would carry out their mission with little to no responsibility for the environment or its inhabitants. Appalachian writer Harry Caudill summed it up most eloquently in his 1962 book *Night Comes to the Cumberlands,* in which he described coal mining as "an extractive industry which takes all away and restores nothing. It mars but never beautifies. It corrupts but never purifies."[5]

By 1914, the race to extract that black gold from the mountains could not be more urgent. Not only was coal the primary source of energy in the United States at the time, but it was also the primary ingredient in the manufacture of steel—and the world was preparing to go to war. By the close of the 1920s, within ten years of opening up shop, the coal mining industry in eastern Kentucky exploded. For example, in Harlan County alone, coal production increased from less than two thousand tons in 1910 to over three million tons in 1918. Likewise, the number of coal miners increased nearly twenty-five-fold, from a paltry 170 workers to a bustling 4,000 men during that same period.[6] This number tripled by 1930, when Harlan County boasted a total of 12,741 miners—double the number in any other county in eastern Kentucky.[7]

Coal companies' first order of business during this period of industrial boom was to establish suitable living conditions for its laborers and their families, for in eastern Kentucky, they were starting from scratch. According to Caudill, before the coming of the coal industry, "the land was without towns in the accepted meaning of the word." With very little modern infrastructure, these communities bore little resemblance to what we would call a city or a town. Instead, "in most counties the county seat was the only 'town' and sometimes its population did not exceed one hundred and fifty persons living in a cluster of log cabins and frame houses about the courthouse and jail."

The explosion of mining activities made Harlan County an overnight niche receiving area, sparking the mass in-migration of tens of thousands of international and domestic laborers and their families. Moving in like settlers on the colonial frontier, the coal companies were interested only in the mountaineers' land, not their labor.[8] Companies instead deployed an army of labor agents to foreign countries such as Poland and Yugoslavia,

Hungary, Italy, Germany, and Greece to recruit the base of their workforce. Oddly enough, these coal mining companies also turned their attention four hundred miles south of Kentucky, to the Alabama black belt. From there they would recruit en masse Alabama's tired and poor—its huddled black masses who yearned to be free.[9]

The Encounter

Harlan County, Kentucky, emerged as the global epicenter for coal production during the interwar period. In the blink of an eye, company-owned coal towns sprang up throughout the peaks and valleys of the county.[10] However, as geologists discovered back in the 1880s, the area in the easternmost corner of the county, where the Kentucky and Virginia state lines meet, had an enormous deposit of the most high-grade bituminous coal to be found in the entire Cumberland Plateau. Much like the rest of the county, this area of a little over eighty thousand acres was undeveloped in terms of modern community schemata, sparsely populated, and unadulterated by commercial entities. There were no roads or railways, no stores or offices. There were certainly people who had been living on the land for generations, but much like the encounter in 1492 between Christopher Columbus and the Americas, it was not until the coming of the coal industry that Appalachia was "discovered."

It was not that companies failed to take interest in this particular parcel of land before the advent of coal mining activities; in fact, the land was first purchased by an obscure holding company in 1876. It was just that instead of developing the land, the absentee landowner chose to lay in wait for decades until a profitable suitor came along to purchase it—which is exactly what happened. Trading magnate Warren Delano Jr. purchased the land in 1907 through a holding company called the Kentenia Corporation, a name inspired by the three bordering states through which the property runs— Kentucky, Tennessee, and Virginia.[11] It was not at all random that Mr. Delano chose that specific parcel, as he had made several journeys to eastern Kentucky with his young grandson Franklin Delano Roosevelt just five years earlier. Further, his appointment to the board of the Louisville & Nashville (L&N) Railroad Company armed him with the knowledge of the company's plans to expand into eastern Kentucky. Through the boom of the early 1900s, Kentenia sold off chunks of land to eager coal and steel corporations, individual investors, and whoever else wanted to try their luck in the mining industry.

This is how central Appalachia was created. Rather than being an obviously carved out region governed by any particular geographic logic, it was invented in the North—in the offices of the rail, oil, and steel barons in Pittsburgh, New York, and Chicago, and at the New England estates of the American oligarchy. In writing about the sensational drama of the invention of Appalachia, Harry Caudill writes, "Its headquarters were at South Yarmouth, MA, where a relief map of 'the Kentenia Country' hung above the paneled walls and Persian carpets of the board room."[12] No different from the European scramble for Africa occurring simultaneously an ocean away, this Appalachian land grab laid the infrastructure for corporations, government entities, and speculative investors to enter into the region and reap the bounty of the land.

The Making of the Coal Towns

First came Benham. The Chicago-based agricultural machinery conglomerate International Harvester Company founded this Harlan County city in 1915, during World War I. The company set up a modest mining operation to supply raw material, namely coal and coke, downstream to its subsidiary, Wisconsin Steel Corporation. Typical of any coal town during that period, Benham offered the basic structure necessary to sustain a stable workforce—company houses for miners and their families, a company store, a post office, some form of school, and a lodge or two to entertain the men with liquor and cards when they were not risking their lives in the deep dark abyss of the mines. Although the company town created the basic infrastructure for community formation and social organization, coal towns in the region were notorious for their decrepit living conditions.

For example, a 1925 industry study conducted by the U.S. Coal Commission reported that the coal towns in central Appalachia were the worst in the nation. According to the study, "Only two percent of the company towns in these states had sewage systems, and in consequence there were serious pollution and health problems in most of them."[13] Typhoid and diphtheria outbreaks spread rampantly in these communities. Miners and their families often lived in a perpetual state of insecurity, as food supply, access to basic health care, a steady wage, and protection from the natural elements were left to the company's whim. Due to the totalitarian structure of the company-owned town, these organizations had little incentive to offer anything more to their employees than "bare life."[14] They intentionally recruited uneducated and unskilled migrant labor. With little to no attractive labor alternatives to be found for hundreds of miles, coal mining companies in eastern Kentucky faced few threats to the general stability of their labor force. Benham, however, would not become one such community. Rather, it did not have the chance to—because of its newfound neighbor.

· · · · · ·

I think from what we hear, they are going to develop a very modern and thoroughly equipped plan with fine housing conditions, and we will lose our supremacy in that regard. It will be necessary for us to watch them closely and keep our conditions as far as possible in hand so that we will not be losing our men to them on account of their offering greater attractions to the families of working men. You are quite right in your steps to co-operate with them in giving them such help as they need along reasonable lines.[15]

In the summer of 1917, just two years after International Harvester incorporated the city of Benham, the United States Coal & Coke Corporation (a subsidiary of United States Steel Corporation) purchased eleven thousand acres of undeveloped land from an absentee holding company out of Pennsylvania called the Wentz Corporation. Geologist L. A. Billips, photographed among his dapper gang of northern industrialists, nominated the three-and-a-half-mile tract of land as the perfect place for U.S. Steel to stake its claim in eastern Kentucky. According to Billips's assessment of the region, he had "found three veins in the Big Black, all of the coal good and most of it excellent for steel making." Better yet, "There was a single tract of the coal of proven title and held by a single owner, the Wentz Corporation of Philadelphia; 14,405 acres contained many hundreds of millions of tons of fuel."[16]

This property was contiguous to the Benham city limits, spanning all the way to the top of Black Mountain. News of its new neighbor was of keen interest to International Harvester, and rightfully so, as U.S. Steel was one of the largest publicly traded corporations in the world at the time. This new neighbor was too close for comfort, as it stood to disrupt inhabitants' taken-for-granted way of life in Benham. Benham and Lynch—two company-owned towns nestled in the eastern corner of Harlan County, covering just a sliver of land, merely five miles long and one mile wide—would become two of the top ten producers of bituminous coal in the United States.[17]

The news was received as both a gift and a curse. Because the mining process had not yet mechanized, coal companies relied exclusively on the manual labor of a legion of able-bodied men to dig coal by the tons. Having U.S. Steel so close posed a real threat to the stability of International

OFFICIALS AT LYNCH, KY   APRIL 27 1919
L.A.BILLIPS   W.N.CLAGETT   F.J.DOOLEY
         D.W ENGR   Const Engr   CHIEF CLERK
F.Y.ALBERT   J.D.JENNINGS   R.J.BONDURANT   W.E. RILEY M.D.
SUP'T.   Cons't SUP'T   Ass't SUP'T

FIGURE 1 U.S. Coal and Coke executives from the North at Lynch, Kentucky |
April 27, 1919. The Southeast Appalachian Archives, Appalachian Archive Online
Exhibit. U.S. Coal and Coke Company Collection.

Harvester's labor force. H. F. Perkins, president of Wisconsin Steel Corporation, responded with haste from his Chicago office: "In relation to the purchase or lease by the United States Coal & Coke Company of the Wentz
property. This has an important bearing on us in several ways; first, it will
give us good support in handling some labor problems, while on the other
hand it will increase the competition in our district. You should watch carefully to see whether they do their preliminary work on an eight-hour day
and find out if they are planning to operate on that basis, as their action
will probably have a very strong effect on what we must do."[18] Coal is a by-
product of steel. Its demand, therefore, was insatiable throughout the interwar period, as all the world powers, Allies and Central powers alike, were
in need of weapons of mass destruction—guns, tanks, planes, and endless
artillery. In response, the eastern Kentucky collieries operated three shifts
to cover a twenty-four-hour production cycle. In this way, the labor supply

was always a prime concern for every company. It would only take one competitor offering superior wages or living conditions in any given territory to throw the industrial complex into disequilibrium. However, the executives at International Harvester were fairly certain that U.S. Steel would not upset the applecart.

From management's perspective, the competition stood to benefit International Harvester in terms of coercing its workers to accept their lot in life. If the two companies could somehow view each other as friendly competitors by sharing information and agreeing to adhere to predetermined parameters around labor matters—including length of workday, wages, and benefits—they might have a chance at thwarting unionization, which was the one social movement that menaced all large corporations during the Progressive Era.

Paternalistic Capitalism as a Response to the Threat of Unionization

The question of labor relations loomed large in the minds of the industrial oligarchy during this period. The first two decades of the 1900s brought the populist era to an end, and elite industrial barons were under national scrutiny for their business practices around monopoly and issues related to labor conditions and workers' rights. The companies involved in the coal mining industry, which included almost every major steel, oil, and railroad company in the country, were under particular scrutiny because of the infamous Ludlow Massacre of 1914 in Colorado.[19] At Ludlow, miners faced the risk of explosions, mine collapses, suffocation, and a host of other deadly exposures on a day-to day basis. However, it was the work conditions that led to the massive fallout between the striking miners and their companies. Coal operators subjected workers to seven-day workweeks and provided filthy work environments, uncapped work hours, unsustainable wages, and no recourse for on-the-job injury or death. Like most coal companies, the companies at Ludlow owned the communities and homes in which the miners lived, which meant that they controlled everything, owned everything, and surveilled everything. Under these conditions, miners were forced to circulate their meager earnings right back to the companies through the company store, rent, and other usury fees that were forced upon them, literally financing their own domination.

In 1913, the United Mine Workers of America (UMWA) began to organize the miners throughout the southern region of Colorado in an attempt to unionize them and make labor demands on their behalf. Employers in this area met this effort with vehement hostility and swift action to thwart any and all efforts to do so by means of intimidation, harassment, employment termination, and physical violence. However, the UMWA steadily gained momentum in the region among the miners and launched a seven-point strike by the fall of the year. Ultimately, eight thousand miners participated in the strike, resulting in all eight thousand being forced to move out of their homes by the coal companies. The UMWA set up a nearby tent colony to house the striking workers and their families in anticipation of mass displacement while they fought for their demands. The coal operators responded to the strike by replacing the striking workers and employing hundreds of private guards to essentially declare war on unionization. The strikers rose to the occasion, responding by openly carrying arms through the coal camps and aggressing guards, coal camp managers, and working miners alike. An estimated two hundred men lost their lives over the course of the strike, which ended in utter tragedy on April 20, 1914, when twenty-four people—including two women and eleven children—were suffocated while hiding under a tent in the UMWA colony during a riot.[20] This event received national publicity and led to a federal investigation launched by President Woodrow Wilson.

For example, although several companies had mining operations in Ludlow, John D. Rockefeller Jr. was publicly shamed for his companies' role in the massacre, and was labeled as a corporate villain in the media. It is an understatement to say that the stakes were high when other high profile industrial companies decided to set up colliery operations in eastern Kentucky in 1917, at the heels of Ludlow. U.S. Steel's goal was simple and unchanging: to achieve maximum profits for the corporation and its shareholders. However, the industrial field had become much more complicated, making the former approach of naked feudalism untenable. Throughout the nineteenth century, capitalist formations emerged in their most naked form, with industrialists staking claims in their fields, maintaining full autonomy over the terms and conditions of labor and settling external disagreements corporation to corporation. At the turn of the twentieth century, however, the issue of labor was at the height of public opinion. As a result, many new actors who had previously been voiceless entered the field of "labor," such as labor unions, politicians and government officials, shareholders, and, of course, workers. Corporations were fully aware of this new context and recognized that they needed a strategy to control the situation in their favor. The question of the day for early twentieth-century corporations was how to maintain control over the production of labor in the era of progressivism. Unionization was perceived as the greatest threat to profit; therefore, a priority was placed on developing strategies to counter these efforts. The change would not be to the content of labor arrangements but to the form. Thus came the rise of paternalistic capitalism.

In an attempt to create docile bodies, U.S. Steel designed its new city of Lynch as a "model town."[21] Beyond creating a bare-bones community to merely maintain a stable workforce, the town was an exercise in subject formation. In a letter to Wisconsin Steel's H. F. Perkins, Benham's mine superintendent, F. B. Dunbar, wrote, "Mr. Billips, their engineer, informs me that they expect to build 1500 houses and expect to complete them at the rate of five per day."[22] With great urgency in his tone, Dunbar underscores that "they are spending large sums of money" and are "sparing no expense" in the construction of the new coal town—what Harry Caudill labeled the "Kingdom of Lynch."[23] The paternalistic relationship that animated the model company town was adopted to instill a false consciousness among laborers.

• • • • • •

This is the context through which Benham and Lynch emerged. It was the era of progressivism, paternalistic capitalism, unionization, and world war. U.S. Steel was intent on creating a corporate utopia, and International Harvester woke up to a behemoth in its bed. The series of letters between F. B. Dunbar and the Chicago-based president of Wisconsin Steel reveal how conscious the company executives were about the climate in which they governed. Yes, they were concerned with the logistics of running an efficient operation to meet their goals, but they were also concerned with matters of employee morale and mood, the company's image, and the sociality of the community they had built.

U.S. Steel intended on building a company town like no other in Lynch. A new experiment in social engineering, company executives wanted to test the theory of paternalistic capitalism. If the company created a utopia, a built environment that provided miners and their families with everything they needed and much of what they wanted, at relative exceptional quality, would workers be disinclined to unionize? F. B. Dunbar was right to take heed of U.S. Steel's intention to "spare no expense" in the construction of Lynch, for it would have great influence on how International Harvester would govern Benham. In a letter sent on September 4, 1917, just one month after U.S. Steel purchased the land from the Wentz Corporation, Dunbar wrote to Perkins to apprise him of the grandeur of the coal town that was to come:

> They expect to build a large steel tipple having a capacity of 10,000 tons, which will be located about a half mile east of our property line. . . . They will also build houses wherever surface conditions will permit, Mr. O'Toole stating that they expect to build about 1500 houses. They expect to build a large department store near the main tipple and have probably two other commissaries farther up the valley. Mr. O'Toole spoke of building a large high school on the plot of ground adjoining our property. Their baseball and amusement park will be at that point also.[24]

Over the following eight months, U.S. Steel went into a building frenzy. The coal tipple that Mr. Dunbar references was completed in May of 1919, and was at that time the largest one in the world. Company houses were erected throughout the seven coal "camps" that made up the city of Lynch—and not just the monochromatic ramshackle homes that were common in coal towns. The homes in Lynch varied in model, with some built as single-family homes and others as duplexes, and they came in a variety of sizes and colors to offer aesthetic appeal to the community. The main department store, U.S. Supply Company—known as "the big store"—was also the largest of its kind. Once completed, miners and their families could purchase everything from food to furniture to tailor-made suits from that company store. And because a true model town would not do without a variety of entertainment and amenities, the company built an entertainment facility for its inhabitants—the Victory Theater—which featured a restaurant with separate sections for its black and white patrons; a luxurious hotel for executives and visitors; and a first-rate hospital to serve all U.S. Steel employees and their families. The company even built a baseball stadium and hired its own semiprofessional baseball team, the Lynch Greys, to entertain the community with sporting events.

International Harvester had no choice but to respond by expanding its amenities to converge the disparity between the two communities. The school is a good example of its effort. As a border state, the Kentucky statutes adhered to the Black Codes, enacted to govern race relations. The state legislature made it illegal for black and white children to be educated in the same schoolhouse. However, it did not mandate that counties offer a high school for black children to receive an education beyond the eighth grade. Therefore, International Harvester had no incentive to offer more than the basic school system required by the state. However, once it learned about U.S. Steel's intention to build a first-class school system for its black and white children, International Harvester had to respond. F. B. Dunbar wrote to Perkins in 1917 concerning this matter after a conversation with a Lynch executive: "I talked with Mr. O'Toole regarding the school for the colored people and he has instructed his man here to get some data on this matter. . . . They want a graded school for their colored people and a graded school for the Americans and a high school for the Americans."[25] Benham already had black and white elementary schools and plans to build a white high school in their community. However, International Harvester's commitment to providing black education was hollow. Responding to Dunbar's request to build a new school building to accommodate the town's growing black population, Perkins was hesitant to consider it for fear that the proposed new building, which included an indoor toilet, would send the wrong message: "I think he is getting something up that is way beyond what we can do for the colored people; in fact it would be so much better than the white school house that I think it would excite uncomfortable comment."[26] If International Harvester executives paused at the idea of an indoor toilet, they must have been utterly shocked when six years later, in 1923, U.S. Steel added two state-of-the-art high schools to their community: one for the Americans and one for the "coloreds." This decision created a frenzy among International Harvester executives and generated dozens of letters between them and Benham about what to do about the fact that Lynch's colored high school offered amenities and resources that white schools throughout the region did not even have at the time. Their first thought was to enter into an agreement allowing the black children in Benham to attend the Lynch Colored Public School. However, due to logistical complications, they decided to build a high school for their black population, which was completed within a year of the opening of the Lynch Colored Public School.

In the end, the workers benefited from this friendly competition. Nevertheless, neither town was a utopia. Although Benham and Lynch were heralded as model towns, company interests were the same as those that owned raggedy roughshod communities in neighboring areas of eastern Kentucky. International Harvester and U.S. Steel employed the veneer of freedom to keep their workers from protesting. Some would argue that it worked. As Italian scholar and Harlan County expert Alessandro Portelli notes, "Harlan County was the last coal county in the U.S. to accept the union-shop clause."[27] However, these companies did not keep the laborers at bay solely with treats and comforts; they used sheer force and domination as well.

Portelli reminds us that "even at the 'model' company town of Lynch, owned by U.S. Steel, company guards escorted all strangers who came in at the train station to the company office, where they were asked to justify their presence in the camp or leave. The town was surrounded by a wire fence, explicitly intended to keep the organizers out."[28] At the time, unionization was the only force that stood between the companies and their aim of profits on profit. However, the mighty army—the United Mine Workers of America—would soon come to Harlan County and wage war on King Coal: Mr. John L. Lewis was coming to town.

This burst of immaculate conception, whereby city and community were established overnight at the enunciation of northern corporate executives, instantiated the mass migration of labor migrants into Benham and Lynch, Kentucky. As a result, thousands of laborers poured in from Poland, Hungary, Yugoslavia, Italy, Greece, and dozens of other European countries, with fewer coming from Kentucky and the neighboring states of Tennessee and Virginia. However, there was another, rather unusual internal migration stream flowing into Harlan County: men and women from the Alabama black belt.

· · · · · ·

This chapter laid out what sociologist Dan Hirschman and Isaac Reed term the "formation story"[29]—the historical formation of a social kind—of the global labor migration into the coalfields of central Appalachia during the interwar period.[30] Alongside a deluge of European immigration into the region during the first four decades of the twentieth century, tens of thousands of African American families settled in coal towns throughout central Appalachia in search of the life, liberty, and happiness that the United States promised its newly emancipated citizens but that their places of origin in the Deep South had so harshly denied them. However, the African American experience in this region of the country is woefully understudied and vastly underrepresented in popular culture.[31] Between 1900 and 1940, the black population in central Appalachia nearly tripled, from approximately 40,000 to nearly 115,000 inhabitants—an in-migration almost solely attributable to labor recruitment by coal mining companies.[32] So acute was this labor migration, according to labor historian Ronald L. Lewis, that "by 1920, 96 percent of blacks living in central Appalachia resided in [one of the] sixteen coal counties" represented in the region.[33] The vast majority of black coal miners in central Appalachia settled in West Virginia, which accounted for three-quarters of the region's black population by 1940—the census year that boasted the region's greatest black population density of the century.

However, eastern Kentucky witnessed its fair share of black labor migration as well. While the majority of the black migrants who settled in West Virginia originated from the agricultural areas of Virginia and North Carolina, those who came to eastern Kentucky emanated almost exclusively from the mineral district of Birmingham, Alabama.[34]

Table 1 shows the total population of Harlan County, Kentucky, during the prime years of the African American Great Migration. As the census records show, the total population in the region increased by more than sevenfold between 1900 and 1940, from nearly 10,000 inhabitants to over 75,000. However, what is most striking are the racial dimensions of this population change. While the white population increased by a little over 600 percent, the black population rose by more than 3,000 percent during the same period, increasing from 226 to 7,534 black inhabitants between 1900 and 1940. However, the black population has never exceeded 10 percent of the total population. This seemingly unnatural rapid demographic change leads one to inquire: What were the biopolitics of this carefully curated black migration?[35] Who were these black migrants, and where did they come from? This influx of black migration was no coincidence; as the data for the following decades shows, they poured out just as quickly as they came in.

Chapter 2 reveals the inner workings of this unusual population change. In doing so, it reconstructs this black migration stream out of the mineral district of Alabama into the coalfields of eastern Kentucky, specifically the migration into the "tri-city" area of Benham, Lynch, and Cumberland. In it we explore the questions that lie at the heart of this phenomenal mass migration: How did they get there? Why Kentucky? What were they in search of? To understand these migrants' plight, the stock from which they came, and the muster that fueled their strivings, we must get a sense of the origin story of this migration. Therefore, in this section I reconstruct what sociologist Rubén Hernández-León calls the "migration industry," a term he defines as "the ensemble of entrepreneurs, firms and services which, chiefly motivated by financial gain, facilitate international mobility, settlement and adaption, as well as communication and resource transfers of migrants and their families across a border."[36] Migration scholars have rightly identified the role of migrant networks and social capital as central mechanisms for perpetuating mass-migration flows. However, here I am concerned with its antecedents. For example, it is difficult to fathom, in this case, that black

TABLE 1 Harlan County, Kentucky, Population Change, 1900–1970, by Race

Year	Total Population	Total White Population	Total Black Population	Percentage White	Percentage Black	White Change	Black Change	Total County Population Change
1900	9,838	9,612	226	98%	2%			
1910	10,566	10,002	564	95%	5%	4%	150%	7%
1920	31,545	28,644	2,901	91%	9%	186%	414%	199%
1930	64,557	58,678	5,879	91%	9%	105%	103%	105%
1940	75,271	67,737	7,534	90%	10%	15%	28%	17%
1950	71,751	66,298	5,453	92%	8%	–2%	–28%	–5%
1960	51,107	47,044	4,063	92%	8%	–29%	–25%	–29%
1970	37,271	34,936	2,335	94%	6%	–26%	–43%	–27%

Source: Minnesota Population Center. National Historical Geographic Information System: Version 2.0. Minneapolis: University of Minnesota, 2011.

working-age men living in post-Reconstruction era Alabama woke up one morning and decided to migrate to the mountaintops of eastern Kentucky. How would they have heard about the coalfields there? Better yet, how did they know that Benham, Lynch, or any of the other five hundred coal towns that sprang up in central Appalachia between 1910 and 1930 would be safe and viable for black life?

These were not light questions for the generation who migrated during the first wave of the African American Great Migration. By 1910, nearly 90 percent of the black population still resided in the U.S. South, primarily in rural agricultural areas. This meant that there were essentially no networks at their disposal: no cousins in Washington, D.C., or Chicago to open their home and help them get on their feet, and little information about what lay beyond the oppressive strictures of the Deep South. Stories of the North and freedom surely circulated within the black community,[37] but information about how to initiate such a journey was largely unreliable. Further, blacks were met with great suspicion when they attempted to purchase train tickets or access other modes of transportation.

In situating the African American Great Migration into the migration industry framework, I argue that for those early movers—those who left the Deep South during the first wave of the Great Migration—the act of leaving was not a migration but an *escape*. Because there is no comprehensive publicly available data source on the Great Migration, and because the majority of people represented in this generation of migrants have long since passed away, I rely heavily on the postmemory of their children to reweave the rich tapestry of this mass movement of black people from the mineral district of Alabama to the coalfields of eastern Kentucky—one of many journeys in what would eventually culminate into what we now call the African American Great Migration.[38]

Let's go to Alabama.

From the deep and the near South the sons and daughters of newly freed African slaves wander into the city. Isolated, cut off from memory, having forgotten the name of the gods and only guessing at their faces, they arrive dazed and stunned, their heart kicking in their chest with a song worth singing. They arrive carrying Bibles and guitars, their pockets lined with dust and fresh hope, marked men and women seeking to scrape from the narrow, crooked cobbles and the fiery blasts of the coke furnace a way of bludgeoning and shaping the malleable parts of themselves into a new identity as free men of definite and sincere worth.

—August Wilson, *Joe Turner's Come and Gone*

My dad came to Lynch with a guy called Limehouse. You are probably going to hear Limehouse's name a lot interviewing people. But my dad came to Lynch on the back of that truck with Limehouse, got a job in the coal mine, and then he went back and got my mama; and they got married.

—William Jackson | Born 1944 in Lynch, Ky. | Currently resides in Los Angeles, Calif.

2 The Great ~~Migration~~ Escape

· ·

Origin Stories

My daddy is from Alabama *(Vyreda Davis Williams)*. They came from Alabama to Lynch, Kentucky, where they needed coal miners, and that's where a lot of blacks came from—the South *(Ernest Pettygrue)*. They were from Alabama; somewhere around Utah, Tuscaloosa, Ellisville, down in that area *(Albert Harris)*. I think my mom and them descended from Alabama to the State of Kentucky *(Samuel Coleman)*. Mama came from a place called Maytown in the northern part of Alabama, and Daddy came from the southern part of Alabama, a farming area called Mosses *(Odell Moss)*. My father was from Tuscaloosa, Alabama *(Virginia Taylor-Ward)*. My grandfather was named Lee Halls, and he migrated here from Alabama to come here to work in the coalfields *(Sanford Baskin)*. My mother, Reila Lee Harris Steward, was from Lowndes County, Alabama; Pintilala, to be specific *(John Steward)*. I was born in Alabama, and I came to Kentucky when I was eight years old. I was born in 1937 *(Betty Powell)*. He was from Frisco City, Alabama *(Leslie Lee)*. My name is Willie Watts Jr., and I was born October 6, 1936, in Docena, Alabama, and I came to Benham, Kentucky, when I was eight months old *(Willie Watts Jr.)*. I was born on November 25, 1934, in Docena, Alabama, and we moved to Benham, Kentucky, in 1936, and we was raised up there until I got married in 1951 *(Betty Jewell Watts Rogers)*. Okay, my father, like I said, was from Alabama, he met my mother here—they dated. She was from Benham, and he went to school in Lynch *(Teresa Austin-Mimes)*. Union Springs, Alabama. . . . Just like many other families, I think that's how we got there—that the patriarch was recruited and actually physically brought up here, and I think sold a house from the company and then sent for the rest of the family *(Dwayne Baskin)*. My father was from Brookside, Alabama, and my mother was from Dolomite, Alabama *(Lena Margaret Jones)*. My dad was born in Coaling, Alabama, and he came to Lynch looking for a job *(Ron Thomas)*. Somewhere down in Alabama. Yes, that's where he was born. And he was a coal miner until he retired *(Vera Garner Robinson)*. She was born in Bessemer, Alabama. And their family moved to Cumberland; they lived on Sanctified Hill *(Janice Brown)*. Now most of the people in Lynch—I refer to them as old-timers—and most of them came from Alabama, but my family came from South Carolina. I don't know of anyone else from South Carolina *(Edwin Gist)*. I know all of them were born in some part of Alabama on both sides *(Barbara Haury)*. I was born in Marion Junction, Alabama, on June 1, 1930. We left Alabama in May '36 and moved to Harlan County, Kentucky, and my daddy worked in the coal mines for U.S. Steel *(Ike Gardner)*. Well, my dad was from Wylam, Alabama, and my mom said she came to Lynch when she was eight years old. So they both came from Alabama; whether they came from the same town in Alabama, I don't know *(Joyce Hall)*. She came from Weirton, West Virginia. And because her father was a coal miner, she moved back and forth between the coal mining camps between West Virginia and Lynch, Kentucky. So she stayed in different areas in Kentucky, and she also stayed in different areas in West Virginia. But her parents originally were from Alabama *(Brenda Thornton)*. And you know certainly he used to tell me the story over and over again. Now, he is from a place called Union Springs, Alabama. His father was a sharecropper in Union Springs, but you know the concept of sharecropping—you never break even, you never make any profit, and most times you come up short *(Brian Cash)*. I'm from Jenkins, Kentucky, and I came from Alabama to Kentucky back in 1930 *(Mother Ferguson)*. They were born right outside Birmingham, in a place called Ensley, Alabama *(Arthur Simmons)*. I came from Queensbury, Alabama, in 1936 to Lynch, Kentucky, and that's where I resided for a long time. I was schooled there and everything *(Nathaniel Fielder)*. Alabama. Lafayette, Alabama, with some growing up in Talladega, Alabama, as well. My father came like other fathers, looking for an opportunity to find wholesome employment; and the coal mines afforded him that opportunity. Migrating from Alabama, you had coal miner opportunities, as I understand, in the Birmingham area, so there was a natural transition of a lot of residents of Alabama. But he came looking for the opportunity to live a prosperous life, and the coal mining industry afforded him that *(Jerome Ratchford)*.

· · · · · ·

They came from Alabama. They took the train; some got a ticket, most just hoboed. Some of the firstcomers even worked for the L&N Railroad Company—laying track from Bessemer, Alabama, up through the hills of southeastern Kentucky—and, after months or years of transitory toil, decided to take root in the burgeoning coal camps in Harlan County. As for the others, they came with Limehouse.

That these men came from Alabama is no coincidence. While there were healthy sources of able-bodied laborers in Kentucky, as well as in neighboring Tennessee and Virginia, the black men from Alabama possessed something that was invaluable to the coal companies: experience. The state of Alabama is resource rich in anthracite coal, iron, and ore, and it was the largest producer of coal and fossil fuel in the American South up until the early decades of the twentieth century.[1] Blacks were used as free labor in those mines both before and after emancipation: as enslaved labor in the antebellum era, and through the convict leasing system from the close of the Civil War up until the 1920s.[2] Corporations operating in eastern Kentucky knew to target their recruitment efforts in Alabama, because they owned those mines too.

The trek out of Alabama was by no means easy or safe for this generation of black migrants, as they were the early participants in what would soon become the African American Great Migration. At the time, the threat of unspeakable violence, disappearance, or dispossession was very real and was demonstrated through a reign of racial terror.[3] Because of the stealthy nature of this early migration wave, primary data on the migration stories into Harlan County are limited. Therefore, I made it a point to ask my participants—the children of the first wave of migrants—to recount what their fathers and mothers told them about life in Alabama as well as their decision to migrate to Appalachia, of all places. Almost all of them knew that their parents descended from Alabama, and many were able to identify a city for one or both of their parents. However, when asked about their parents' lives back then, the most common response was, as William "Bo" Schaffer Jr. of Lynch, Kentucky, recalled, "He never would tell." Upon further pondering, Schaffer's curiosity drifted with my own: "And the funny thing is, my dad never went back to Alabama after he left; he never went back. And he never talked about nothing concerning Alabama." Participants repeatedly offered the same perplexed recollection when asked if their parents ever shared any stories about life in Alabama: "As far as I know, they didn't talk about their roots too much" (Arnita Davis-Brown).

That this form of repression was a direct response to the racial traumas they experienced growing up in the Deep South can only be a claim of my own speculation. For this generation, there is no family tree or migration record to tell them where they come from, no Ellis Island, and no family story to pass through the generations about the horrors and hardships of life growing up black in the American South at the turn of the twentieth century. Instead, their parents left shards of their shattered lives for their children to piece back together, to make beauty out of brokenness, like a stained-glass window. This has been the only way for them to get a glimpse from whence they came.

"Hey, Nigger!"

These glimpses sometimes resurfaced in moments of vulnerability, when parents' pasts haunted their present. Although she described her father as a man of few words, Cynthia Brown-Harrington recalled a vivid memory of her father's migration story:

> He used to get drunk. And he basically told us the same story when he got drunk about how he hoboed (we call it "hitchhike"). He said he hoboed from Alabama because he had heard about the jobs in the mines in Kentucky. I think he was in his thirties at that time, I'm not actually sure. But he said he was hoboing and he was walking and these white men saw him one day and they said, "Hey, nigger! Where you going?" So he told them that he was going to Kentucky to get a job, and he said they continued to taunt him for a while and they said to him, "We heard that niggers can preach." So they said to him, "Nigger, preach." And I asked him, I said, "So, what did you preach?" He said he only knew one book in the Bible. So he preached the book of Job. So he said he had to do it because he was a little afraid and then he said after he preached they said, "Well, we heard niggers like to dance." He said they said, "Nigger, dance." And I said, "Did you dance?" He said, "Sure, I danced." And you know, once he danced and they taunted him some more, they let him go.

> —Cynthia Brown-Harrington | Born in 1954 in Lynch, Ky. | Resides in Greensboro, N.C.

Those words—"Hey, nigger!"—hurling from the mouths of those white men, a random group of strangers, hailed Brown-Harrington's father.[4] The social force of four hundred years of racial domination and hegemony, slavery, bondage, and unadjudicated violence claimed his body. With the wretched understanding that he could do nothing to protect himself from whatever fate his interlocutors chose to visit upon him that day, he obliged them with a timid response: He preached the book of Job.

Those were the times that this generation would have liked to forget. Not only did the thought of revisiting those memories pose the potential to unleash volcanic emotions within, but no parent wants to pass down a narrative of fear, helplessness, and humiliation to their children when simply asked, "Who are we?" or "Where do we come from?" However, some children

pieced together their migration story through concerted efforts at historical excavation. For instance, some participants took on the endeavor to dig
up their past later in life by returning to Alabama in search of clues. In an
attempt to unearth his roots, Albert Harris sojourned to Alabama after his
father had passed away:

> I had the opportunity to meet one of my great aunts in Tuscaloosa, Alabama,
> and I sat at her feet being curious and trying to get some family history . . .
> and she just told the story of her, especially her brothers and the men in our
> family, how they just didn't take it. And then she gave me some insight because
> here in the South too you will see a lot of the [black] Masonic Freemasonry,
> and she told me how instrumental they were in Alabama. That a lot of times
> the Masons and the guys in the death business would put blacks in a casket
> and transport them across the state. Why? To get them out of the area and
> keep them from getting apprehended or killed.
>
> —Albert Harris | Born in 1950 in Benham, Ky. | Resides in Sunrise, Fla.

Conditions of Exit

What was the Alabama from where these soon-to-be black Appalachians
came? And why didn't this generation of mothers and fathers talk? It goes
without argument that the political conditions for blacks throughout the
Deep South during their time were hellish. In Alabama, these conditions
emerged through the convergence of a declining plantation economy and a
bustling extractive industrial complex. This is what migration scholars refer to as "conditions of exit," meaning the "political conditions of exit [that]
have significant bearing on subsequent patterns of settlement."[5] Post-
Reconstruction Alabama presented its own peculiar set of political conditions for its black inhabitants.

The post-Reconstruction era was a period of resurrection for the South.
Slavery had been abolished, the Confederacy had been dismantled, and the
modern world no longer suckled at the teat of King Cotton. In exchange for
southern Democrats' resigned acceptance of the inauguration of Republi-
can Rutherford B. Hayes as the nineteenth president of the United States,
the two parties made a tacit agreement that called for President Hayes to
abandon the federal occupation of the South and to turn a blind eye to
matters concerning the welfare of its African American citizens.[6] Up until
that point, federal troops and agents of the Freedmen's Bureau were being
sent from the Department of War to "reconstruct" the South and reunify

the nation. The Reconstruction era ended with the Hayes compromise.[7] Recapping this epoch moment in southern history, the inauguration of what is termed the "Redemption era,"[8] historian C. Vann Woodward states: "The phase that began in 1877 was inaugurated by the withdrawal of federal troops from the South, the abandonment of the Negro as a ward of the nation, the giving up of the attempt to guarantee the freedman his civil and political equality, and the acquiescence of the rest of the country in the South's demand that the whole problem be left to the disposition of the dominant Southern white people."[9] As a result, white southern elites were left to reestablish order according to their standards, mores, and ideologies. With the explicit forms of the "peculiar institution" of slavery and the plantation system dismantled, this new version of the old order was accomplished through law, custom, and terrorism. Although slavery was officially off the books as far as the federal law was concerned, it persisted in the South through a new set of more implicit institutions and practices.[10]

One immediate action following the departure of the Union troops was the adoption of the Black Codes into state legislatures, also known as Jim Crow laws. While this period witnessed a variety of interracial solutions to the "Negro problem," by 1901 the entire South had committed to the wholesale disenfranchisement of African Americans from the political and social sphere.[11] This manifested in the proscription of voting rights and representation in political office, the emergence of new forms of economic domination used to re-enslave black labor, and the rise in lynchings and other forms of racial terror as a tool for social control. The majority of white society was willing to do all it could to reestablish the racial order that slavery had for so long maintained. Sharecropping and convict leasing were the two main systems instituted for the re-enslavement of southern blacks. In his writings on the emergence of these oppressive systems, W. E. B. Du Bois referred to them as the "spawn of slavery." In a 1901 essay on the topic, he wrote, "Two systems of controlling human labor which still flourish in the South are the direct children of slavery, and to all intents and purposes are slavery itself. These are the crop-lien system and the convict lease system."[12]

Sharecropping was a farming tenancy arrangement that allowed black families to contract their labor out to landholders in exchange for a percentage of the profits earned from the year's harvest.[13] These contracts were on unequal terms; white landowners set the standards of the agreement and maintained control of all the accounting throughout the contract term, while black laborers were in control of only their hope that the contract would be fulfilled when it was time to make good on the promise at hand.

This hope was most often traded in for a heap of disappointment, as it was common for the black farmers to end up indebted to the landholder at the end of the harvest.[14] Worst yet, blacks were hard-pressed to adjudicate these contracts, as the Black Codes in Alabama made it nearly impossible for a black person to sue a white person in court. In essence, the sharecropping system bound black farmers and their families to plantations much like chattel slavery did.

The Black Codes also made African Americans subject to arrest for just about anything, and the slavery loophole in the Thirteenth Amendment of the U.S. Constitution, which legally abolished slavery or involuntary servitude "except as a punishment for crime whereof the party shall have been duly convicted," created a profitable incentive for southern states to lock them up. Herein lies the policy origin leading to the contemporary mass incarceration of black bodies in the United States.[15] Ambiguously worded laws related to loitering and vagrancy were popular, as were laws for petty crimes—such as stealing a chicken—which could subject a black person to months or years in jail.

The convict leasing system became crucial to southern states in the post-Reconstruction era when the landed gentry attempted to reconstitute its wealth base.[16] With chattel slavery abolished, the convict leasing system emerged as its postbellum rearticulation. Nowhere was the convict leasing system more deep-seated than in the state of Alabama. Whereas Georgia abolished the system in 1908, Alabama held on to the practice for more than another decade, until it was finally made illegal in 1920. This is because the system was crucial to the economic stability of the state treasury. In an 1893 manuscript written about the unique character of the convict leasing system in Alabama, abolitionist Frederick Douglass wrote, "The state controls and supports the convicts who are hired out by a Board of Inspectors. Of the state convicts, the best of them physically, are leased out under contract, and worked in coal mines and on lands, Corporations being generally the lessees."[17] Corporations, especially coal mining companies, profited handsomely from this arrangement with the state and therefore made heavy investments in the system, such as building prisons, company towns, and company burial grounds. The Tennessee Coal, Iron and Railroad Corporation (a subsidiary of U.S. Steel), for example, built the state of Alabama a prison—right on the site of Pratt mines in the mineral district of Birmingham, Alabama.[18]

Unlike plantation slaveholders, who were responsible for the livelihood of their enslaved persons, small business owners and major corporations operating within the convict labor system were only leasing bodies. Thus, they were relinquished from the operational expenses of owning a human being. So if a convict was killed in a labor-related accident or simply worked to death while under contract to a lessee, the state would simply replace the commoditized body with another convict at no cost.[19] Thus emerged a new form of legal slavery based on the backbreaking cycle: lease, break, replace.

Under these conditions, lessees had no incentive to maintain decent work conditions. To the contrary, the mines were decrepit; tuberculosis and typhoid outbreaks were rampant; and living quarters were dark, dank, and always moist, leaving prisoners' skin shriveled and peeling and their bodies welcome hosts for disease—so much so that in 1902 the governor of Alabama threatened to ban coal companies from using convict labor due to the poor labor conditions. In an action approved by Governor Jelks, the State Convict Board announced that "no state convicts will be leased to coal mines of Alabama. About seven hundred convicts are leased to the Tennessee Coal, Iron and Railroad Corporation and the Sloss-Sheffield Company in Jefferson County."[20] This decision came about at the recommendation of Physician Inspector Shirley Bragg, who cited that a "change in conditions is necessary to preserve the life and health of the convicts."[21] Unfortunately, this order did not apply to the eight hundred convicts under the purview of the county, which was deemed to be beyond the state's jurisdiction. So singularly vile were the conditions in the mines in Alabama that this order made explicit that this charge would not affect "leases by farmers, lumber mills, and turpentine companies, as their treatment of convicts is satisfactory."[22] Alabama was notorious for its cruel treatment toward its convicts.[23] Not only were black convicts physically debased by their conditions as leased hard labor, but the system also attempted to strip them of their sense of dignity. Many of the state's black convicts resisted such treatment by attempting to escape from prison, appealing their cases, and appealing to the moral conscious of the state administrators. For an example of the latter strategy, in 1884 two black convicts at the Pratt mines in Birmingham, Alabama—Ezekiel Archey and Ambrose Haskins—jointly penned a letter to the president of the Alabama Board of Inspectors of Convicts, Reginald Dawson. Excerpts from the six-page letter follow:

> We write you looking to get your kind attention in this case. We have bin treated very cruel lately by the Board and we wish to find out what we have done to cause such treatment. . . . [We know] that you bring colored men that have not the chances of white men and we at the same time know that we are the greatest in number. We are the men

who do the work. We pay for kind treatment and fail to get it. Look at the white men and see how Avery [is] cutting 5 or 4 tons of coal a day. They [the white men] are few. They are the men that cause the present trouble. Every state officer tries to hold us accountable for their actions by denying us the privilege of allowing our families to come see us. . . . Could [you] consider for one instance if you were by law or violence been taken from your families and led to court and go[ne] without speaking one word to them. Sir it is heartbreaking to our families and to us. We all wanted to serve our time but the times are getting very hard daily without ceasing. . . . We are whipped for dirt and rock-soot, and if they run a half day, we are whipped if we fail to get our task of [the company].[24]

Unfortunately, the prayers and pleading and sorrows of men like Ezekiel and Ambrose would go unanswered, for the company wanted cheap labor, and the state needed a check. Convict leasing was too often a death sentence, as any minor infraction could result in an extension of the sentence for those who survived their initial term. According to historian Ronald L. Lewis, "Ninety percent of all the crippling accidents and nearly all deaths among Alabama convicts occurred during sentences in the coal mines."[25] Quoting Reginald Dawson, Frederick Douglass noted that in 1880, the prison mortality rate in Alabama had reached 41 per every 100 convicts.[26] Worse yet, the disappearance of black men, women, and children haunted black communities all throughout the South: Were they lynched or killed? Were they sent to the mines? Did they migrate? The disappearance of black bodies was a "ghostly matter" indeed.[27] In writing about Alabama's transformation from plantation slavery to that of convict leasing—a system that he calls "slavery by another name"—historian Douglas Blackmon writes, "Alabama's slave system had evolved into a forced labor agricultural and industrial enterprise unparalleled in the long history of slaves in the United States. During 1906, the state sold nearly two thousand black men to twenty different buyers. Nearly half were bought be the two biggest mining companies, Tennessee Coal & Iron and Sloss-Sheffield."[28] These are the conditions of exit from which these black migrants from Alabama migrated escaped to eastern Kentucky.

While sharecropping and convict leasing served an economic imperative for the South, lynching provided the psychological terror necessary for southern whites to keep the Negro in his or her place. There were a recorded 2,805 lynchings in the Deep South between 1880 and 1930, and Alabama claimed nearly 10 percent of the reported black lives lost to lynching during that period.[29] This five-decade period in the post-Reconstruction South was marked as the "lynching era." In their comprehensive study on lynching in the Deep South, Tolnay and Beck found that "targets for violence included politically active or successful African Americans, northern carpetbaggers, and southern scalawags."[30] However, these public and publicized events were carried out to induce a sense of terror throughout the black community, as the victims were emblems of what could befall black people who did not stay "in their place."

Not only were lynchings carried out with impunity, but the justifications were random and baseless.[31] While rape and murder were by far the most cited reasons used to justify lynchings, infractions such as "acting suspiciously," "throwing stones," "suing a white man," and "quarreling" were also cited as cause for a spectacular murder.[32] Lynch mobs resorted to this form of extralegal violence not because they were unsure of the court system's propensity to find the accused guilty or sentence them to death; rather, it was the need to make a public spectacle of the "sassy" Negro.[33] It was an act of terror employed to maintain the racial order of white supremacy and to squelch any thought of protest, mobilization, or justice.

As Figure 2 depicts, lynching was a community event, a celebration, and a ritual to inculcate the racial order across generations. White fathers brought their sons, mothers stood to the side and brought their young daughters, and the accomplishment of the day's event was often captured in a photograph. This image of the lynching of sixteen-year-old Lige Daniels was taken on August 3, 1920, in Center, Texas. The description accompanying the image notes that "one thousand men stormed the Center, Texas jail, battered down the steel doors, wrecked the cell, chose a courthouse yard oak, and lynched Lige Daniels." We can see from their collective posture that this was a prideful event. So much so that this photograph was reprinted onto a postcard and mailed to family members in other lands. The back of this particular postcard reads, "This was made in the court yard, in Center Texas, he is a 16-year-old Black boy, He killed Earl's Grandma, She was Florence's mother. Give this to Bud. From Aunt Myrtle." Revisiting that fateful moment in Cynthia Brown-Harrington's father's journey, we can see how he very much understood that hearing those two words—"Hey, nigger!"—was a moment of life or death.

The black migration from the mineral district in Alabama to the coalfields of eastern Kentucky was no coincidence, as the companies that controlled the extractive industries in Alabama were the very same ones that

FIGURE 2
The lynching of
sixteen-year-old
Lige Daniels in
Center, Texas |
August 3, 1920.
J. Allen, H. Als,
J. Lewis, and
L. F. Litwack.
*Without
Sanctuary:
Lynching
Photography in
America*. Santa
Fe, N.M.: Twin
Palms, 2000, 13.

owned the coal towns in eastern Kentucky. For example, the largest collier in Alabama—Tennessee Coal, Iron and Railroad Corporation—was a wholly owned subsidiary of U.S. Steel Corporation, the same company that controlled the mining operations in Lynch, Kentucky. A newly "discovered" region for mineral extraction, coal companies were in dire need of a stable labor force to dig that black gold out of the mountains during the World War I era, and at the time, coal was still extracted manually. Therefore, companies valued two qualities above all: a strong back and a special kind of desperation that would keep a man returning to the mine, risking his life and filling his lungs with black coal dust, day in and day out, without complaint.

Getting There, 1915–1930

They called him Limehouse. The few who are old enough to bear witness to him describe him as "just a common looking old white man with a big 'ole straw hat. I could remember he used to bring sugarcane and I love sugarcane, and daddy would always buy me sugarcane when Limehouse came" *(Lorene Clark)*. However, his role in bringing black families from Alabama into Lynch is legendary among the black community.

· · · · · ·

Well my grandfather used to talk about how he worked out in the fields in Alabama and then they had a man that would come to Alabama because coal mining was booming in Lynch during that time. . . . So this man named—I think it was Limehouse or Lemehouse or something—came and got a lot of men, so that's how he got a chance to move up to Lynch and start working in the coal mine. I think my grandfather was about seventeen years old when he started working in the coal mines. Yes, they were out in the fields picking cotton and all of that when they heard about this coal mining *(Cheryl Baskin-Brack)*. He said that when he came to Lynch, there was another friend of his and he was a man by the name of Limehouse. They used to bring men up from Alabama and their families to get a job because he knew that they were hiring up here, and that there was also blacks and Hungarians and Germans and people all over this world coming in and getting jobs, and he would get up here to get a job *(Lena Margaret Jones)*. But you see every year, every New Year, it was a white guy that used to bring people there from Alabama—Limehouse—and he would go to Alabama and anybody who wanted to come back had to pay a fare. And sometimes they didn't have no money but he would bring them anyway, and they would come to get a job and they would pay him because he came in every two weeks *(Jessie Willis)*. Yeah, Limehouse was an ole' funny looking hillbilly. I've seen him . . . he used to be up there every week in a big truck that had corn and stuff on it, but he had the blacks in the back . . . corn in the front, blacks in the back. And he used to go up there, and you used to see him sitting right up there in front of the big store. That's where he used to be sitting every payday. There were new guys coming out that he had brought up there, and he'd be sitting there and he would roll call and then they had to pay. He had a book, and I guess he'd show you [what you owed]. But that was the deal with Limehouse *(James Stevens)*.

Of all of my 153 oral history interviews, only two participants remembered being brought to Lynch as children by Limehouse:

I was born in Plantersville, Alabama. Then my father and my mother moved to Ensley, Alabama. It got so bad down there [pause] the company U.S. Steel hired a man they called Limehouse. He was bringing all the coal loaders up here to Lynch. And, that's how I got here. And I've been here ever since. . . . And the way I got up here I had to ride on the back end of a truck. Me and another boy. I don't know his name, I don't know where he went to, or what.

—William H. Morrow | Born in 1922 in Plantersville, Ala. |
    Resides in Lynch, Ky.

Well at that time at I didn't know anything about Limehouse. . . . My daddy left the farm and went to Birmingham, and then they [the police] tracked him to Birmingham and so he had to leave down there. And he got with Limehouse and they come up here—one of my uncles had got him a job here in the mine. So after a year or so, he contacted Limehouse, and Limehouse contacted us in Anniston, Alabama, to tell us that my dad had made arrangements to bring us up here. But he didn't come to Anniston to pick us up, to bring us up here. One of his stops for picking up people was in Birmingham on Eighteenth Street. So we went to Birmingham and stayed with my aunt for about a week. And one day he came by—I guess my mother knew him . . . and we left and came up here. . . . He would pick people up that wanted to get out of Alabama that worked for people on the farm, or owed people money, or was hiding from the law. And he had certain areas that he would go through at certain times and pick up people like that. But the car that we come up here in, he wan't [sic] bringing no men to work, he just had some women—wives of these men that he'd already brought and their kids. There were just some women and kids, there was three women—my mother, Miss Baskin, and another lady and her kid and, just some women and some kids though. . . . Well, we got here at night and I seen all these lights [and] I thought I was in a nice place [laughs]. But the next day I got up and didn't see nothing but mountains and said, oh lord, and I cried for about a week.

—Gean Austin | Born in 1930 in Munford, Ala. | Resides in Lynch, Ky.

· · · · · ·

While labor agents like Limehouse played a significant role in initiating the black migration into Harlan County, they were not the only way that black men discovered opportunity in the Kentucky coalfields. The proliferation of the railways throughout the United States was also a central protagonist in opening new pathways of mobility for southern blacks, as they established access to layover stops like eastern Kentucky and beyond. Many firstcomers worked for the railroads. Much like the Chinese rail workers of the U.S. Pacific in the nineteenth century,[34] this labor was largely conscripted. As Betty Parker Duff points out, "The Louisville and Nashville Railroad (L&N Railroad) brought in thousands of black laborers, many of them convicts, to build the railroads. But unlike the chain gangs of convicts who were forced into labor to build the railroads, black tenant farmers came to work the mines willingly."[35] Under the former condition, black labor was leased to rail corporations through convict leasing agreements, peonage arrangements between debtor and company, or through kidnap. One participant illuminates the threat of conscription for black men during that time in Alabama in reflecting on his memory of his father's migration story:

> The only thing he told me was about working on the roads and moving up. He moved up because he didn't want to work on no highway roads and he didn't want nobody whooping him and all that kind of stuff, so he decided that he could not take it. . . . He stayed in Kentucky until 1957 before he went back to Athens, Alabama. And the only reason he went back to Alabama was because his mom died, and he went down there to bury her.
>
> —Willie French | Born 1940 in Lynch, Ky. | Currently resides in Lexington, Ky.

Although documented in southern history scholarship, traces of the lived experience of this woeful episode of black labor history largely exists in African American music, art, plays, and family lore. Mississippian soul singer Sam Cooke archives this experience in the lyrics of his 1960 song *Chain Gang*, which reached No. 2 on the U.S. Billboard chart that year. In this song, Cooke sings:

All day long they work so hard
Till the sun is goin' down
Working on the highways and byways
And wearing, wearing a frown
You hear them moanin' their lives away
Then you hear somebody say

That's the sound of the men
Working on the chain ga-aaang
That's the sound of the men
Working on the chain gang

Can't you hear them sayin', mmm (Hoh! Ah!)
I'm going home one of these days
I'm going home, see my woman
Whom I love so dear
But meanwhile, I've got to work right here

These are the unsung sorrow songs that these men—the fathers who just wouldn't talk—kept suppressed deep down in their souls so that they and their children might, in fact, "dream a world."[36] Once they arrived in eastern Kentucky, whether by way of laying track, hoboing, or Limehouse, opportunities for paid labor were plentiful. As described earlier, coal companies entered Harlan County similar to the scenes in Perry Miller's *Errand into the Wilderness*.[37] Like the early New England settlers, the coal mining companies chartered the land to build towns, cities, governments, and a new culture. For those tens of thousands of poor and weary migrants, coal mining offered the opportunity to transform anew.

Coal mining companies historically practiced a recruiting strategy called "judicious mixture," designed to construct their workforce along ethnic and racial lines.[38] Under this policy, companies targeted a fixed percentage of "native" white, immigrant white, and black workers to live and work in the company-owned towns that were under their purview. The purpose of creating these artificial multiethnic communities was to thwart unionization efforts through ethnoracial differentiation. Each group came to the coal town with its own set of languages, cultures, motivations, and political conditions of exit, making it less likely for workers and families to effectively organize around similar issues. As Harry Caudill notes, the early coal towns resembled "turbulent Babels set in a wilderness."[39] In this way, these isolated coal towns, nestled in the Appalachian mountainscape, were quite cosmopolitan, similar to urban hubs in New York, Chicago, and Philadelphia at the time.

Recruitment was an international enterprise. Companies partnered with labor agents to recruit men to eastern Kentucky, sending some agents across the Atlantic to places like Yugoslavia, Hungary, and Italy with a promise of a better life as a coal miner in America, while others traveled a mere four hundred miles south, to Alabama, to convince the black men in the area of the same. These labor agents operated under the old "padrone system," an Italian term that translates into "boss" or "manager." A popular actor in the migration industry during the height of European immigration to the United States, the padrone was "a labor contractor who imported his country-men and provided them with jobs in America."[40] Padrones provided a dual service, both to industrial employers, as they were instrumental in helping labor-intensive companies meet their demand for workers, and to their fellow citizens, as they were instrumental in helping newcomers adjust to their lives in America. In most cases, the padrone shared similar lingual, national, and cultural backgrounds with his recruits and acted as a cultural resource and advocate for his people. In addition, Peck points out that "the padrone also exploited his intermediary position by charging fees to all immigrant workers for getting and keeping their industrial livelihoods."[41] Although the term was originally coined to describe labor recruitment from Italy to America, U.S. corporations relied heavily on labor agents of all ethnic backgrounds, including Japanese, Greek, Hungarian, and Polish.

This system is how the vast majority of African Americans got to Harlan County, Kentucky. In his analyses of the role of the labor agent in recruiting southern blacks to central Appalachia, historian Ronald Lewis states, "The labor agent received as much as ten dollars per recruit, and all able-bodied men were accepted." In fact, "many agents made arrangements with local jailers to empty the cells of those prisoners who agreed to migrate."[42] This was true for the men who came to work the mines in Benham and Lynch for International Harvester and U.S. Steel. However, unlike the traditional padrone relationship, which relied on kinship and a shared ethnoracial background, Limehouse—the labor agent who snuck the black men out of Alabama—was white.[43] This makes sense given the racial landscape in Alabama at the time, for a black man with access to transportation, money, and the authority to dole out promises and dreams to his countrymen would not last long in the Deep South.

There was no shortage of work for firstcomers, even before the mining operations began. In an early correspondence between the Benham mine superintendent and Wisconsin Steel president H. F. Perkins, Dunbar warned:

> The United States Coal & Coke people have about 450 men working on construction work and the L&N have about 50 men in here on construction work. . . . Mr. Billips, their engineer, informs me that they expect to build 1500 houses and expect to complete them at the rate of five per day. They hope to have the railroad track and temporary tipple in shape to begin to ship coal by January 1st. Due to the strike they are getting quite a lot of the native labor and are shipping

FIGURE 3 Photograph of a temporary shantytown at Lynch, Kentucky | circa 1917. The Southeast Appalachian Archives, Appalachian Archive Online Exhibit. U.S. Coal and Coke Company Collection.

carpenters in from all over the country. . . . They expect to begin construction of a large hotel pretty nearly opposite the large rock where the natives used to hold school.[44]

Figure 3 is a photograph of the temporary shanties built in Lynch to house the building crews and rail laborers during the period when the construction of the city was underway. U.S. Steel promised permanent housing to those who were willing to stay in Lynch once the mining operations opened up. Single men were offered company housing in boardinghouses, typically sectioned off by ethnicity, and men with families were given priority for single-family homes or duplexes. Figure 4 is an aerial image of the building site for the hospital and the sawmill, which were set to be built in the center of camp Number Four, in the heart of the city of Lynch. Both images were taken around 1917 and show just how undeveloped the land was when U.S. Steel and International Harvester came in to eastern Kentucky.

FIGURE 4 Photograph of sawmill #1 at the hospital site at Lynch, Kentucky |
circa 1917. The Southeast Appalachian Archives, Appalachian Archive Online
Exhibit. U.S. Coal and Coke Company Collection.

Labor, Then Race and Migration

Once the towns were built, they were ready to get to the business of operating high-capacity coal mining operations. Between 1910 and 1940, the
census years capturing the period from when mining operations began
in both towns through the peak of mining productivity in the region, the
population in Harlan County increased sevenfold, from a little over ten
thousand to well over seventy thousand inhabitants (see Table 1). The
black population in Harlan County exploded during that same period,
increasing from a recorded 564 black inhabitants in 1910 to 7,534 in 1940,
doubling the black population density from 5 to a little over 10 percent
within the short span of three decades. By 1930, Harlan County alone
employed a reported 12,741 coal miners, working throughout the county's fifty-seven operating mines. The county hosting the second largest

worker count reported 6,091 coal miners—less than half that reported in Harlan County.

The 1940 U.S. Census is telling with respect to race and migration in and through the central Appalachian region of eastern Kentucky. According to the Appalachian Regional Commission (ARC), there are fifty-three counties represented in Kentucky's Appalachia. With the exception of the handful of counties bordering the ARC line—that is, counties closer to urban centers within the state, such as Lexington and Louisville—few eastern Kentucky counties boasted a black population of more than 3 percent. Mapping on to popular conceptions of the region, Appalachia—or at least eastern Kentucky—was white. However, five of the eight counties with substantial mining activity were the same ones boasting a black population density exceeding that 3 percent. It is no surprise that Harlan County, the county with the lion's share of mine workers, was also the one that had the greatest black population density, at 10 percent.

The black "Bamas" choice to migrate to certain counties in eastern Kentucky was determined by labor. They migrated to Harlan County because they were recruited and because the coal mining industry in eastern Kentucky presented a labor market that was open to black workers. Without the latter condition, it would not have mattered whether or not jobs were plentiful, as "Whites Only" signs were not only reserved for bathrooms.

"Give Me Your Tired, Your Poor": And We Will Make Them Miners

This was the first stop. When men arrived from Ellis Island, by way of Yugoslavia, Italy, Hungary, Poland, or any of the other twenty-eight recorded countries from where the first wave of European immigrants originated, or from the southern plantations; iron, ore, and coal mines; or the cold dank cells of the county jails from where the black men traversed, their first stop on the road to becoming a miner in Benham or Lynch was a medical examination with the company physician. The doctor needed to confirm that their joints, lungs, and backs could endure the work that would eventually break those parts.

Without even having the chance to be fully indoctrinated into the American racial order, the assortment of soon-to-become white immigrants intuitively knew to cluster together, assuming the three available seats in the group examination room, with the rest clustering behind them, as can be seen in Figure 5.[45] In the same way, the black men self-segregated off

FIGURE 5 Photograph of employee physical examination at Benham, Kentucky | circa 1920. The Southeast Appalachian Archives, Appalachian Archive Online Exhibit. U.S. Coal and Coke Company Collection.

in the right-hand corner. This was not new or unusual for them; through a lifetime and more of subjugation through slavery and Jim Crow, they surely knew their place. Although all these migrants were likely coming from dire straits—leaving behind a homeland rife with various combinations of political, ethnic, religious, and economic strife—and seeking refuge and a better life for themselves and their progeny, this photograph shows traces of racial inequality, produced and reproduced on these men's bodies at this moment of becoming.

It is sartorial. Although their suits were ill cut and cheaply made, the white men could at least access a tailor or haberdashery and had access to the economic or social capital necessary to purchase or borrow one. This group of men came to the job interview dressed to impress, while the black men came wearing their overalls and jumpsuits—clothing that told the story of their accumulated history: *They are farmers. They are laborers. They are slaves.* Even if they could afford it, we cannot take for granted that there were stores that would sell blacks what might be considered luxury goods, such as suits or other fashionable wears—lest they be considered uppity

FIGURE 6 Photograph of employee physical examination at Lynch, Kentucky |
circa 1920. The Southeast Appalachian Archives, Appalachian Archive Online
Exhibit. U.S. Coal and Coke Company Collection.

Negroes. Under their conditions of exit, it may have been unwise to attract
attention to themselves on the eve of their departure, as many of these men
escaped in the middle of the night with Limehouse, fleeing peonage, bondage, and imprisonment.

Reading the preceding two photographs together allows us not only to
get a better sense of the historical context through which this generation
of miners entered the company-owned towns of Benham and Lynch but also
to peer into this particular process of subject formation through the company gaze. The photograph in Figure 6 was taken in 1920 in Lynch. These
images were taken for two different companies, in two different company-
owned towns, yet we see similar content and composition in each frame. In
both situations, men were brought to the medical examiner in groups. They
had no privacy as they were poked, prodded, ordered to remove their shirts,
made to publicly answer questions about their medical history, and deemed
fit (or not) to be assigned a position in the mines.

Racial markers exist in both photographs. With all the men in the second image shirtless, we can see how race is also embodied. Read their chests.

FIGURE 7 Coal loader in Mine Portal #31 at Lynch, Kentucky | circa 1930.
The Southeast Appalachian Archives, Appalachian Archive Online Exhibit.
U.S. Coal and Coke Company Collection.

Notice the definition of the black man's muscles, likely from years of toil sharecropping in the field, working from sunrise to sunset—or like my own grandfather would repeat over and again about the hardships he experienced during his childhood growing up in Alabama: "They worked you from cain't to cain't—cain't see when you start and cain't see when you get off." The black man in the photograph is an outlier in his choice of dress. The only one wearing jeans, his pants are at least three times his size, to the point where he has to roll the waistband over to make them fit around his torso.

For all these men, irrespective of race, this scene is a clearinghouse of bodies rather than a visit to the doctor's office. However, it is in this moment of receiving a clean bill of health from the company physician that black men transformed from peasants to proletarians; from convicts, peons, and conscripts to wage earners, to men who could send for their wives and provide for them and their children, black men who could vote and carry guns—they were truly New Negroes.[46]

· · · · · ·

Escaping the throes of the Deep South did not just present an opportunity for greater social and economic mobility for black migrants in the early decades of the twentieth century; it also inaugurated a transformation in their personhood. Reflecting on his observation of the influx of blacks to urban spaces during the early grumblings of the African American Great Migration, fin de siècle philosopher Alain Locke wrote,

> The migrant masses, shifting from countryside to city, hurdle several generations of experience at a leap, but more important, the same thing happens spiritually in the life-attitudes and self-expression of the Young Negro, in his poetry, his art, his education and his new outlook, with the additional advantage, of course, of the poise and greater certainty of knowing what it is all about.[47]

In his final comments in this short lyrical essay, Locke states firmly, "In the very process of being transplanted, the Negro is becoming *transformed*."

"Hey, Nigger! Where You Going?"

This first generation of black migrants came to the coalfields of eastern Kentucky not only in search of a new life but also for a new mode of being. In that four-hundred-mile journey from Alabama to Kentucky, they carried with them their hopes for a chance in life, for an opportunity to earn a decent wage in order to provide for their families, for the right to protect their children's lives from being disappeared through the physical and spiritual violence of racial terror. What they were reaching for were what W. E. B. Du Bois articulated in his 1897 essay as "our spiritual strivings."

Their decision to migrate to the coalfields did not come without sacrifice. Coal mining was and still is one of the most perilous occupations in the world. Although most men would escape the fate of death in a mining accident—albeit that mine collapses, explosions, and deadly methane gas leaks were everyday occupational hazards—none would escape the slow death of black lung. The black women who accompanied their husbands on this journey sacrificed their freedom by wedding themselves to a life as a coal miner's wife. With the exception of the role of schoolteacher, these single-industry coal towns offered no employment opportunities for women, and birth control was not available to them. Therefore, this generation of women were saddled with multiple children—some bore sixteen or seventeen babies—constrained with the doubly patriarchal structures of marriage and a company-owned town.

However, in exchange for their sacrifice, these adults hoped that they could offer their posterity a clean slate. In that migration, they attempted to break history: they did not want to pass on their particular legacies of racial slavery and social death to the next generation. Instead, this generation of migrants hoped that their children would experience the freedom, liberty, and equality that their own parents had hoped they would taste with emancipation. Although this generation did not get to experience it, the combined sensation of hope and disappointment was enough to fuel their quest in search of another world. Grasping for words capacious enough to express what this journey meant, one participant echoes Locke:

> And our black culture is not just the people from Alabama; most of them came from the South, but they came and started anew, so that's our connection—the rebirthing of a hope—you see what I'm saying? It's just like a cradle.
>
> —Teresa Austin-Mimes | Born in 1958 in Lynch, Ky. | Resides in Lynch, Ky.

· · · · · ·

This chapter dealt with the black migration into Harlan County during the first wave of the African American Great Migration, with the purpose of laying the "formation story" upon which this transformation in African American subjectivity emerged.[48] The remaining chapters center on the lived experiences of the second generation—the coal miners' sons and daughters—and their collective experience growing up as black Appalachians. Kentucky was not the Deep South, but it was still a Jim Crow border state. It was not quite rural yet by no means was it urban by the standards of a Chicago, Philadelphia, or New York. However, like all children, where they were was where it was at. For them, their black social world emerged in the mountains of Harlan County, Kentucky. Appalachia was home.

Our histories are inscribed in home, "recorded in the landscape";
our origin stories are in the land. It's a living, age-old family tree.

—Yi-Fu Tuan, *Topophilia*

The mountain has a way of defining who you are, your character.

—Jeff Turner | Born 1959 in Lynch, Ky. | Resides in
  Indianapolis, Ind.

3 Home

· ·

You know Lynch is a coal mining town. And from years ago there were people that lived in different areas; they named them camps. You would have Number One, Number Two, Number Three, Number Four, Number Five, Number Six, so forth and so on, and a place called Garbage Knob; that was a place back up on [the] hills of the mountain. *(Norman Thompson)*

At the height of Eastern Kentucky's coal production, during the interwar period, Lynch was the largest, most modern, and most densely populated company-owned coal town in all of central Appalachia.[1] Incorporated in 1917 by U.S. Steel Corporation, the city comprised seven coal "camps"— analogous to what would be referred to as neighborhoods in a present-day urban setting—and boasted a little over ten thousand inhabitants. The majority of black folks lived in Number One, Number Three, Number Five, or the small in-between zone referred to as "Garbage Knob." Each camp had its own flavor. The boys in Number One thought they were the toughest, the girls in Number Five were rumored to be the finest, and those in number Three thought they were the coolest, because their section was home to the movie theater and the black boardinghouse. Also, like most historical urban industrial neighborhoods, their ethnoracial compositions varied over time. The camp with the highest concentration of black people was Number One, the community located on the westernmost edge of the city. It is here where the redbrick Lynch Colored Public School stood tall for all the city's black children to attend, from first through twelfth grades, and where the residential streets were laid into the side of the mountain like railroad tracks—from Main Street, which sat flat at the bottom of the hollow, to First Street, Second Street, all the way up the side of the mountain to Sixth Street. While Main Street was strictly reserved for "whites only," only a few white families lived on First and Second Streets in the early days. In Number One, the higher up the mountain, the blacker the neighborhood. Number Three and Number Five were more diverse in that they were composed of various ethnic enclaves established to accommodate the needs of

U.S. Steel's deluge of European immigrants. While no camp was exclusive to any group, the company made sure to set aside social, religious, and sometimes residential areas to foster some sense of ethnic identification. These included Greek Orthodox, Catholic, African Methodist Episcopalian, Southern Baptist (one black, one white), and Pentecostal churches; ethnically oriented social clubs, in which the miners could drink and gamble; and, of course, the boardinghouses.

"The blacks had what we called the boardinghouse that was for single men that worked in the mines. Now where the whites lived, in their boardinghouse, we called it the 'hunkey stand.' . . . Maybe we didn't know exactly at that point when we were younger, but they were Hungarians" *(Humes Perry)*. These boardinghouses mainly served as temporary housing for newcomers, primarily single men who had been recruited by a labor agent—whether it be Limehouse or a padrone who shared their same homeland—to come and work in the mines for U.S. Steel. These newcomers would live in the boardinghouses until they established themselves, which meant paying off their recruitment fee, sending for their wives and children (or finding a new wife), and receiving an assignment for one of the most coveted commodities in a coal town: a company-owned home.

Benham too was a company-owned town with its own stock of company homes. However, International Harvester took a more straightforward approach to the allocation of homes along ethnoracial lines. In Benham, there was a white camp and a black camp, and they were separated by a bridge. White Benham boasted street after street of sturdy homes. Ensconced there were also the white elementary and high schools, the post office, the company store, and the white YMCA. East of the bridge was black Benham, where every black family lived. Black Benham was subjected to the environmental racism that face so many black and brown communities today,[2] as International Harvester saw fit to designate all operations related to industry and labor, including waste, to the neighborhoods black folks called home. Born in Benham in 1941, the Reverend Edgar James Moss remembers that "the coal mines were in the black community, the coal trucks were in the black community, the coal car repair shop was in the black community—we call that Smoky Road—where all of the dust and the dirt and whatever would all filter out, and blow out into the community."

Like U.S. Steel, International Harvester established a segregated schooling system for the black and white miners' children to attend. While each company adopted its own approaches to regulating how benefits and privileges were to be allocated along racial lines, they both followed the law of the land: Kentucky was a Jim Crow state. The main statute to which both companies adhered was the legal segregation of schools. Cumberland, on the other hand, was an independent city. Thus, there was no company to mediate race relations or to provide the amenities that come along with a company-owned town. In many cases, miners and their families would settle in Cumberland because the company-housing stock in Benham and Lynch was filled to capacity. In addition to residential property, Cumberland served as the commercial business district for Benham and Lynch. Anything one could not get at the company store in Benham or Lynch could be found in Cumberland. Because of its independent status, racial tensions in Cumberland were not mediated by the mining industry, making it a far more precarious place for people of African descent to live and thrive.

Whereas chapter 4 attends to the awakening of the next generation's racial consciousness—how they came to understand themselves as *black children*—the remainder of this chapter offers an invitation to enter this generation of coal miners' children's black social world of pre–civil rights era central Appalachia, from the perspective of their childhood. The string of quotations laced throughout the chapter illuminates the structure of memory that emerged from more than 150 individual oral history interviews that I conducted with African Americans who were born and reared in the coal towns of eastern Kentucky.[3] The point of the long, multivocal soliloquies that follow is to bring you into the world in which these people's selves emerged, so we may know the social types that constituted the black community: "the black father," "the black mother," "the black child," and "the village." In this way, they attend to the universal, as opposed to the particulars, of individual families. They also situate the participants of this research as "protagonists of their own histories,"[4] a distinguishing virtue of oral history methodology. Selected themes and accompanying quotes reflect those aspects of childhood that were most common for the participants. There is no better way to peer into the interiority of what it meant to be black *and* Appalachian during the pre–civil rights era than through the subjective reflections of those who experienced it.

This form of presentation is quite unusual, and it requires a different type of work from you, dear reader—work that I can only characterize as a certain level of intimacy, vulnerability, and collective responsibility to engage with them through their stories. In the sections that follow, you will get to know these people—the inner workings of their spirit, their pain and their humor, as well as their strivings. The origin stories presented here root this text in the souls of these Appalachian black folk.

Let's go home.

· · · · · ·

Well, I remember the freedom of it. I remember the mountains, friends and families and mothers and fathers. Everybody's father was a coal miner; everybody's mother stayed home unless she was a nurse or a teacher. I remember snowy days, having snow rides on 2nd Street, stealing tires from the white people's yard to make us a fire. I remember going to the Pool Room to warm up when it snowed *(Cynthia Brown-Harrington)*. I can remember playing marbles, running around in an open area free with friends, just group games: spring-board, jump board, riding a bicycle that I can't remember anybody else having in the neighborhood; my little 3-speed bicycle up and down Liberty Street *(Jeffrey Ratchford)*.

There were a lot of children in the community, yes. And we didn't have a lot of toys, we played a lot of, you may call them homemade games. . . . What we would do after dark is we would catch lightning bugs; they would light up and we'd catch them and put them in a jar, and we also used to break them in half and put them on ears and we had earrings. We'd put them on our fingers for jewelry. Can you believe I broke a bug in half and put them on my ears?! There was also a bug called a June Bug, and we'd catch the June Bug and tie a string around his leg and we'd hold on to the string, a long string, and this June Bug would fly around and we'd run around behind him until finally he would fly away from us and all we'd have is the string, and a hip. That was cruel, but it was fun *(Clara Smith)*.

Well, growing up when I was a little guy, there were tons of kids, and one of the things that we loved to do as little boys, we always played cowboys and Indians. We used to climb a lot of trees; we had broomsticks, and we made like they were our horses, and we would run up and down the street with the broomsticks like they were our horses. We would get a stick and break it off and that was our gun; it's like we were shooting, but that was the biggest thing that we did. And typical of boys we liked to play sports; we would ride our sleds, play softball, football, basketball, stuff like that *(William Jackson)*. Right and see, I will never forget. . . . My dad brought a big old board home—it was like ten feet long, might be a foot wide, about two or three inches thick. And we would get a railroad tire, and we would play spring-board in the backyard. And my sister Ethel, I mean she could send you to the moon! She could absolutely just about send you to the moon, and we would play on that till from the time we got our homework done until it was time to come in the house *(George Massey)*.

· · · · · ·

Wild fruit was all over the place; just walk out of your backyard right up on the hill there, and there they were. They were all in different places, and when you go blackberry picking in the morning, you would see a lot of your buddies, "Hey, I'll see you later man!"; everybody would go different ways. We would have sacks if we were going to do apples, or we would have these big buckets if we were going to pick the blackberries; and that is how we did it. Same thing with hunting; my dad taught us and brought me into hunting with a little .22 rifle, and we used to kill squirrels and groundhogs. And take them home, skin them, cook them up; rabbits, the whole thing, and fishing; we would do a lot of fishing *(William Jackson)*. On one mountain there was a wild apple orchard, and we would take a cloth of sack up on the mountain and fill it with apples and roll it down. We would also walk along the railroad tracks and pick wild strawberries and those kinds of things; we would bring them home, or mother would can them. We also had hogs up on the mountain; I never saw them because the girls wouldn't go up there; my brothers had to feed them *(Harriet Callaway-Hill)*. Well at that time, growing up in Lynch, my dad would come home from work and he would make us go up on the hill. So many men—they would pick them out a spot on the side of the mountain, and we would dig it up and make a garden. Yeah, I hated that, and then we would step in and clear out all the weeds and had to dig it all up by hand. And some people used mules. But we didn't have a mule. We were the mules! *(George Massey)*. Daddy didn't hire anyone to come in and plough that garden. We had to do that garden ourselves.... You might say it was a good 35, 40 yards— yeah, somewhere in the neighborhood—long and about 30 yards wide. And we would plant the vegetables; we would plant collard greens, tomatoes, onions, potatoes—Irish potatoes—okra, hot peppers, all those different things. Oh, we also had large chicken yards in the backyard.... We'd have meat everyday. Because the hogs that we would kill, we'd start eating off of those pretty regular 'cause we would kill them in November; it's always the week before Thanksgiving, that's when the average family would kill the hogs *(Odell Moss)*. And so in the fall, my father would bring two hogs down. They had a big iron pot. They would make a fire and put this pot over the fire and boil the water, and I believe those hogs knew that it was "slaughtering" time because they went "oink, oink, oink" all around the yard there. And so they'd wait until we went to school, and my dad and maybe four or five other men in the community, they'd stand around smoking their cigars and whatever; after we'd left and gone to school, they would shoot the hogs right in the middle of the forehead . . . right between the eyes. And they slit them open and they'd hang them up so that the blood would drain down, and put them in a big tub of—a big iron pot—and they would, you know . . . pull the hair off. But I would be in school and I wouldn't know anything about it, so when I would come home from school my mother and maybe four or five ladies in the neighborhood, they would be there at the kitchen table cutting up all that fresh meat, and it was red and fresh and smelling like blood, and that was the time of the year I hated *(Clara Smith)*.

· · · · · ·

It's very hard sometimes to really get to know a coal mining father. When I was growing up, I knew more about my mother than I did with my father. My father because he worked on a night shift, he would be sleeping most of the day. So if you ask me about my father, I think of him as "be quiet" or "don't you all have something to do like go outside and play?" I think that's because my father was more intent on getting his work and tried to keep his family together more so than he was on entertaining his kids *(Brenda Thornton)*. No, he was not really an affectionate man. I mean, you can see that he loves and cares about you, but he was not really affectionate *(Richard Chapman)*. He was a quiet man *(Vera Garner Robinson)*. Yeah, and he didn't do too much talking *(Mullins Siblings)*. And see my daddy, he was not a talker or anything like that; but if you watched him, you learned a lot. Now, that took me until my later teenage years to figure out *(Leslie Lee)*. Well, the problem was my father was very . . . he would keep a lot of stuff to himself. He wouldn't tell you a whole lot unless he was drinking *(Richard Brown)*. He was just a hardworking man; he worked *(Arthur Hauser)*. Quiet, he was there and I knew he was there, but he worked a lot *(Terry Mason)*. Very quiet man, very very quiet. My daddy got up, he went to work, he came home, he'd watch a little television, he'd go to sleep, and he'd get up and go to work and that was kind of his routine *(Porter G. Peeples)*.

And one thing I do remember was that on the weekends Daddy used to drink. Mother used to have to go get him his nip—anytime she'd go to Cumberland she would have to bring him back his bottle of whatever he was drinking *(Wanda Davis)*. Daddy was a hard drinker, drinking that moonshine. . . . Starting Friday night, boy look out! They're going to come out there and drink up half a gallon of moonshine. And Saturday they would do the same thing. But come Sunday night at about ten thirty, they'd go to bed because they're going to be up in the morning at five on that job. And they did that every single weekend *(Willie French)*.

I can't remember my daddy spanking me but once. And that's because I sassed him and knew I was going it get it because I had pushed the limits. And what happened was that when I would get a spanking, I would run. So he knew I was a runner, so he locked the screen door and he was chasing me around the house, and I was getting ready to exit through the door and I hit the screen door and bounced back and broke my tooth off. I blamed him for that! *(Virginia Taylor-Ward)*. He hit me one time in my life. And I cried for days because he had never put his hands on me; he had never spanked me in all my life *(Vera Garner Robinson)*.

Mama would always pack an extra sandwich in Daddy's lunch bucket. And it was such a treat for him to come back from work and get that sandwich. And it'd be smelling like the mines—you know, be all musky smelling. I doubt if I would eat one now, but boy that was the biggest thing in the world *(Leslie Lee)*. I just remember my dad going to work before I got up in the morning, coming home late at night and falling asleep on the bed with his clothes on. I also remember coming home from school and we would be sitting on the porch waiting for Daddy to come home . . . and he would walk down the street and we would go meet him and we would get his lunch bucket for us—a piece of cake, whatever it was, he always left something in it because he knew we wanted it *(William Jackson)*. And every day when he got out from work I could see him walking up the road, and I would run down the road . . . and every day he gave me his lunch bucket and he had a boiled egg and snowball cake *(Belinda Napier)*. He would never bring his bucket home empty. And he always had something for us to have, and we thought it tasted so good—because it was coming out of his bucket. I mean, that was the mind of a child and the love of a parent *(Lena Margaret Jones)*.

· · · · · ·

Sit around? No way. They could not sit around. I have never seen Daddy sit around in a pair of pajamas—he got up, he put his clothes on, and if he was not going to work, he was going to his garden *(Arnita Davis-Brown)*. Oh gosh, I can just remember waking up Saturday morning and seeing all those older men in their gardens *(Katina Akal)*. Gardens. I mean we just had yards and yards of gardens. . . . Wherever you see a spot that's clear and you want to make a garden, you just make a garden *(Ernest Pettygrue)*. Oh, a huge garden. My father raised all kinds of vegetables; corn, cucumbers, tomatoes, squash— he was pretty green thumbed . . . but he had us out there helping him work it *(Raven Whitt)*. They believed in their gardens at the time. And you had to

FIGURE 8 U.S. Steel miner tending to his backyard garden at Lynch, Kentucky | circa 1968. Michael Davis Papers, EKAAMP Collection, Southern Historical Collection, Louis Round Wilson Special Collections Library, University of North Carolina at Chapel Hill.

work their garden *(Chuck Rodgers)*. And the sons always went to the garden with Daddy. After school Thornton, Michael, and Kenneth would go up in the garden and help Daddy with whatever needed to be done in the garden *(Arnita Davis-Brown)*. And that's why Thornton doesn't have a garden 'til this day—Daddy wore him out! *(Patricia Davis Liggins)*.

Because our parents used to—there was a phrase that I daresay . . . you are going to hear from lots of us. Our parents did not want us to have to do what they did, which was, in the case of our fathers, working in the coal mines. So they would say to us, Get your education, and that's what your job is; because I want you to have the opportunities that I didn't have *(Jerome Ratchford)*. I wanted to go into the mine. Daddy would not let me. Oh, we had our biggest arguments about that *(Leslie Lee)*. Daddy told me when I was young, he didn't want us working in the coal mine. Because I told him, when I graduate, I'm going in the coal mine. He was like, Uh-uh, no *(Katina Akal)*. We never talked about what coal mining was like for him but he always—he and Mama—always pushed us to get an education. And one afternoon Daddy and I was walking back home from the store and I said to Daddy—"Daddy, once I get sixteen years old I'm going to quit school" . . . and he said, "Well, son, the day you quit school you better have yourself a job." I said, "But, Daddy, I am your son!" He said—"That's why." *(Edgar James Moss)*. No, he never talked about it. He preferred you to grow up and get an education *(Geraldine Brown-Kirkland)*. They'd always say "Get all the education you can get." That's what Daddy would say. No, my dad told me to get as far away from this mine as possible—he would tell us that "I want the best for you. I don't want to see you have to go up under this earth every day not knowing whether you are going to come out or not" *(Jack French)*.

My father didn't say many words. But when he did, it's like you'd have to hear him. You had to listen because when he spoke, he meant what he spoke and there was no beating around the bush. He was very stern, I would say *(Mike Mason)*. He didn't whip us. If he tried to whip us he would be tickling us and he would say, "Here, Naomi, you do it" *(Mullins siblings)*. She would almost have to make him whoop us. It was not an "I want to whoop you" but a "your mama said you did this and you are going to get this whooping" *(Raven Whitt)*. Dad really didn't—he really didn't say a lot. Mama did all the discipline and did all the talking, and Daddy just sat back and watched, and he really didn't say a lot. And now and then if Mama could not handle the situation, Daddy might step in, but that was very, very rare because Mama was the disciplinarian and she didn't take no stuff. She didn't care how small you are or how big you are, she put it on you. And so you got to know that Mama was in control *(Lee Arthur Jackson)*.

· · · · · ·

She was more of a homemaker. She didn't work outside the home. Very disciplinarian; made sure you do what you had to do. If you didn't, that little lady would wear you out. And if you thought you was getting away, she wouldn't chase you or nothing. She'd just say, "You got to come to eat, you got to go to bed, you have to do something in this house; I'll get you then." And you think she done forgot about it *(Chuck Rodgers)*. Now, Miss Marie was the disciplinarian. I mean she was everything to the family because my dad worked all the time, but Miss Marie was about maybe five foot two inches tall and maybe a hundred pounds. But she demanded a lot of respect, and she got a lot of respect. Now my brothers, all of us pretty good-sized guys, that is when we were teenagers and stuff, we thought we were big tough guys, but she would break us down. And my mother, and probably a lot of other mothers, would use whatever was close, whatever she could grab; the poke iron, the broom

FIGURE 9 Mothers sitting at the kitchen table at Lynch, Kentucky | 1967.
Karida Brown personal photograph.

handle, the pot on the table, it didn't matter, whatever—she would hit you with it. She would throw her shoe at you, and that was life, that was the way it was *(William Jackson)*. Now my mom whooped on a daily basis. Daddy didn't have to whoop but every now and then—but you didn't want my mom when it came to the whooping *(Roy Stevens)*. Her name was Dorothy Chapman, and she was a very disciplined person. You had to listen to what she said, and if you didn't listen to what she said, you would end up getting the consequences that she gave you. For instance, we were sitting in the living room watching TV and she was eating, and she told me to do something and I kept on ignoring her, and the next thing I knew she threw that fork at me. They were not going to kill you, or nothing like that, but you better listen. And the thing about it is that you had to respect them, and you did what they said because they meant what they said *(Richard Chapman)*.

[She was a] stay-at-home mom. She didn't really have a job or anything, just taking care of us *(Debra Oden-Williams)*. She was the one that was home with us while my daddy was working, so my mom didn't work *(Jacquelyn Ratchford)*. But I remember distinctly how it was the mother who would run the money in our house. My father never had no damn money—Miss Punkin ran the show in our house when it came to money! My daddy would always say, "I make the money and the old lady, she pays the bills." And my mother would say, "Earl is my mule, he in the barn, he is my worker." My parents had eight children, so my mother never worked a day in her life; she never held a job (*Jeff Turner*). She raised a bunch of children, and there were twelve of us. She said it was more than that but this is the twelve that I know you know. I am sure she had probably had some miscarriages or something like that, you know. . . . She said she had seventeen, but I can only call off names up to ten (*Lacey Griffey*). I don't know how she did it, but she raised ten children plus my nephew. And I think my mother was ahead of her time because they are trying to tell us what we are supposed to eat now, but my mother cooked from scratch; there were no preservatives, [and] we did not eat fast food (*Patricia Davis Liggins*). Sweet lady, funny, cursing. Just a sweet woman. And nobody that met her knew that she cursed a lot. But fourteen kids would make you curse, I don't care who you are! And I remember she used to get up in the morning, my father would get up first and he would start the fire and put on a cup of coffee. Then my mom would get up and she would immediately start cooking; yelling, "You all better get your asses up!" And nobody would move. And then she would be down there cooking all that food. And she would cook about two hundred biscuits in the morning. I'm telling you! And had to cook five chickens. You could feed a hotel when fourteen people are coming to eat. And my sisters ate just as much as my brothers. And it was just like feeding a hotel. Every day we were scrambling for food and then we would be all out of pans and the plates would get broken—and we could not all sit at the table (*Richard Brown*).

My mother would probably start cooking early in the morning before the sun came up. . . . She would get up early and my father would go to work, and she would stay up and begin her chores, which we would get up and help her [with] until we got ready to go to school, which probably started at six o'clock in the morning, so we walked to school by seven; we then carried in buckets of water to go wash our clothes (*Raven Whitt*). She'd make up rolls. Boy, and I'd be so mad because she'd be sending me all over town giving folks rolls. And Lord knows I love me some rolls! I didn't want to give up no roll (*Leslie Lee*).

Just a good ole homemaking hard lady. She was something. She was a very religious woman, just the opposite of my dad. My dad was no religious man at all—well, I shouldn't say it that way; he would be there on Sunday morning after a night of drinking his booze and doing his thing—but she was just a real Christian lady that kept us all in line (*Willie French*).

· · · · · ·

This was the village. And a lot of times if you got in trouble and they saw you in trouble they'll spank you and send you home and tell your parents; and then you'll get another one *(Chuck Rodgers)*. I heard a term a few years ago about "it takes a village to raise a child"; well, that village, that is all I have ever known my whole life. Everybody in that town, it was like their child, and they were like your parents. And I still can't understand how the word got around: I could do something at the ball park and my mother knew about it before I got home; I mean, I'm like, "How did she know?" The word passed but people were just so kind. . . . We knew everybody, we knew everything, and we knew our limits. And we were good kids, we were malleable, we didn't talk back; our parents told us to do something one time, and that was it; that is how we were raised *(William Jackson)*. Well, I think it was a fun time. It's a time really you would like to go back to. Growing up, everybody was like family. . . . It was big families everywhere. The Brown family seemed to [have] had fifteen, my family had about fifteen, the Pettygrue family had about fifteen, so it was children "coming out the woodworks," as my mother would call it, you know. And so it was a fun time, it really was; some people look at it [as] "Oh, coal mining camp"; yes, it was a coal mining camp, but it was a loving camp and everybody shared *(Arletta Andrews)*. Oh gosh, everybody was your parent. I mean everybody could tell you what to do, when to do it, and when not to do it, you know, and if you did something wrong, they could actually spank you and oh gosh, you were really in trouble when you got back home. If you walked around the street a hundred times you had to say "hello" to everybody sitting on their porch, in their yard, a hundred times. Even to this day, you still have to do that. Everybody knew everybody, and everybody watched out for everybody *(Brenda Clark Combs)*. If another adult saw you doing something wrong, they would stop you from doing it. And they would tell you "Come here, I don't want to see you doing that no more," and if it is bad enough they would spank your behind, call your parents and tell what you did. And then you would get home and get another spanking. Do you hear what I'm saying? . . . And then if you went home and said, "Oh, I didn't do that"—oh, then that so-and-so is lying? Oh, no, I'm not. . . . I don't care if she was lying or if she was not lying *(Lena Jones)*. Oh, you're calling the grown up a lie [*sic*]?! Oh, you wouldn't dare. Even if you knew that teacher was wrong or any adult was wrong you could not—you're calling them a lie [*sic*]?! You didn't—oh, you could not say that, oh, no. If you thought that, you didn't go through that, oh no. You're calling another adult a lie [*sic*]?! Oh, no, that wouldn't fly. They were the adult, they were the authority, and your parents fully believed that they had your best interest at heart. And like one of the phrases my grandmother would say, if she'd tell you something and you question it. . . . Her phrase is "You're 'sputing my word? You're 'sputing my word?" In other words, "Are you questioning me?" *(Albert Harris).* Oh no, no, that was just a no-no, you didn't use any curse words to my dad or to any adult. Oh, that was a curse word. You could not say "lie." You had to say, "She told a story on me." You could not tell your sisters and brothers, that's just a "lie." You had to say, "You're telling a story on me, I didn't do that, he's just telling a story." You had to say a "story." You cannot say "lie." You could not say anything like that *(Clara Smith).*

· · · · · ·

This was their home, a community where race fully determined group membership, ordered by the inculcation of rigid gender, age, and class roles, and maintained through a hermetically sealed code of social closure; this was what Du Bois called their "black social world."[5] Populated by hardworking, moonshining, silent-yet-stern daddies; nurturing, take-no-mess disciplinarian mamas; and free-flowing yet obedient children of the land, within the confines of this lifeworld, everyone knew their place. Mothers, fathers, and children; blacks and whites; miners and bosses—they all had a role to play in the company-owned towns in Benham and Lynch, and also in the neighboring unowned city of Cumberland. In this particular context, two structures conditioned this generation's subjectivity: the patriarchal structure of the company-owned town and their blackness.

They Owned Everything . . .

There is no privacy in a coal town. Families with five, eight, and up to seventeen children were placed in five-room company-owned homes. These were often duplex homes built to fit two families, rivaling in size, each on the other side of a thin sheet of drywall. Typical homes consisted of one kitchen, one living room, and three bedrooms—girls on one side, boys on the other, mother and father downstairs. The bathrooms were located in the backyard, in the outhouse. However, there was always a slop jar sitting in the corner of each bedroom, just in case it was too cold, too dark, or too urgent to make it outside to go. Children everywhere, paper-thin walls, and shared everything, there could be no privacy within the home. Outside was no different.

The coal camp was a place where everybody knew everybody, and where everybody watched. Neighbors watched as the miners went to and from their shifts, as children played in the ballpark and wandered into the wilderness of the mountainscape, and as mothers sat on the porch resting their weary feet before returning inside the house to prepare the next meal. Watching more so than anyone, however, was the company.

The company-owned town was a socially engineered space, and no facet of private or social life was beyond its purview. As Jerome Ratchford recalls, "They owned every thing":

> For example, you could not live in housing without abiding with the standards that United States Steel established. And if by chance a husband was deceased, that lady could no longer live in those houses. . . . They owned the houses, they owned the mineral rights under the houses, they owned the commercial outlets. And the same thing was also true of Benham, [though] it was International Harvester, which was also a major top five hundred company at the time.
>
> —Jerome Ratchford | Born 1940 in Lynch, Ky. | Resides in Atlanta, Ga.

Not only did the companies own everything, but they appointed the clergy, hired the teachers, and even deputized their own police force to handle matters of social life within the confines of the coal town. They surveilled everything, from community members' actions and bodies to their ideas, notions, and discourse. Further, any person deemed a troublemaker could be expelled from the town without warning, along with their entire family. In the company-owned town, political mobilization was intolerable, as it would threaten to destabilize the workforce. This included the social movement of labor unions, such as the United Mine Workers of America, as well as terrorist organizations, such as the Ku Klux Klan. In the company-owned coal town, there was little separation between the private, the public, and the industrial. Coal was the raison d'être.

This totalitarian industrial complex led to the formation of a distinct identity as the child of a coal miner. To this day, in their golden years, participants proudly sport T-shirts and hats with "My daddy was a coal miner" boldly imprinted on the front. It is also not unusual for them to have a lump of coal somewhere in their home, as a tell-all symbol of who they are and where they came from. The coal mining father therefore presents an ideal site from which to illuminate the extent to which coal and industry permeated the very being of everyone who lived in the company-owned town.

My Daddy Was a Coal Miner

The coal mining father embodied labor. When he was away from home but not working in the mines, he was on the side of the mountain working in his garden or out in the streets from Friday night to Sunday morning, working on a bottle of moonshine, only to come home in the midnight hour to work his wife's nerves by "raising hell." When he was home during the week, he was resting, because he was tired from work. Work was the entrée through which children came to relate to their fathers.

As a young girl, Clara Smith accompanied her mother on a walk to the Big Store in Lynch. Along the way, her mother took up a conversation with an eerie man. Shy and obedient, Clara dared not interject into a conversation between adults; however, her silence did not preclude her curiosity: "I was looking up at this man and I was wondering, 'Who is this man my mother's talking to?' . . . He was pitch black from head to toe. All you could see was his eyes." Perplexed, her body language gave her away:

> I guess he saw me staring at him. And he looked down at me and my mother looked at me and she said, "Clara, do you know who that is?" and I said, "No"; [then] she said, "That's your daddy." I looked at him and I said to him, "Daddy, that's you?!" And then my hand was black, and my mother had to get some Kleenex and scrub my hand because I could not believe that was him. That's just how dirty they were when they came out of the mines. You could not see anything on him that would make me know that that was father.

> —Clara Smith | Born 1942 in Cumberland, Ky. | Resides in Southfield, Mich.

So much were those men *in* and *of* the earth while digging that coal that they emerged from the mines unrecognizable to their family and friends. After work, the miners went straight to the bathhouse to wash away any reminder of their labor so that they could enter their households simply as fathers and husbands. However, the sight of an unwashed miner was stunning.

> Some of the miners would come home with those dirty clothes, but my daddy changed at the bathhouse . . . but I never saw him in his mining clothes *(Ernest Pettygrue)*. They had a bathhouse, and we'd go there sometimes . . . and they'd be in there and they'd be so black; you could not tell a white man from a black man *(Arthur Hauser)*. But I remember being up near where they came out of the mine. And you would see the guys coming out, and going to the shower.

It's at Number Two or Number Three up to that part; they would come out of the mines *(Mullins siblings)*.

Even for those who never witnessed their fathers faces dipped in black coal dust, industry pervaded every facet of their lives. It was in them. Children made homemade toys out of old mining straps and railcar tires, two-by-fours, and even industrial waste.

We used to play what was known as the slate dump and from what I gather, the slate is something that comes off of the coal and they usually dump it in the wayside. And if you can imagine one—maybe, gosh, ten or twenty stories high—and we would take garbage can tops, and they were aluminum, and the slate material was very slick *(Dwayne Baskin)*.

With aluminum garbage can lids under their feet, they surfed down the sludge and waste on an imagined tidal wave of fun. The company whistle blew three times a day with a screech that alerted the entire city to the inauguration of each shift; freight cars brimming with blocks of coal chugged through the heart of town on the L&N Railroad to their final destination at the steel mills in Gary, Indiana, or Chicago, Illinois; and a gray mist of coal dust constantly floated in the air. In this way, all their senses were animated by the workings of the mining industry; the company-owned town shaped their lives and identities as coal miners' kids.

Children were also hyperaware of the possibility that a mining accident could befall their fathers any day. Their fathers' generation was that of manual extraction, which entailed coal loading, dynamiting, and pick-and-shovel digging. Mine safety procedures were not yet an industry standard, and a human life was still considered cheap and easily replaceable to employers at the time.

Well, Daddy was in the mines in the late twenties and thirties. And at that time, what they would do . . . every man would have their own little tunnel; and what you would do, you had the little pick and shovels that were short and had a long handle on it. And you dig the coal and rake it back behind you; and as you went in, you would pin the ceiling so it didn't fall in on you. And what would happen is that they would weigh out your coal, and you get paid accordingly.

—Leslie Lee | Born 1948 in Lynch, Ky. | Resides in Harlan, Ky.

The possibility of a mine collapsing and killing one or all of their fathers was real, and as children, the unspoken understanding that their family could be the next one to get "the call" is the tie that binds all mining families. Memories of the ambulance sirens, broken and dismembered parts, and gurneys and hearses were just as everyday as the sound of the red robins chirping and the sight of the blackberry and apple orchards blossoming.

When you'd hear the ambulance going down the street, you never knew whose father was in that ambulance. And sometimes it was my father, like there were several times he got his leg broken in the mines (*Arthur Hauser*). The danger came when they had cave-ins; because that's what happened to my grandfather (*Betty Williams*). And that's where my grandfather got killed in the coal mines. A rock or something fell on him and killed him in West Virginia (*Roland Motley*). My father's cousin—Theodore Jones was his name— he got his hand cut off in the mines. And I remember going to the house he lived in and Dad, he took the hand and wrapped it up in some newspaper. He took it to the church, at Mount Sinai church, and put the hand in the furnace.... And I would say that it was dangerous, but they didn't talk about it (*Mullins siblings*).

They were also at the center of some of the most violent labor wars in American history. Harlan County was the last battleground in the central Appalachian region in the fight for unionization through the United Mine Workers of America (UMWA).[6] Conversations about the ongoing labor wars and UMWA president John L. Lewis were a constant in every miner's household. Further, dozens of individual laborers, both black and white, were casualties of this infamous labor war:

Oh, yes, I remember vividly about United Mine Workers of America. He loved John L. Lewis; he loved the union. Daddy said it used to be so dark in the mines and the rats would be big as dogs. And they'd be crawling into that mine and they'd be below all day long (*Arnita Davis-Brown*). It was not nowhere as good until John L. Lewis came in. Then they had to pay you, they had to write you a check and you could go to the bank and get your cash and all that.... Don't get me wrong, it was a good living for our fathers, but they had to spend it all here (*Bennie Massey*). One of the reasons why they started calling us "Bloody Harlan" was because people would get killed over there. It doesn't seem real, but it happened (*Raven Whitt*). In the '50s they had a strike in the coalmines, and I had heard about the strikes and all that, but this was right in our neighborhood. Somebody blew a car up (*Betty Williams*). They had a strike one day and we had to get under the bed because the union and the coal miners were shooting each other. They were shooting across the mountain, people over here were shooting, people over there shooting—one of my aunt's boyfriends got shot; he was a coal miner *(Robert Pollenitz)*.

• • • • • •

The hyper-surveilled company-owned town was a double-edged sword. On one hand, miners provided their families with guaranteed housing, food, and protection from external economic shocks. Even in situations in which there was not enough money to cover the household expenses, miners and their families could use credit at the company store.

> It was company-owned, so U.S. Steel owned the mines and everything. So U.S. Steel saw that we had food, clothing; our parents had to pay them back when things got better but we never went hungry *(William Schaffer Jr.)*.

In fact, up until the mid-1950s, International Harvester and U.S. Steel paid their workers in company scrip instead of U.S. currency. A mechanism to keep laborers tethered to their jobs, the scrip system lent a false sense of security.

> We had a good life because we had the company store and we had scrip. And it was just a beautiful upbringing because it was kind of a Utopia during World War II because coal was King; it was our main source of energy. So we had it made pretty well *(Ike Gardner)*.

However, scrip and other measures of control functioned to create a paternalistic relationship between the company and its laborers in hopes that the laboring class would gradually forfeit their own sense of agency and come to view the company as omnipresent and in control of their destinies. In his analysis of paternalistic capitalism in Harlan County, Kentucky, oral historian Alessandro Portelli observed, "The subordinate subjects of a paternalistic relationship have no rights, but they may receive gifts—the replacement of the right to a safe mine with the gift of a sack of flour."[7] The concept of giving was inextricably linked to that of ownership in that no one *owned* the material conditions of their livelihood; instead, the company *gave* it to them. In most cases, awareness of the extent to which the seemingly benevolent company controlled their lives arose only when there was a direct experience with disruption, such as a death or other dislocation. Only through these moments of discontinuity did participants become aware of how disposable they were to King Coal, for just as the company giveth, the company taketh away.

While these coal camp blacks were in many ways removed from the racial landscape of overt domination and terror that articulated their parents' subjectivity, at this time they were still not quite "African American" in the sense of their right to make claims to full citizenship in the eyes of the law or in public opinion. So how did this generation experience and make sense of their blackness at the time? And how did these free-flowing mountain kids come to understand themselves as *black* children as opposed to children in the unqualified form? These cultural formations of the self were just as influenced by the racial landscape in the coal towns of Harlan County as they were by the context of the company town. Chapter 4 theorizes from within the veil to demonstrate how black and white subjectivities are co-constitutive, particularly in the Jim Crow South.

But after all that has been said on these more tangible matters of human contact, there still remains a part essential to a proper description of the South which it is difficult to describe or fix in terms easily understood by strangers. It is, in fine, the atmosphere of the land, the thought and feeling, the thousand and one little actions which go to make up life. In any community or nation it is these little things which are most elusive to the grasp and yet most essential to any clear conception of the group life taken as a whole. What is thus true of all communities is peculiarly true of the South, where, outside of written history and outside of printed law, there has been going on for a generation as deep a storm and stress of human souls, as intense a ferment of feeling, as intricate a writhing of spirit, as ever a people experienced.

—W. E. B. Du Bois, *The Souls of Black Folk*

We wondered that and said "why?" But we couldn't get an answer at that time, you know our parents couldn't give us a good true answer to that: "Why do we have to be here and they're there and they got quality things that we don't have?" And we wondered that but we never could figure out "why?" And we knew one thing "why"—because of the color of our skin.

—Sanford Baskin | Born 1948 in Lynch, Ky. | Resides in Benham, Ky.

4 Children, and Black Children

· ·

On the Ordinariness of Everyday Racial Violence

The formation of Jim Crow societies, which refer to states and communities that subscribed to legal de jure segregation, was a state-sanctioned racial project. It not only explicitly licensed discriminatory practices on an entire group of the American citizenry but also implicitly created the conditions under which white citizens could visit terror, at their discretion, on black citizens with impunity. In this way, the institution of Jim Crow did not just sanction racial violence; it was racial violence in and of itself. Its function was to legalize and to normalize the subjugation of a people. In his essay "Of Masters and Men" in *The Souls of Black Folk*, W. E. B. Du Bois articulates both the material contours of de jure segregation and the intangible "structure of feeling" that anointed southern living at the turn of the twentieth century.[1] The sheer cloak of the veil shrouded the hearts and minds of all, rendering mutual recognition between racial groups nearly impossible. However, it is mutual recognition—the ability to see yourself in another—that is constitutive of a democratic society and of the very sense of one's own self. Put differently, mutual recognition presupposes humanity. Of the intangibles, Du Bois writes, "In any community or nation it is these little things which are most elusive to the grasp and yet most essential to any clear conception of the group life taken as a whole."[2] This chapter takes up "these little things" to provide an analysis of the ordinariness of American racism within the context of the Jim Crow South, paying special attention to how this institution fomented the formation of the racial self.[3] Centering the experiences of eastern Kentucky's young and gifted, I examine how they came to understand that they were also, indeed, black.[4]

In internalizing the uneven structures of society, even little children embody racial ideologies and come to know themselves as little *white* children and little *black* children. At a certain age, it is no longer acceptable for them to play together or to freely associate as friends. The cultural geographies of a single community become legible only through a racial lens, and at some point, each subject encounters that fateful moment of interpellation—

the white child learns to call out "Hey, nigger!" and the black child knows exactly to whom he or she is speaking.

Herein I seek to illuminate the ways in which the generation of black children in the coal camps of eastern Kentucky made sense of themselves as racialized subjects within the broader structures of American society. While there is a substantial body of literature on Jim Crow as a racial formation and its lasting legacy on the life outcomes of white and nonwhite populations,[5] there is little on the ways in which this institution structured racialized subjectivities. Here I am adopting anthropologist Sherry Ortner's dynamic definition of subjectivity: "By subjectivity I mean the ensemble of modes of perception, affect, thought, desire, and fear that animate acting subjects. But I always mean as well the cultural and social formations that shape, organize and provoke those modes of affect thought, and so on."[6] Throughout this chapter, I attend to both the particular and the universal— examining their specific experience as black children in central Appalachia as well as the general genre of black subjectivity that is conditioned by the context of living in the Jim Crow South.

The Racial Self

The Self is a social construction.[7] We come to know ourselves through our experiences with others. According to social theorist George Herbert Mead, the Self "becomes an object to himself only by taking the attitudes of other individuals toward himself within a social environment or context of experience and behavior in which both he and they are involved."[8] If this is so, the question of the *racial Self* cannot be anything but a social problem. If the individual only becomes an object to him- or herself by assuming the attitudes of others, then how does a black person come to see his or her Self? Particularly black folks living in the Jim Crow South, where both public opinion and law explicitly affirmed their status as inferior beings of questionable humanity? Du Bois's conceptualization of second sight, twoness, and the veil are essential for considering how processes of racialization distort the formation of the racial Self. In *The Souls of Black Folk*, he wrote:

A sort of seventh son, born with a veil, and gifted with second-sight in this American world—a world which yields him no true self-consciousness, but only lets him see himself through the revelation of the other world. It is a peculiar sensation, this double-consciousness, this sense of always looking at one's self through the eyes of others, of measuring one's soul by the tape of a world that looks on in amused contempt and pity. One ever feels his two-ness—an American, a Negro; two souls, two thoughts, two unreconciled strivings; two warring ideals in one dark body.[9]

Taken together, what these theorizations illuminate is that the self is an amalgam of the thoughts and feelings of others in society, what Mead calls a "structure of attitudes," cognitively mapped onto the individual's perception of his- or herself. However, this process is distorted for the black person who receives no mutual recognition from what Du Bois calls "the other world" but instead only "contempt and pity." He asserts that the American Negro is "born with a veil," an inescapable perception of what is really going on at the checkpoint into the broader structures of national life. Unpacking Du Bois's formulation of the veil, scholars have argued that it "structures the lived experiences, self-formation, and perception of the world for both racialized and racializing subjects."[10] Central to the conceptualization of the veil is that it *precedes* these material manifestations of racialization, such as segregation, differential treatment, Jim Crow laws, or racially hegemonic iconography. It is first a cognitive phenomenon. Of this seemingly intangible level of analysis, Du Bois points out, "We feel and know that there are many delicate differences in race psychology, numberless changes that our crude social measurements are not yet able to follow minutely, which explain much of history and social development. At the same time, too, we know that these considerations have never adequately explained or excused the triumph of brute force and cunning over weakness and innocence."[11]

A particular genre of the veil emerged in the New South after the death of plantation slavery, the strange Redemption era, and the emergence of the Jim Crow laws (Black Codes) at the close of the nineteenth century.[12] While the codes structured the material conditions of life across racial dimensions, they also structured a racial subjectivity of a particular kind. These dimensions of black subjectivity that emerged in the pre–civil rights era Jim Crow South, Du Bois argued, "must be answered, not by apology or fault-finding, but by a plain, unvarnished tale."[13]

· · · · · ·

Down there, there were areas you could not go, you could not go to the pool. If you wanted to swim you had to go to a swim hole around the river. There was a beautiful pool in Cumberland, but you could not swim in it; there was a playground, but you could not go to it. You knew your place, and you knew not to go to those areas. Your parents told you you're not allowed here, you were not allowed there, so you didn't cross the line *(Virginia Taylor-Ward | Cumberland)*. Black girls could not take ballet, not in my town *(Brenda Nolan | Cumberland)*. It was very racist, but we were unaware of it. I mean, we rode the back of the bus, and there were neighborhoods you didn't go in and you didn't live in. . . . The racism was institutionalized—there was a little store in Lynch—now the institutionalized things said that if you were black and were in line to pay for your groceries and somebody white came in, they got in front of you. I mean, that was just the way it was. But none of that mattered because we had our own fun, you know? *(Leslie Lee | Lynch)*. But behind the track it was black, and the white folks lived on Main Street, but they got along pretty well together. They had baseball teams. The whites had a baseball team, and the blacks had a baseball team. But I don't ever recall them playing each other, you know? They were segregated, but it was in a kind of way that "you don't bother us and we don't bother you," you know? *(Ernest Pettygrue)*. It was hostile, but we didn't notice that, and I think it was because of the coal mines. It was separation. Now when you got close to where that bridge was, blacks would be on one side of the street and whites on the other because that was the dividing line *(Betty Williams)*. I didn't know black and white. We went to a black school. . . . We stayed in a black area. We had two or three camps, so you didn't know it. . . . We also had so much fun playing and all that that you didn't see it. And when we were playing sports we just played other black schools. And you just felt that's it, and you didn't worry about it *(Ron Thomas | Lynch)*. Black kids could not go into those type of places; we could not go up to the Lynch country club pool *(Jeff Turner | Lynch)*. I remember the theater—you know, it's segregated in Benham theater too. So you come and pay and then you go upstairs; you could not sit down with the white people. But in Benham I didn't realize it, even though I knew whites went that way and blacks went that way. But all of them worked in the coal mine together, but when they came out they went that way *(Robert Pollenitz | Benham)*.

That's Just the Way It Was . . .

Racial segregation is one of the fundamental techniques for reinforcing racial difference, inextricably linking the relationship between race, space, and place. As it relates to racial consciousness, it is not only the fact of segregation but also the way it is practiced and performed in everyday life. This everydayness, the very ordinariness of racialization normalized difference, while the ongoing interaction between the way things are and everyday human action, legitimizes it. The result of these dual conditions is a taken-for-grantedness. As children growing up in Harlan County, few were aware of the racial prejudice embedded in the act of separation; instead, that's "just the way it was":

> No, no, because I knew that that was just segregation and all that . . . because they didn't use the same bathrooms as we did during those times and things like that. You know, wherever you go, there was one side for the white and one side for the black and you know, no, I never questioned why.
>
> —Arthur "Three-Knots" Simmons | Born 1937 in Lynch, Ky. |
>   Resides in Chicago, Ill.

> Well, I never paid too much attention to it growing up because we always had the same personality, you know; we had special days and well I knew that about the segregation part, we had special days that we could go to the show and we had to sit in the balcony. But we didn't pay too much attention in that you know; we just took it for whatever it's worth because that was the way it was.
>
> —William "Bo" Schaffer Jr. | Born 1926 in Lynch, Ky. | Resides in Chicago, Ill.

> I think there were but I can't really recall now because I was so young when I left. I don't know if I just knew that that was what was supposed to happen, you know growing up there, and that's all I knew. I knew to go to the back of the bus, and I knew to go through a certain door. I think it's from going to the store with my parents. I learned what to do and what not to do.
>
> —Clara Smith | Born 1942 in Cumberland, Ky. | Resides in Southfield, Mich.

Although ostensibly benign, this taken-for-grantedness is by no means inconsequential on black psyche. As children, every time they walked into separate schools, took their seats in separate sections of the movie theater, walked home to separate neighborhoods, they came to embody the racial ideological structure. Political theorist Anthony Bogues points to this feature of racial domination, what he calls the "ideological weight of colonial domination," arguing that "it was not just a matter of the ways in which dominant ideas worked by setting limits or establishing horizons that were then taken for granted. Instead, those ideas were inhabited and then came to map our social world."[14] These moments of active separation birthed in the minds of young children an ideological cartography of the racial order of things.

The three preceding excerpts are illuminating, as they demonstrate how we inherit the world into which we are born. This generation's unawareness did not stem from a biological understanding of their own racial difference; it was always there for them to inherit, from historical ideological structures into which they were born. Although their explanations differed—with Simmons's through embodied practice, Schaffer's through cultural affirmations of "us" and "them," and Smith's through intergenerational transmission of knowledge—what links their experience is that they were all "born with a veil." The level of their racial consciousness in terms of their oppression was in large part explained by the extent to which they shared amicable, albeit removed, social interactions with whites. In his attempt to distinguish the character of the racial landscape in Lynch from that of his neighboring communities and the Deep South, Jerome Ratchford explains:

> And things were *loosely segregated* in Lynch. And this is a term I'm formulating here, *loosely segregated*. There was not the rigid strict segregation that you know to have occurred in the Deep South and some other places and so forth. So we . . . for example, I don't remember separate water fountains, except when I went to Harlan and you could see the signs. I don't remember that, okay. I daresay that [there] was nothing like that in Lynch.

Indexing Lynch and the Deep South is a discursive slight of hand that runs through many participants' accounts of race relations in Benham and Lynch. This is natural given that the markers of what counted as "racial oppression" in their parents' generation—that is, lynching, abduction, convict labor, and open rape—were not visible in the lives of the children. In this sense, the distinction "We were not like Alabama or Mississippi" was a signal of progress for this generation of Appalachian children. As Lynch, Kentucky, natives explain, "I mean we understood the prejudices were there, but it was not as pronounced as it was say in the Deep South like Alabama, Mississippi, or some parts of Tennessee" *(Ike Gardner)*. "But then in Lynch we grew up with a system of separate but equal. And most blacks did not have to deal with the racial deal as in Alabama, so to speak. Usually we were not aware of it, you know, so that was a little bit different there in Lynch to me growing up, you know" *(Sam Howard Jr.)*.

However, normalizing current oppression in this way against the backdrop of historical oppression in the name of progress is a common theme of modernity. Our conversation continued, and I pressed Ratchford on his assertion that Lynch was an exception from the city of Harlan, just twenty-one miles away, and the Deep South writ large. Aware of the many sites of segregation in Lynch, I prompted, "Now, I have heard accounts of the movie theater . . ."

Yeah, but there were—that's what I mean—but there was a balcony, obviously, in the movie theater. And blacks sat in the balcony, and whites were at the lower level. There was also . . . bus travel; I learned, having grown—having lived for a period of time—in the Deep South, there was strict enforcement, which is ridiculous, but where you could see it and so forth.

In Lynch, there was an understanding that you cannot sit beyond a certain point; but there was no intervention if someone sat somewhere that they were not "supposed to sit." And if I can go back to the major department store; there were absolutely separate counters in proximity of each other that blacks sat on for their sodas and their ice cream cones and so forth; and whites. But that was like an imaginary line; there was no "this is for colored, this is for whites." There was no such signage there. So there were some things that were understood and so forth, and then there were some things that were sort of orchestrated and cemented, such as a balcony and what have you. So there was a loose— things were loosely segregated. But now if you went outside to Harlan, you saw a manifestation that you would equate with the Deep South, yeah.

—Jerome Ratchford | Born 1940 in Lynch, Ky. | Resides in Atlanta, Ga.

Upon further reflection, Ratchford illuminated for us the various ways in which Lynch was in fact segregated in the same manner that one might find in downtown Harlan or even in Selma, Alabama. However, for him it was the *politeness* of it all that made this brand of racism tolerable, largely due to the sense that he was in many ways able to maintain his dignity—albeit as long as he did not cross that "imaginary line."

So ingrained were the hegemonic structures of racial domination, few participants were even able to recall if there were in fact signs that restricted their actions. What they remembered instead was that "they knew their place."

Oh, you could not sit in the front of the bus. I'm sure the bus driver would have said, "You need to get back in your area." But you knew not to do that. I mean, why would you when you see "colored" back there? And I rode the bus a whole lot. I can go on and tell you after everything was integrated what hap-pened with that, but you knew your place.

—Virginia Taylor-Ward | Born 1949 in Cumberland, Ky. |
 Resides in Dayton, Ohio

This politeness, or civility, is at the core of what historian William Chafe conceptualized as the "progressive mystique." In his *Civilities and Civil Rights*, Chafe argues that "civility is at the cornerstone of the progressive mystique, signifying courtesy as the value that should govern all relationships between people."[15] Civility for black people in the tri-city area of Harlan County, like in so many other southern communities, simply meant knowing and staying in one's place. Chafe elaborates how this "progressive mystique" of knowing one's place operates within the veil: "Yet blacks also understood the other side of civility—the deferential poses they had to strike in order to keep jobs, the chilling power of consensus to crush efforts to raise issues of racial justice. As victims of civility, blacks had long been forced to operate within an etiquette of race relationships that offered almost no room for collective self-assertion and independence. White people dictate the ground rules, and the benefits went only to those who play the game."[16] Sound familiar?

Friendship as a Proxy for Mutual Recognition

I often used questions about friendship in the oral history interviews as a proxy for mutual recognition. Beyond interracial contact, which really does not require true communication or intersubjective understanding, friendship signals a mode of knowing somebody. On the surface, responses to the question "Did you have white friends?" varied, as respondents' conception largely depended on the extent to which their neighborhood, or "camp," was segregated; however, when pressed with follow-up questions about the quality of those relationships, it became apparent that their social world, no matter the level of interracial contact, was completely black.

> I had white friends living right beside me growing up, but we didn't go to their schools, we didn't go to their recreation facilities *(Sanford Baskin | Lynch)*. I grew up with white friends, and most of my classmates would say that they had white friends, if not acquaintances; played sports together; et cetera. The main segregation was the schools *(Jerome Ratchford | Lynch)*. Not in Kentucky. In Kentucky they had different areas that were designated, like Number Five had a street that was totally White. The hillbillies were White, and I was friends with them but they were not really close friends. The closest that I came to as far as seeing a White person in my life was the milk guy; he was very friendly and he was White. And he would come every week and he would deliver the mail and ice cream and sometimes he would give us free samples and whatever and he was always glad to see us. So it was like he was the

only White person that we knew outside that would come in our community all the time *(Brenda Thornton | Lynch)*. Not 'til we integrated school. I mean, there were some who would speak to you *(Leslie Lee | Lynch)*. Oh, no, not down there. The schools hadn't integrated, because that's what brought about that, once the schools integrated *(Betty Williams)*.

These friendships were limited in the sense that they did not lend themselves to the same "village"-like familiarity that they were used to within the black community. That became apparent when I asked those who claimed to have white friends if they ever shared meals in each other's homes:

We didn't. I can't remember going into their houses to eat *(Sanford Baskin | Lynch)*. No, that was not common. That would be a select instance where that occurred. So, yes, I did do it once or twice, but that was unique to our respective families. That was not something that routinely occurred. What did occur that was interesting is that while we could not go to white social events, say a dance or something of that sort, whites frequently came to black social events *(Jerome Ratchford | Lynch)*. Well, we may not have gone to each other's homes to eat. . . . We were good friends in the classroom and in the neighborhood, but, no, we didn't share homes. They didn't come and sit on your porch, it was still segregated in that way, but you could walk to the store and see each other and talk *(Arnita Davis-Brown | Lynch)*.

The reality was that the veil of the color line demarcated two discrete worlds of blacks and whites. The blueprint of de jure segregation was so well crafted that it even functioned to adulterate children's play. More violent than the physical isolation that legal segregation produced were its psychosocial effects. It ingrained difference within their cognitive frameworks, so much so that children simply inherited the racial logics undergirded by nearly five centuries of historical events. No one had to explain the long history of imperial conquest, the transatlantic slave trade, four hundred years of chattel slavery, Reconstruction, Redemption, and the subsequent emergence of Jim Crow to these children. They simply "knew their place" in the world, a world that did not include the predetermined "Other."

Thank God That I Knew How to Run . . .

Those who claimed not to have experienced prejudice in their daily lives as well as those who had been unaware of the racist structure of their lived environment were still vulnerable to unadulterated, sublime encounters with the veil in all its omnipotence. Like a bolt of lightning, these flashpoints made hypervisible what they subconsciously understood all along: the precarity of blackness. Brenda Thornton was born and raised in camp Number Five in Lynch. As she shared in an earlier excerpt, the only white folks she had encountered as a child were the "hillbillies," who were kind of her friends but not really, and the milk man; other than that, her social interactions were experienced within the veil of the color line. Only from time to time would she and her siblings venture out of their community on their own and leave the ostensible safety of their segregated world:

> When we were walking sometimes we would go through the white community and sometimes somebody would come out and call us nigger or whatever. But the other thing that I remember too is that it was not directly in the area where we lived at because it was segregated. But when we went to the big store we had to travel through some of these areas that were white. Before we reached the hospital—and I think it was on Church Street—these people would always sic their dogs on us, they were boxer dogs. So we actually really had to run for our lives with these dogs. . . . And still to this day, if I see one I still have that fear. *Thank God that I knew how to run very fast.* Sometimes they were mostly kids, but sometimes the adult father would egg the kid on. And there was always one particular house at the end, before you got to the hospital, that would do that. They would think it was funny, and they would wait until we got up there and sic that dog out there on us. And we were kids. It could have killed us, but they thought it was funny. I remember that. And we used to always take something with us to protect us, either pick up a rock or something like that. But as far as passing people on the street, coming out of the store or even being in the shopping area with them, there was no problem. And I could not understand it, I said to Mama, I said, "Why is it that we could go into the big store and we could be in the area up there buying anything else and they walking around but as soon as we go into the area that's considered to be segregated then they start picking?" Lynch was weird. And you're not going to understand why when they were underneath the ground in the coal mine—I mean, and they all got out and they all had black faces, they all looked alike and they were all down in that hole. And there was no difference. If you got hurt down there and you're a coal miner, the other one would help the other one out. They were brothers in the coal mine, but they were enemies outside. It's just weird. I don't know.
>
> —Brenda Thornton | Born 1950 in Lynch, Ky. | Resides in White Plains, N.Y.

Thornton and her siblings somehow understood that when those men and boys loosed those boxers, it was their personal responsibility to save their own lives. No officer would come to their assistance, no white neighbor would chastise the perpetrators for their actions, and those dogs would consider it a reward of service if their teeth and tongue could rip into the flesh of one of those black children. In Thornton's explanation, there was no indictment on whites, because she understood that the onus for her life was on her. For that, all she could say was, "Thank God that I knew how to run very fast."

Running for one's life was a recurrent trope used to describe the moments when the foil of politeness was exposed and the veil laid naked in all its horror. In describing race relations in Cumberland at the time of his childhood, George Taylor remembered:

> Well, we experienced a lot of it. . . . When I was maybe eight or maybe nine years old, some of us would go downtown to the new area and we'd be heading back and some of the older white people come up and would say "Niggas what are you doing downtown?" and "You know you better not come down here!" and all that stuff.
>
> *Karida:* To kids? . . .
>
> Yeah, to kids. We was eight, nine years old, and we would go to this railroad track and we would have to go walk at the railroad track and those guys would say "You better get to running!" And we would have to run all the way home because they would come and act like they were running after us, something like that. I know a number of times at night they would really run at us because they knew there was not nobody out to see what they were doing to us, you know, stuff like that.
>
> —George Taylor | Born 1950 in Cumberland, Ky. | Resides in Dayton, Ohio

The accounts by Thornton and Taylor are examples of racial flashpoints, encounters when the niceties of civil society are suspended and the unvarnished power of racial domination materializes at the whim and fancy of its beholder. These were not acts that resulted in physical harm or death; instead, they exemplify what sociologist Kathleen Blee refers to as "the communicative nature" of racial violence. According to Blee, "It is not only that acts of racial violence communicate fear to others beyond the immediate victims, but that the communicative aspects of racial violence are themselves acts of terrorism."[17] Glares, epithets, sicced dogs, threats, silence, chasing, hyper-surveillance, being lied on, suspicion, insults, and slights; these are all common props in the repertoire of ordinary, taken-for-granted, "that's just the way it is" racial terror. While it may not effectuate direct physical harm, communicative racial violence "broadcasts the potential for racial violence; they are acts of racial violence because they communicate messages of racial empowerment and racial vulnerability."[18] Entire generations of black children grew up within the Jim Crow context and were socialized to understand the world through the lens of their black bodies. To go without this racial navigation system was potentially life threatening, not only for them individually but for every other person in the village.

Desire, Envy, and Moments of Inferiority

African American psychologists Kenneth and Mamie Clark devoted their scientific research to the emergence of consciousness and racial identification among preschool-aged African American children. From the late 1930s through the 1940s, Clark and Clark conducted a series of experimental studies to test black children's perceptions of racial difference, famously known as the "doll experiments." During the experiments, the Clarks presented black children with two dolls, identical except that one was brown with black hair and one was white with yellow hair. They proceeded to ask the children a series of value-laden questions: "Which doll is the smart one?" "Which one is pretty?" "Which doll is the bad one?" and so on. The study showed conclusively that African American children had internalized societal racism, especially children who attended segregated schools. The Clarks published several influential articles on their findings in major psychology journals, and they were called by Thurgood Marshall to present expert testimony on this work during the landmark 1954 *Brown v. Board of Education* Supreme Court case.[19] Their findings ended up being the linchpin in Chief Justice Warren's ruling on the decision.

While much of black culture is full of tradition, pride, and joy, the omnipresence of racism escapes the hearts and minds of no one. Earlier sections showed the ways in which the segregationist Jim Crow laws and customs functioned to normalize racial hierarchies and to instill notions of "us" and "them" among black children in the coal towns of eastern Kentucky. However, their effects are far more reaching than the material distribution of space and resources along racial lines. They also distort the black psyche, so that they can, as Du Bois states, "only see themselves through the eyes of the other."

In the eyes of the blacks . . . I believe it always as being, "If you're black stay back, if you're brown stick around, if you are white you're all right." And that's the way it was even in the black neighborhood; to be a dark complexioned person was not too good for that particular person. They'd have their problems, and by the same token, being too light you were told about your complexion too!

—Sam Howard Jr. | Born 1942 in Lynch, Ky. | Resides in Louisville, Ky.

Race is a sociohistorical construction. One of the main ways in which we interpret racial taxonomies, both between and within groups, is through skin color.[20] As catchy and playful as it sounds, the childhood saying that Sam Howard offered to describe how skin color played a role in the lives of black children in his community still holds true in most societies across the globe.[21] Colorism favors those within a group who have lighter skin over those whose complexion is darker. Like the white doll in the Clarks study, lighter-skin blacks were associated with beauty, intellectuality, good behavior, and other innate positive qualities. This worked on a gradient; however, there was a clear difference in the way dark-skinned participants experienced and navigated perceptions of and experiences with beauty, especially dark-skinned women. Dark girls struggled with being perceived as ugly, less bright, or "fast."[22]

I was always black and ugly, you know; the saddest part of my life was [people saying,] "Hey, you little black thing"—I mean by black people! You know, you are bow-legged, and you are ugly, and you are fat, and you are a whore, or you this and you that.

—Brenda Faye Nolan | Born 1958 in Cumberland, Ky. | Resides in Dayton, Ohio

These notions of pigmentocracy were reinforced by media, institutions, peers, and unfortunately sometimes by community leaders. Desire also functioned to reinforce difference across racial lines. Those who had exposure to white children could not help but notice the inequality between their lives:

They can go and buy what they want to buy. They bought all the candy and all that other stuff and we'd see a white boy that was somewhat our friend and all of a sudden I am trying to get candy from him and stuff like that (George Taylor | Cumberland). I used to want to be like Charmaine; I used to want to be white. I envied something about her. I envied the fact that she had everything. She had all the dolls and clothes and the beautiful house, and I wanted that. . . .

In fact, I can remember that Christmastime came, and my mom bought me a black doll, and I didn't want it. I threw it across the room because I wanted a white doll *(Virginia Taylor-Ward | Cumberland)*. You know because back then we didn't call Negroes "black." Those were fighting words *(Vera Robinson)*.

In a child's eyes, that envy was conjured at moments when the smallest of things were made to seem like luxuries—all the dolls, all the clothes, and all the candy. It was not only in the not having of the thing but also in the tacit feeling that those things were not for you. The objects of their desire too often seemed to have a "Whites Only" sign on them. As these examples show, desire functioned as a key mechanism to perpetuate white supremacist logics of racial difference and inferiority—ideologies that were reproduced within the black community.

The Spectrum of Whiteness

Consolidated whiteness is a twentieth-century formation. Up and through the 1950s, there were dozens of phenotypically white "races" in America: Irish, Italian, and French, as well as Slavs, Teutons, Cossacks, and Iberics. American studies scholar Matthew Jacobson calls this categorical conundrum the "epistemological crisis" of whiteness.[23] The 1920s marked the beginning of "Americanization," an assimilationist movement aimed at transforming the European immigrant into a "new man." Efforts to accomplish this newness included forsaking the use of ethnic cultural symbols in public, as well as such markers as native languages and dialects, ways of dress, and foodways.[24] Even by the 1960s, the structure of whiteness had not yet tempered itself to the point that the privilege of whiteness was extended to groups on the basis of phenotype or continent of origin.

This epistemological crisis was especially pronounced in the "cosmopolitan canopies" of Benham, Lynch, and Cumberland,[25] where the coal companies made intentional efforts to recruit a diverse European immigrant population of laborers through the judicious mixture policy. Contrary to the assimilationist sentiment that was championed among American citizens at the time, International Harvester and U.S. Steel were invested in reinforcing transatlantic ethnic solidarities, and they did so primarily through space and ethnocentric institutions.[26] For example, U.S. Steel intentionally built ethnically centered boardinghouses and churches throughout the community to ensure that the Greek, Slovenian, Hungarian, Italian, and other highly represented ethnic groups continued to identify as miners first, their "fellow countrymen" second, and some gradation of white third. This form of ethnocentric social engineering was inculcated by company-sponsored events, such as concerts that hosted famous entertainers from their homelands. These measures to reproduce an obscured "we" were taken in order to keep unionization efforts from mobilizing throughout the labor force.

What this meant for black people, particularly black children, was that their racial selves emerged not only within the context of a white–black binary, as their parents had experienced in the Deep South, but vis-à-vis a spectrum of whiteness.

And there were those who were equal and probably some white families who were more superior. But at that time you would have to realize that they were foreigners, and if they were from the Boot—you know, that's one of the ways of learning geography—you learn very young that the Boot is at the bottom of Italy and those people are dark Italians and so they are different than the English and the French or the Germans, so they are not supposed to be with the upper-crust white folks; and not only that, the Hungarians, the Slavs, the Czechoslovakians too. There were people who came to work in the mines from those countries and who lived in the community, not necessarily in Sawmill Hollow but in Cumberland period, and they were just a step—and in fact in some instances they may not have been equal to the Negro or treated as the same as Negroes or colored people. And many of the white people of a certain class didn't fraternize or socialize or even go into their businesses.

So . . . there was a class difference both economically and otherwise. And as an example in Cumberland—there was a place you called New York. Well, in New York that's where the business-class white folk lived. And if you wanted to make some money washing windows or washing walls or cutting grass, then that's where you would go, and you go down the street and you knock on doors [and] say you have any work to be done. And so they were the upper-middle class of Cumberland, and they had attitudes about Catholics. There was a Catholic church in Cumberland. . . . And I think they had a school, a small school at the church, but it was not—they were not treated the same, and you know they didn't have the same status as the white people.

—John Steward | Born 1942 in Cincinnati, Ohio; reared in Cumberland, Ky. | Resides in Aliso Viejo, Calif.

Whiteness was constructed on an origin-class continuum and institutionalized through spatial ordering, where the "real white people" lived in the completely segregated upper-echelon neighborhoods, while the as-yet white folks lived among the element. Those who shared ethnic origins with countries such as Hungary, Poland, and Yugoslavia were considered to be white folk of a different class.[27] Even as children, blacks were aware of these ethnoracial distinctions of whiteness; they also understood that their blackness anchored the spectrum of the racial order. One way that racial knowledge was affirmed was through geography, both real and imagined. John Steward points to both "the Boot" of Italy but also the cultural geography of his own childhood neighborhood in Cumberland, where the "upper-crust" whites lived in one section, and the "Othered" whites lived among the blacks. Knowing little to nothing about Europe, let alone Italy, Steward mapped the symbolic meaning of otherness onto the geographic landscape of Italy as he saw it manifest in his own neighborhood. Another more intersubjective way that black children were able to classify the social hierarchy of whiteness was by whether or not an ethnic group was known to socialize with them. Speaking of Hungarians, Virginia Taylor-Ward remembers that "they would socialize with Black people because they were not wanted there, I mean, they were foreigners. And the White people didn't treat them well either." What black children like John and Virginia Taylor-Ward understood was that the element that created the possibility of mutual recognition across racial lines—the nonetheless tenuous relationship between Hungarians and blacks—was the one characteristic that they agreed they shared in common: their unwantedness.

Ironically, the group that occupied the space of the ultimate Other existed as the uncounted in the imaginations of all inhabitants of the mining community. These were the descendants of the people who had settled the land centuries ago. In a similar way that they had stripped the native peoples from their claim to belonging to the land generations ago, the coal mining industry transformed the Scotch-Irish mountaineer into a persona non grata. Today, scholars refer to them as mountaineers, but back then, folks called them hillbillies.[28]

The Great Equalizer

Economic markers were the prevailing empirical way in which black children evaluated racial difference. To them, it just seemed as though the white kids had everything: homes on Main Street, nicer clothes, dolls that looked like them, and, echoing George Taylor's earlier observation, "all the candy." Yet that perception of difference was greatly mediated by the industry. Coal mining is a very fraternal occupation in the sense that in the mines, under the earth, everyone's lives are on the line. Coming out alive depended on trust and cooperation among miners. Similar to the type of brotherhood mentality that is associated with other dangerous occupations, such as firefighting, crabbing, the military, and law enforcement, coal miners stick together. The fact that their fathers shared the same occupational status as everyone else's in the community had an impact on how black children perceived their status vis-à-vis their spectrum of white counterparts. In Chicago or New York City at that time, neighborhoods were highly segregated by race and ethnicity, and labor markets were segmented, with African Americans occupying the positions at the lowest rung of the economy. This was not true in the coal towns of central Appalachia.[29] There, almost everyone's father was a coal miner, and their mothers were homemakers. There was one boss, and his name was King Coal. And no strife— be it racial tensions, labor disagreements, or organized crime—would come before the coal company's interests.

In discussing inequality, participants were sure to distinguish their perception of differences of race from those of class. Common responses pointed to the coal mining industry as "the Great Equalizer":

Well, the mines were the Great Equalizer. Everybody was buddies, you know? That's the way they were, they were buddies" (*Leslie Lee | Lynch*). The fact that your father worked in the mine, that made you equal across the board—black and white—so I, maybe I think I was naïve in that way that I didn't really know that kind of order (*Arnita Davis-Brown | Lynch*). When I was growing up, the company owned all the homes in Benham; everybody worked with the coal mine; everybody was making the same amount of money; there was a mother and a father in the home, otherwise you didn't live there (*Harriet Callaway-Hill | Benham*).

Black and white miners worked together, organized together, and even lodged strikes against the company together. They knew each other's plight, were all controlled by the same paternalistic corporations, and were all breathing in that black coal dust that was slowly taking their lives. In the end, these miners and their families were all striving for their children to attain a role in the American dream—education, the opportunity to thrive economically, freedom, success, safety, choice—they wanted them to have a chance at the good life. However the ideals of brotherhood, camaraderie, and mutual recognition broke down outside the field of labor. Race relations in the mines at Benham and Lynch can be summed up with two recurring statements within the body of oral history interviews:

He would oftentimes talk to me about the black and white side of the coal mines. And he would say when you go in that hole every day you go in even and when you come out you are dark. You can't tell a white man from a black man when you come out because you are dirty and you are completely sandy.

—Jeff Turner | Born 1959 in Lynch, Ky. | Resides in Indianapolis, Ind.

They would work side-by-side with the whites every day. But when they came out [of] the mine, they had to go on their section of the bathhouse, and the whites had to go to their section of the bathhouse. They would then go to the restaurant, [and] they would go into their side, the black side. And they would go on the white side. After they worked all day together.

—Lena Margaret Jones | Born 1938 in Lynch, Ky. | Resides in Louisville, Ky.

They would go in every day as equals, and if they were lucky enough to come out at all, they came out black. Yet the entrance to the bathhouse was a threshold of subjecthood; with one step those men would transform from miners to black men and white men—and never the two shall meet.

The coal companies also involved themselves directly in racial matters. They took measures to regulate behavior by proscribing interactions that were deemed intolerable to their company's mission or to public opinion. For example, fear of miscegenation loomed large in the white psyche, and to deter white community members from taking matters into their own hands, the companies stepped in to censor that behavior.

U.S. Steel had strict laws up there. Because I remember a case—Willie Mike—Willie Mike Powell on the choir was dating a white girl; everything was consensual but he got caught and so the girl didn't say he raped her; but they had an unwritten law that he had to leave Lynch or his daddy could not work there anymore.

—Ike Gardner | Born 1936 in Marion Junction, Ala.; reared in Lynch, Ky. | Resides in Chicago, Ill.

If a father lost his job, it meant that everyone had to go. With ten, eleven, fifteen, or sixteen mouths to feed, that was no small threat. The companies also intervened in supporting sites of cultural production along ethnoracial dimensions. For example, they sponsored lively Fourth of July celebrations every year, replete with games and competitions in the baseball park, free ice cream doled out by the company store, and parades up and down the streets of the several coal camps. Although everyone acknowledged the holiday, it was generally understood as "white folks Independence Day." However, the companies would sponsor an equally spectacular celebration one month later for the Eighth of August—Independence Day for the blacks.

The coal company's role in affirming and destabilizing racial epistemologies cannot be ignored. Being a coal miner's kid generated a strong sense of pride and dignity within the hearts and minds of the black children in the tri-city area of Harlan County, Kentucky. For them, while the white and black social worlds may have been segregated, and whiteness was somehow a proxy for economic status, whites were by no means in a class of their own. The black community had its own culture, mores, traditions, celebrations, and sources of pride. As their testimonies, in all their variety, have shown, that's just the way it was back home. However, no black person in America escapes the veil of the color line. We all have our moment.

Second Sight and the Emergence of Racial Consciousness

There is a moment in every black person's life when they discover what their blackness means to the world. This is not a discovery of phenotype but of history. It is the moment of awakening when they realize that their blackness signals an accumulation of processes of racialization, a moment when the encounter of 1492 and the present collapses on their black body.[30] This moment inaugurates the emergence of one's racial consciousness. Different from the taken-for-granted acceptance of racial segregation, iconography, discourse, or gratefulness that the Lord blessed us with fast legs with which to run from vicious dogs, racial consciousness gives the racialized subject the ability to see the injustice of it all. Du Bois called this "second-sight"[31]—a "gift" that affords the racialized subject the opportunity to "suspend the optics of the veil and see other possibilities of organizing the world."[32] Du Bois animates the concept of "second-sight" in his allegorical essay in *The Souls of Black Folk*, "Of the Coming of John," in which he tells the story of John, a young black man who grew up in the rural southern town of Altamaha, Georgia. Like the children in the tri-city area of Harlan County, Kentucky, John grew up happy and unaware of the violent structure that Jim Crow was imposing on his body and mind. However, after leaving his hometown for college, John's second sight comes upon him in a transformative way. Du Bois writes:

> Thus he grew in body and soul, and with him his clothes seemed
> to grow and arrange themselves; coat sleeves got longer, cuffs

appeared, and collars got less soiled. Now and then his boots shone, and a new dignity crept into his walk. And we who saw daily a new thoughtfulness growing in his eyes began to expect something of this plodding boy. Thus he passed out of the preparatory school into college, and we who watched him felt four more years of change, which almost transformed the tall, grave man who bowed to us commencement morning. He had left his queer thought-world and come back to a world of motion and men. He looked now for the first time sharply about him, and wondered how he had seen so little before. He grew slowly to feel almost for the first time the Veil that lay between him and the white world; he first noticed now the oppression that had not seemed oppression before, differences that erstwhile seemed natural, restraints and slights that in his boyhood days had gone unnoticed or been greeted with a laugh. He felt angry now when men did not call him Mister, he clenched his hands at the "Jim Crow" cars, and chafed at the color-line that hemmed in him and his.[33]

Like John, several participants cited their first encounters with new cities and communities as the first time that they "saw" race, in part because the onus was on them to pick up on the "thousand and one little actions" that made up the social fabric of a new surrounding[34]—including the racial etiquettes and orders—thus making them conscious of the labor that came along with "performing" their race. Travel also sparked this awakening, because the contrast of racial landscapes gave them a new set of criteria with which to evaluate their own home setting. Speaking of his own racial awakening, William Jackson recalls:

That is interesting because, early on I didn't even—that was no big deal to me. I didn't know anything about blacks and whites separating; this is the way of life. This is how we lived and it was fine, but I think as time went on, you started becoming aware because you got older. For the summer you might go to Chicago or New Jersey or somewhere, and then you would pick up little things about race relations, then you would come back to Lynch. Then you start thinking like, "Why don't black people live in Main Street? We all live over here"; so I think as I got older, I became aware of a lot of stuff. I do not to this day remember anybody ever in Lynch calling me a nigger. I do not remember that.

—William Jackson | Born 1945 in Lynch, Ky. | Resides in Los Angeles, Calif.

Du Bois wrote of his own racial awakening when, as a young child, a little white girl refused his offering of a decorative card during a group game. Her refusal was subtle at best, but he recognized beyond a shadow of a doubt that her refusal, along with her particular look of contempt and disdain, was due to his race. From that moment on, he went from not noticing race to seeing it everywhere. Of this encounter, Du Bois wrote, "Then it dawned upon me with a certain suddenness that I was different from the others; or like, mayhap, in heart and life and longing, but shut out from their world by a vast veil."[35] This last section of the chapter attends to how that sudden moment is experienced in all its force and subtlety.

· · · · · ·

Again like I said we lived on Church Street. And I used to play with the Miller brothers. So what happened was the family next door to the Millers, they moved, and this other family moved in there. So one day I was going down, and I was looking for Jim. So I went in the yard and all I heard was a voice say, "What are you doing down here?! Get'on back up there where you belong?!" And I'm going like, [to himself] "Who said that?" So I stopped. And he said again, "Didn't you hear what I said? Get'on back up there where you belong!" So again I didn't move. I'd never heard that before. I'd gone on down and knocked on Jim's door a bunch of times before. So this guy comes out the house. A grown man. "You better get your so-and-so out the street! I'm talking to you!!" But there was a guy, a neighbor of my parents heard this guy, and he came out and said, "I know one gotdamn thing, you better not touch him!" So the guy went back in the house. So I left. . . . And so, that was it. That was my first experience. I was in elementary school. That's what got me, I just remember hearing that voice—"You better get back up there!" And I froze. . . . What got me, now that I think about [it,] is that I froze. And I still ask myself, Why did I freeze? Personally, that was my awakening.

—Victor Prinkleton | Born in 1944 in Lynch, Ky. | Resides in Lexington, Ky.

Why did Victor Prinkleton freeze? What did his unconscious mind know that he did not at that moment in time, and why did his body respond by entering into a temporary state of paralysis? Is there such a thing as a racial atavism, where the specters of racial violence visit black children's consciousness to remind them of what lay behind that man's "What are you doing down here?!"—was it the ghost of "Hey, nigger's" past? While we can only speculate why he knew to freeze, we can see traces of how this second sight continued to map Prinkleton's social world, as it did for other black boys and girls in his community. Again he returns us to the site of the yard:

> And some of that stuff you just picked up on, ain't nobody had to tell you. I'll never forget once when I—there were two sisters that lived behind us—their grandmother used to talk to my mother all the time. And she would keep these girls, and they had to move in temporarily. And I used to take a shortcut, I used to go to the creek; and I had a habit of cutting through this yard to get over to Looney Creek. And these girls one day, they were out there in the yard. And as usual I started going out through the yard, and something told me, [he says to himself] "Oh . . . there's Pat and Martha." Right away the light goes off— "Don't cut through the yard. Pat and Martha are out there." I guess I was about fourteen or fifteen. And so I just took the long way around. 'Cause I knew. There's some things people ain't got to tell you. You just knew as a young black.
>
> —Victor Prinkleton

Unfortunately, second-sight does not provide an escape from the reality of the sheer and utter violence of the veil. It grants consciousness, a knowing awareness of what is really determining the scene; however, it does not provide the tools to break down, jump over, or transcend the wall of the veil. Beyond anything else, it is a tool of survival—mental and physical. Yet the cries of these black children went unanswered.

> We wondered that and said "Why?" but we could not get an answer at the time. You know our parents could not give us a good answer to "Why do we have to be here and they're there, and they got quality things that we don't have?" . . . And we knew one thing "why?"—because of the color of our skin *(Sanford Baskin | Lynch)*. And why are we treated so mean? But God never did answer me, you know? And that was the question that I just wanted the answer to *(Ernest Pettygrue)*.

Conclusion

On the surface, the racial landscape in which this second generation grew up seemed different from that of their parents; however, the structure was the same. The difference was the way in which race relations in the tri-city area were performed—that is, through politeness and knowing one's place. As long as the terms of the old racial contract were maintained, there was no reason for exerting overt, repressive measures to maintain order. Instead, the ideology of white supremacy and the structure of separate and unequal were internalized into the habitus of everyone living in the Jim Crow South. As long as they had internalized these overt structures, there was no longer a need for signs and lynchings; all people knew their place. However, the veil of the color line would expose itself in moments when the racial contract was breached, and in others reinforce its durability. Forbidden acts, such as miscegenation, were cause for the force of the veil to shine bright, while other instances of unambiguous racism ignited simply to reinforce the racial order, such as loosing dogs on neighborhood children. There was a general consensus that the racism in Kentucky was much better than that experienced in the Deep South—"it's not like we were in Alabama or Mississippi." This was what racial progress looked like on the ground in the Jim Crow South.

They want a graded school for their colored people and a graded school for the Americans and a high school for the Americans.

—William H. Perkins | President, International Harvester Company

And we had pride in our school. We were taught pride, which is interesting.

—John Steward | Graduate of Benham Colored School | Class of 1958

5 The Colored School

· ·

Chapter 4 explored the ways in which racial consciousness emerged in the minds and souls of black children in Harlan County within the overlapping contexts of Jim Crow segregation and the company-owned town. Both contexts structured the conditions under which racial ideologies took shape in all the people in the communities, irrespective of their race or ethnicity. Within the confines of their segregated social world, black children became aware of the veil of color line at a very young age—through racially coded messages about skin tone, not having, and the tacit knowledge about "knowing their place." They also downloaded messages about how their black skin would shape their lives from the other side of the veil, in the white world. These signals were more blatant—"Whites Only" signs, looks of disdain and contempt, and, of course, boxer dogs.

However, their racialized subjectivities did not survive on notions or interpersonal interactions alone. Whereas chapter 4 offered an exploration of the interior dimensions of how, as children, this generation of black Appalachians came to understand themselves as racialized people and the ways in which they coded and decoded their racial landscape, chapters 5 and 6 examine the ways in which their blackness was articulated through embodiment—taken-for-granted practices, habits, and dispositions—and institutions—policies and material structures that pressed on their beings. These black youth came of age along the generational arc of the pre- and post–civil rights era, a period of political transformation in American history. The bounty of the civil rights movement opened a new horizon of possibilities for African Americans in terms of educational access, occupational and residential choices, and the sheer aspirations that black people were allowed to have for themselves.

However, the progress brought about by the civil rights movement also brought dislocation to the local black community. Under de jure segregation, black people lived in close-knit legally segregated communities, with their own black religious institutions, black neighborhoods, black schools, and black businesses. An unintended consequence of the civil rights era, therefore, was that the organizational structure of the southern black community would change dramatically. It marked the eve of an era, as it brought an end to the way things were.

The following chapters trace this transformation in the black community along the grain of the civil rights movement, with a specific focus on the effects of the landmark *Brown v. Board of Education* decision. During the period of de jure segregation, inequality between the black and white populations was ensconced and reproduced through explicit racial projects, including institutions, physical and geographic structures, and policies that intentionally allocated resources along racial lines—separately and unequally—in order to maintain power and advantage within the white majority.[1] *Brown v. Board* was the first of a series of federal civil rights legislation that would begin to fell the giant, bringing the "strange career" of old Jim Crow to an end.[2]

In addition to reshaping the political landscape, the expansion of civil rights for black Americans reshaped them as a people. For example, on their birth certificates, research participants had been legally identified by the state as "colored" or "negro." By young adulthood, they had *become* "black" and "African American." Let us explore the meaning and experience of this transformation of selfhood through a close reading of the rise and fall of one of the institutions most beloved by the black community in Harlan County, Kentucky—the colored school.

Through this analysis, I will show how the black segregated school, the prototype of what sociologists Michael Omi and Howard Winant famously termed a "racial project,"[3] institutionalized and reproduced racial ideologies within the black community. At the same time, I will show how the colored school was a proud site of black cultural expression. Ironically, much of my participants' collective pride, dignity, and love for one another was generated within one of the very institutions that was created for their subjugation.

The History of Education in Eastern Kentucky

Like most southern states, public education in Kentucky was legally segregated by race. Section 4363-8 of the Kentucky statutes reads: "It shall be unlawful for any white persons to attend any school or institution where Negroes are received as pupils or receive instruction and it shall be unlawful for any Negro or colored person to attend any school or institution where white persons are received as pupils or receive instruction or school; provided, the provisions of this law shall not apply to any penal institution or house of reform." District boards of education were responsible for furnishing and maintaining public schools that offered first through twelfth grade education for their given territory; however, it was not until 1936 that the statutes were amended to explicitly mandate a full twelfth grade education for nonwhite children.

Given the mountainous, sparsely populated, underdeveloped condition of the Appalachian region of Kentucky, William T. Gilbert wrote, "Maintenance of twelve grades of school service for Negro children in districts where the Negro population is sparse has become a serious problem in eastern Kentucky."[4] At the time, high school enrollments ranged from "six pupils in Pineville High School to 288 pupils in the Lynch High School."[5]

A Tale of Two Schools in Harlan County, USA

"They want a graded school for their colored people and a graded school for the Americans and a high school for the Americans."[6] This is the condition under which the segregated black schools in the towns of Benham and Lynch came into existence—one school for the "colored people" and another for the "Americans." Lynch Colored Public School opened its doors in the fall of 1923, and, within a year, the Benham Colored School opened as well. Although there was some disparity in the size, enrollment, and faculty salary scales between these two schools, Lynch and Benham were considered the finest colored high schools in the region. Both schools graduated over four decades of black coal miners' sons and daughters.

All the teachers at Benham and Lynch came with at least a bachelor's degree, and several went on to continue at the master's level during their tenure in the colored school system. Former teacher Rose Ivery Pettygrue remembered how impressed she was with the caliber of teachers at the Lynch colored school when she arrived in 1958

> because they had a better high school than we did in my hometown. And they had really qualified teachers. . . . A lot of their teachers already had master's degrees. I know Miss Knight did, Miss Gregory did. But they all had degrees and see and in the county, there were some county teachers teaching there with just two years of college.
>
> —Rose Ivery Pettygrue | Born 1937 in Greensburg, Ky. | Graduated Kentucky State College 1957 | Former teacher at the Lynch Colored Public School

Part and parcel of the companies' social engineering project to create a model town, the companies deputized its black principals—Professor Matthews (Benham), Professor Shobe (Lynch), and his successor, Professor Coleman (Lynch)[7]—to go out to colleges throughout the southern and midwestern regions, much like labor agents were doing at the time with future miners, to recruit the top performing black graduates to come and teach up in the hills of Appalachia. Thus, each black principal had tremendous license to handpick his teaching staff in line with his vision of what the flavor and texture of pedagogy should be for his school. Although the schools in Benham and Lynch were segregated, the coal companies—in striving to create "model towns"—offered resources, salaries, and amenities that were superior to their neighboring competitors in the central Appalachian region.

Armed with the authority to make hiring decisions and to offer teaching salaries that were often more competitive than the going rate in major cities, the black principals at the colored schools recruited what they considered the best of the best. These new teachers at Benham and Lynch—an unusual destination with a dearth of college-educated teachers, black or white—primarily got their jobs through the principals' personal or alumni networks. Mrs. Pettygrue recalls her excitement about being recruited by Professor Coleman during his visit to Kentucky State:

> And so I never really had an interview; I never wrote a resume for a job. And so what happened, Mr. and Mrs. Coleman came by and it was in the summer and that was before you could not go to a restaurant and eat. You didn't go to a hotel and stay, so they just came to our house, and my father worked in Louisville at the country club in the summertime. And so my mother was not at home when they stopped by and I had just finished Kentucky State . . . and also, I had a job offer in Lexington and Elizabethtown. And then when Mr. Coleman told me what I'd be making in Lynch, it was going to be more than what Elizabethtown or Lexington paid! Because Lynch was independent. It was not a county school. So, buddy, I got busy. I killed a chicken, I picked the chicken, I cut the chicken up, I fried the chicken, I mashed potatoes, I made a salad. I did all this to fix him dinner. And he was so impressed!

Lynch ran an independent school system, and U.S. Steel paid teachers handsomely instead of subjecting them to county rates. This was partly because of the company's desire to create a model community and partly because it had to incentivize professionals, such as teachers, physicians, attorneys, and engineers, to move to the isolated mountain region of Kentucky rather than pursue opportunities in nearby urban centers, such as Lexington, Louisville, and Frankfort. Another teacher, Mrs. Vergie Mason, recalls going to Lynch after graduating in 1941 from Wilberforce University in Ohio. She too was recruited through the John V. Coleman grapevine:

> My sister was a teacher, and her principal knew the principal of Lynch [Mr. Coleman]; he told my sister, and that's when I applied for the job. I went up for an interview. I didn't know where Lynch was. I went up for an interview and thought, "I don't want these mountains. I don't want this job. I hope they don't call me" . . . but after I got there, I realized it was a lovely place.
>
> —Vergie Mason | Born 1923 in Mt. Sterling, Ky. | Graduated Wilberforce University 1941 | Former teacher at Lynch Colored Public School and Lynch High School (integrated)

Even those teachers who did not have a direct personal connection with the principal were recruited based on their affiliation with the principal's alma mater. They were graduates of the commonwealth's black college, Kentucky State, where the lion's share of the teachers in the tri-city area came from. Charles Price was one such recruit. A native of Louisville and a Kentucky State graduate, Mr. Price had his eye set on migrating to Chicago to join his family and friends who had previously journeyed to the Midwest in search of better opportunities. Poor and out of the loop with the black elite network, Price understood that he would have to cast his own lot in life, so he planned to start off as a substitute teacher for the Chicago public school system until he could find a permanent position. That is, until Professor Matthews called:

> Yes, I was not of the system. But and that's how I ended up in the mountains of Kentucky, because they offered me a job. I did not apply for a job, but I was offered a job in Benham. I was on my way to Chicago and I was going to go to Chicago and substitute until I could find a permanent job, but I was offered—I was called by Jay Matthews and he said, "I need a music teacher and I heard that you were available, would you come?" I have no idea how he found out about me . . . his connection with where I went to college I guess.
>
> —Charles E. Price | Born 1933 in Louisville, Ky. | Graduated Kentucky State University 1955 | Former teacher and last sitting principal of Benham Colored School

Teachers such as Mrs. Mason, Mrs. Ellison, Mrs. Sweatt, Mr. Price, and Mrs. Knight stayed at the colored schools in Benham and Lynch for over thirty years, long enough to teach at least two generations of black children in Lynch, Kentucky. They came from the leading historically black colleges and universities (HBCUs) in the South and Midwest—Wilberforce University, Hampton College, Tuskegee University, Tennessee State College, and, of course, Kentucky State College. These institutions mattered in terms of the type of training and educational ideology the college supported. For example, although now a liberal arts university, Kentucky State College was originally founded in 1886 as the State Normal School for Colored Persons. Kentucky State was established under the auspices of the Hampton model,[8] with the mission of training black teachers for black schools.[9] The college's ethos of industrious work ethic, rote learning, and black respectability emanated from the teachers and largely shaped the school context for the colored schools in Harlan County. Before we turn to the Benham and Lynch colored schools, let us lay the groundwork by sketching outlines of the ideal pre–*Brown v. Board of Education* "black teacher" and "black principal." This profile work is important because the black segregated school emerged out of a peculiar sociohistorical context, making the black educator at that time a very specific type of figure within the African American community.

The Black Teacher

Black teachers embodied the ideology of racial uplift.[10] They were like missionaries, sent out to the rural hamlets of the South to educate the black masses, to expel impulse and instill in their souls a spirit of thrift and providence, and to awaken the benighted young Negro to the ways of the modern world. In the early decades of the twentieth century, most HBCUs pressed their students to become teachers, both because the black masses were in dire need of basic education and because the veil of the color line occluded blacks from most professions in the American occupational structure. Whether the young gifted and black desired to be engineers, accountants, or concert pianists when they entered college, a teacher they would be by the time they graduated.

Even W. E. B. Du Bois was influenced by this steering during his time at Fisk University in Nashville, Tennessee, where students were encouraged by the faculty to go out during their vacation months and find a country school where they could enlighten the black masses. Reflecting on that time in his life in the essay "Of the Meaning of Progress" in *The Souls of Black Folk*, Du Bois recalls, "Once upon a time I taught school in the hills of Tennessee, where the broad dark vale of the Mississippi begins to roll and crumple to greet the Alleghanies. I was a Fisk student then, and all Fisk men thought that Tennessee—beyond the Veil—was theirs alone, and in vacation time they sallied forth in lusty bands to meet the county school-commissioners. Young and happy, I too went."[11] Reveling in his memories of the "hunt" for a Tennessee country school in need of a teacher, Du Bois relays, "I learn from hearsay . . . that the hunting of ducks and bears and men is wonderfully interesting, but I am sure that the man who has never hunted a country school has something to learn of the pleasures of the chase. I see now the white, hot roads lazily rise and fall and wind before me under the burning July sun; I feel the deep weariness of heart and limb as ten, eight, six miles stretch relentlessly ahead; I feel my heart sink heavily as I hear again and again, 'Got a teacher? Yes.' So I walked on and on."[12] This generation of educated Negroes—the men and women of Fisk and Hampton and Kentucky State and Wilberforce and Spelman and Morehouse—were groomed to be the "talented tenth," idealized as the best that black society had to offer the world.[13] However, they were trained that their position in the upper crust of the veil came with an almost divine responsibility—to lift their fellow soul mates, who occupied the lowly status of the "black masses," out of poverty, illiteracy, and strife so that they could assume their rightful place at the center of American life. It is for this reason that many of the black graduates who embraced this mantle—those educated young men and women—did not mind relocating to small rural towns, distant from all the action of city life, to assume their calling as teachers in the Jim Crow South.

Even those who set their sights on other aspirations were steered by their institutions to pursue teaching. Vergie Mason, a former teacher at the Lynch Colored Public School, was one such person:

Actually I didn't want to become a teacher; I really wanted to be a secretary. I worked in the office in the high school, just doing things in the office, and I liked it; and [I] wanted to go to college to be a secretary. But after getting to college, and I took so many secretary courses, my counselor called us and the others that were aspiring secretaries to take five educational courses so that we would be able to teach, because they were not hiring a lot of black secretaries. And so I took the five extra courses and then I graduated—I tried to get a secretary job but they were not hiring. So they needed a business teacher and I thought I would just augment business education in Lynch, Kentucky.

—Vergie Mason | Born 1923 in Mt. Sterling, Ky. | Graduated Wilberforce University 1941 | Former teacher at Lynch Colored Public School and Lynch High School (integrated)

Preceding the wholesale integration of higher education institutions, the majority of college-educated African Americans attended historically black colleges, where choices were limited in terms of degree concentration. Even the few who did earn degrees from predominantly white institutions were shut out of the elite labor economy and channeled back to black schools in the South to uplift their race.[14] It was common for young black college students of Mrs. Mason's generation to have to recalibrate their dreams and aspirations. Three regimes of domination were influencing those choices at the time: the veil of the color line, which had always been determining the life outcomes of black folks; the patriarchal labor market, which delineated men's and women's work; and the institution—the HBCU—whose mission was to produce black teachers for black students. In the end, Mrs. Mason resolved to make the best of her situation; if she could not be a secretary like she had dreamed, she would sure enough, as she stated, "augment business education in Lynch, Kentucky."

A Class of Their Own

Preachers and teachers were the only members of the black community occupying a middle-class status. For this, they were exalted by black parents and children alike, as they held the key to unlocking opportunity's door. However, Jim Crow saw to it that their social capital as educated middle-class Negroes did not translate into access to the broader economic, political, or social spheres of society. In this way, black educators in the early twentieth century occupied what historian Adam Fairclough refers to as "a class of their own."[15]

They lived behind the veil, in the segregated community among the children and parents to whom they felt responsible, taking leadership roles in church and community, socially interacting with parents and friends, and living their everyday lives within the black social world. The black community trusted their black teachers and depended on them to be leaders both in and outside the classroom. In her role as a teacher in Lynch, Vergie Mason remembers this mantle all too well:

> They expected it. Back then teachers were looked up to, and they were sort of leaders. People looked up to us; the parents all looked up to teachers, and so you had to discipline yourself so that you can set a good example for the children. And so we went to church—yes, and whatever it was to be done that they wanted the teacher represented if they would call on them. And we were

FIGURE 10 Teachers chaperoning dance at Lynch Colored Public School | circa 1950. Lynch (Kentucky) Colored School/West Main Alumni Assoc. Collection, Southern Historical Collection, Louis Round Wilson Special Collections Library, University of North Carolina at Chapel Hill.

at different—all of the activities at school; we sold tickets, we chaperone[d,] and we just did everything at school for the kids, and they expected it. And we had fun doing it.

With this expectation came a heightened sense of awareness in teachers of their own social position within the community. As a result, teachers had a reputation of being omnipresent, caring, and intimately involved in the lives of the black families in the community, while also being somewhat removed and even aloof. However, in small close-knit segregated communities like Benham and Lynch, lines between the personal and professional were sometimes blurred.

And I remember Mr. Matthews who was our high school Principal; he deterred me from dropping out of school. This is the way our teachers taught us; he said, "I want you to be the first one to graduate," and I will never forget that. He called me into his office before graduation. But I don't know— you are too young—but he preached to us all the time; our instructors did

FIGURE 11 Teachers sitting at Lynch Colored Public School with students |
circa 1950. Lynch (Kentucky) Colored School/West Main Alumni Assoc.
Collection, Southern Historical Collection, Louis Round Wilson Special
Collections Library, University of North Carolina at Chapel Hill.

and took a personal interest. Integration is coming, you can't be just as
good, and you have to be better. And they really took their time; sometimes
I could come home from school and one of my teachers might be sitting at
the table eating. We shopped at the same stores, went to the same church,
everything.

—Harriet Callaway-Hill | Benham Colored School | Class of 1960

The teachers talked to the students; disciplined them if they saw them mis-
behaving in the street; and sent them on little errands, like going into Cumberland to pay a bill or to pick up a sundry from the store. They invited the

children into their homes and visited with their families in the community, gave rides, patched up scratches with gauze and Band-Aids, looked them in the eyes, and greeted them with a smile. The teachers, the parents, and the children *belonged* to one another.

Fess

Inculcated with the principles of self-help, thrift, industrial labor, and rote learning, the black teacher embodied a particular habitus that was reproduced within local black schools throughout the country, particularly in the South. This particular mode of black pedagogy was perpetuated by the black principal—universally referred to in the South as professor, or fess, by the black community—who acted as the broker between the white power structure of the local board of education and the inner workings, pedagogy, and mode of black learning that the black teacher was to adopt.[16] In addition to being responsible for maintaining order within the colored school, fess was responsible for recruiting qualified black teachers, managing their teaching style, vying for additional resources and expanded curricula from the white school board, and placing students at colleges.

> I remember Mr. Coleman, especially when my senior year came he was very instrumental in seeing that I got to college. And then I think the first year after I completed that year he was principal over here at the high school and I worked in the office with him and he had me typing letters to schools concerning getting other students into college.
>
> —Clara Clements | Lynch Colored Public School | Class of 1955

Both colleagues and students remember the principals as being no-nonsense disciplinarians. Principals were at the top of the food chain in the black community, and they commanded respect from everyone.

> Professor Matthews, oh my God! He was one that you just didn't cross. He always chewed his tongue for some reason, I didn't know why. But you knew not to act up or he would paddle you.
>
> —Virginia Taylor-Ward | Benham Colored School | Class of 1967 |
>   Integrated in 9th grade
>
> Called him "Fess," that's what they called him. You know I have seen him do a little thumping and paddling but I got [a] different experience you know. . . .

He was—he was a disciplinarian. He commanded respect from the teachers and from the students.

—Charles E. Price | Born 1933 in Louisville, KY | Graduated Kentucky State University 1955 | Former teacher and Mr. Matthew's successor as the last principal of Benham Colored School

Black principals and teachers were often active participants in regional and national black professional organizations, such as the Kentucky Negro Education Association (KNEA), which paralleled the white associations from which they were excluded. These organizations were subversive channels through which black faculty and administration disseminated information, organized strategies of resistance, and set the agenda for how best to educate their black children, irrespective of the unequal mandates that the white boards of education may have put forth.[17] For example, the organizations set the standards for parental involvement in supporting school activities; incorporating "off the books" courses, such as Latin or literature, into the curricula; and even children's hygiene.

The segregated school system in the tri-city area of Harlan County operated within this broader structure. Both Benham and Lynch had their own colored schools, while the black children in Cumberland, in absence of a segregated school, attended the school in Benham. From 1923 to 1963, black children in this area spent their entire primary and secondary educational careers, from first through twelfth grades, in one school building, where the same black teachers who had taught a student's elder siblings, and in some cases their parents, taught them. Teachers, students, and parents shared a familiarity and intimacy that extended far beyond the classroom, and in this way, the colored schools in Benham and Lynch were as central to the black community in terms of cultural production as the family and the church.

The Interiority of the Colored School

So what was it like to attend a colored school? What seems like such a long time ago is in fact recent history, an experience that is only one or two generations removed from the present day—so much so that every participant in this study matriculated through the colored school system at some point in his or her first through twelfth grade education. In the segregated South, the family, the church, and the school constituted the trifecta of the black community. In few other spaces could blacks escape the regulating gaze of white society. These were the spaces in which they collectively constructed their social world, the place where they were their blackest. Therefore, before moving on to the analysis of the transformation from segregated to desegregated schooling, the subject of chapter 6, it is necessary to ground our inquiry in "the way it was," or at least the way they remember it being.

Let's go to school.

$$\bullet \bullet \bullet \bullet \bullet \bullet$$

Well, we had the most fun school you could possibly ever imagine. We had some fabulous teachers, and they would really wear you out to make sure that you got what you were supposed to get *(Willie French)*. Strong, strong disciplinarians. All of the teachers had their own ways. But you know discipline was all that they did there. And it was the same with the Janitor; anybody who was seen as a responsible adult was to be respected. That's just the way it was, you know *(PG Peeples)*. We had one beautiful time going to school there; of course schools were a lot stricter then than they are now, and you were not told too many times what to do because if they had to tell you three or four times, you caught it *(Odell Moss)*. And mother told us that if she had to come to school because of us, we were going to be automatically wrong until we could prove ourselves right. So we didn't want that to happen *(Raven Whitt)*.

I think everybody who went through school with them teachers got a whooping. And they were saying, they wouldn't spare no rod, because they were saving the kid. That's what I thought about it. They wanted to make sure that everybody that they taught would have a very good education. Or had the basics to get that good education. Because they had been in college and they knew what they—what we—were going to come up against when we got there. So they did a real good job of doing that *(Chuck Rodgers)*. We used to have some good times down at West-Main. Back then, the teachers cared, because they lived in the community and their main thing was to get you an education. And they would bust your rump back then. And Lord, I got my tail tore up! Miss Mabel Smith, I will never forget... before they tiled up the floor—they used to have wooden floors—and they would clean them, shine them up with oil, and I will never forget: Mom sent me into school, I had a pair of white pants on—and then you would break for lunch, you walk home for lunch and then you come back—when I went home for lunch, you could not tell what color of them pants was, because she had mopped that floor with me! But what she was trying to do was teach you, show you different things, and I just was not ready—but we had some good teachers *(George Massey)*.

They did not play, and you understood that, and that is the way it was. You accepted it and you moved on. As I look back on Miss Jackson, when you are

FIGURE 12 Lynch Colored Public School faculty | circa 1950. Lynch (Kentucky) Colored School/West Main Alumni Assoc. Collection, Southern Historical Collection, Louis Round Wilson Special Collections Library, University of North Carolina at Chapel Hill.

in the classroom it's time to be serious, at noon you could play, when school is out you could play; in that classroom dot your I's, cross your T's, use proper language, sentence structure, that kind of stuff *(William Jackson)*. Yeah, no child was to be called dumb or be dumb. And if it took you staying in that lunchtime because you didn't get it, they would keep you in there, you know. . . . There was one time for me with fractions. I just could not get no sense of this fraction stuff. And Ms. Mason said, "Oh, honey, you can do it." So, I had stayed one day till 12 because I could not get my fractions. And so she came back and she said, "Did you get it?" And I said, "No, mam." And she said, "Let me help you out," and she kind of gave me a little spanking, you know. Then she went over that problem again, and I got it. I really got it. And not only that, you can wake me up in the middle of the night and I could work fractions. Short ways, long ways, which ever! *(Lena Jones)*.

And so—but now having said all of that; there's no substitute for teachers, in this case for us of color, who believed in our capabilities or who saw the future and what we could bring to the future in teaching us in a serious mode and holding us accountable for our capacities to be able to learn whatever we sought to learn *(Jerome Ratchford)*. And the teachers were just exceptional because all of our teachers, you know, they were genuine teachers. Most of them had the label of being professors. There were no young teachers like you would say just graduated from college. All of these teachers had experience, you know. . . . And there was no such thing as [a] parent-teacher meeting because after school it was nothing for you to see the principal come by your house because he's visiting with your grandfather or going hunting with your grandfather or your math teacher is a friend of your mom or whatever *(Albert Harris)*. To be honest, I think we had some of the best teachers around. . . . Miss Smith, this one right there, she was my second grade teacher; and I enjoyed her. Because when you did your work, she always tried to find a way to tell you, "You did a good job and keep it up." And sometimes she would reward you and sneak a sucker around over to you or something *(Chuck Rodgers)*. She just took a lot of time with you. When she saw that you were interested in something she would just . . . she would take a lot of time with students. She really would. She was more like a mother to you too. Yes, Miss Knight was very nice *(Cheryl Baskin-Brack)*. They all cared; I think that was the main thing. They wanted you to learn, to know things *(Delores Mason)*.

I would give nothing for it. Because from what I can see when I think back, these people prepared us for the world because we were in a small coal mining town in Lynch, Kentucky, but they knew we would go out into the world so therefore they tried to prepare us for the world. We could not use improper English or things of that nature. And I think they were doing their best with everything that they had to prepare us for the world, and I think they did a good job. Because when you think about [it] on a whole, the people that came from these schools and in that town and in that community, a lot of them have done well. And it's because of these people on this picture *(Cynthia Brown-Harrington)*.

• • • • • •

The black children that attended the colored schools in Benham and Lynch, Kentucky, share strong, vivid memories of their experience with "their" school. Although the institution itself was created to damn them—as

it existed solely to carry out a project of racial subjugation and to perpetuate an ideology of racial inferiority—the black community members
in Harlan County reappropriated the colored school as a site of social ordering, cultural production, and pride within the bounds of their own
segregated world. Themes of value, care, and self-making are by no means
limited to these eastern Kentucky colored schools, as studies of segregated
black schools in other areas—such as North Carolina, Florida, and Washington, D.C.[18]—demonstrate how blacks in America *valued* their colored
schools in spite of the relative material deprivation they faced vis-à-vis
their white counterparts.[19] What has emerged from this recent body of literature is an ideal type of black school. Individual case studies of black
schools throughout the South reveal a striking resemblance in terms of
cultural approaches to pedagogy, organizational structure, and social interaction among black teachers, administration, parents, and children. In
her synthesis of all published works on segregated African American
schools in the South from 1935 to 1969, educational historian Vanessa Siddle Walker characterizes the meta-description of black schools in the literature by four themes: (1) exemplary teachers, (2) curriculum and
extracurricular activities, (3) parental support, and (4) leadership of the
school principal.[20] These findings are analogous to the ways in which
other institutions within the black community that were born out of oppressive segregationist structures, such as the black church, emerged as
the primary sites of cultural expression and political organization in the
nineteenth and twentieth centuries.[21]

Recent studies using current oral history data on former African American teachers, administrators, and students who formerly attended these
schools reveal strikingly similar narrative frames used to describe their
memories of the black school.[22] While these studies do not overlook the
gross inequality, financial and structural deprivation, and social forces of
racism upon which segregated schools were predicated, they do shed light
on the cultural mode of African American pedagogy that emerged within
this oppressive context. The resemblances in memory and experience are
uncanny. Quoting an excerpt of an oral history interview from Shircliffe's
2001 study on the function of nostalgia in oral history narratives as they
pertain to the segregated black school, one participant recalled:

At Middleton as a student we were indeed a family. We were embraced
by teachers, protected, taught everything that they thought we would
need to get out there and improve the world, as such. Whatever you did

in school, everybody knew it, your Mom also knew it. When you got home you were obedient. The worst thing you could do was probably skip a class or throw a spitball or something of that sort, because everybody really just took care of everybody. We were a *proud, proud, proud* group; a *proud* group of kids.[23]

The oral testimonies of her participants in Hillsborough County, Florida, echo, almost verbatim, those of my participants in Lynch, Benham, and Cumberland, as do the testimonies from other studies I have come across, focusing on the colored schools in North Carolina and Washington, D.C. This structure of feeling that I have traced throughout this chapter is prototypical of the *genre* of blackness that pervaded the segregated South.

Black Pedagogy

It is clear that the teachers saw themselves as role models, but it is just as important to note and illuminate the ways in which their students perceived them. One of the perceptions consistent throughout the entire body of oral history interviews is that the students felt that their teachers *cared* about them. In spite of all the strict oversight and punishments, rigid rules, and high standards, there was no doubt in their minds that their black lives mattered in the eyes of their teachers. As we are experiencing in our contemporary moment in colleges and universities across the country, the issue of care and belonging is central to creating a learning environment where students can thrive. It cannot be measured or quantified in the same way that other measures of academic environment can; instead, it is a feeling that can only be validated by those on the receiving end. Inherent in the intersubjective experience of giving and receiving care is trust, responsibility, and vulnerability. How did the black children in Harlan County, Kentucky, know that their teachers cared? They knew because their teachers spent time with them, affirming good behavior and redirecting them when they were wandering astray. They did not have to *do* anything to receive it; they were care-worthy just as they were.

> Miss Mady Knight, she was down there at the black school. She was always teaching us. She was a music teacher; I think she was the history teacher too. And she would . . . always talk to us, especially young men, always make something up, you know, so she could spend time with us. And when we didn't do what we were supposed to during school hour[s,] they stayed up there at school, I don't care if it take two hours or three hours, and kept us there in

class teaching us. . . . They used to spend all the time with us, and they didn't get the money for it.

—Sanford Baskin | Graduated Lynch High School | Class of 1965 |
   Integrated in 11th grade

They had high expectations of them. The black teachers did not lower their standards for their black children. They believed in them and knew that they were capable of performing in society. To those teachers, black was not a disability.

Yes, I thought they cared. Because they had it hard, as far as getting an education. And they were trying to make sure that you didn't have that hard a time getting an education. You would be prepared when you go to college, to know something, and then you can compete with other kids. And that's what they were about. As far as I was concerned, that's what I thought they were about.

—Chuck Rodgers | Lynch High School | Class of 1974 |
   Integrated in 6th grade

And she said, "I'm going to make you learn. You're going to learn here or you're going to stay here the next year; you're not going to get out until you learn it." And that's what she did. And she cared for you. Because if you're Black, I'll care for you. Evidently, she saw how things were back then when she was growing up, so she said she had to make a difference. And evidently, she did.

—Richard Chapman | Lynch High School | Class of 1973 |
   Integrated in 7th grade

They extended themselves beyond the classroom and let their students get a glimpse of them as human beings. Despite their position as esteemed teachers, those boundaries of respect were ever present, but they were vulnerable enough to let their students see more than one side of them.

Miss Ellison was a home economics teacher, and she taught a lot of girls how to cook and sew and how to be young ladies, that was her thing, and I love Miss Ellison. We used to go to her house all the time, and she was just nice. She was just, she was like I won't say mom to girls but she was like, she was ready to care about how to become a young lady and know how to take care of yourself. . . . Yeah, then our teachers cared because if you didn't do your work and you was failing they would contact your parents, they would let your parents know. They would call them to come to the school, believe me.

—Vera Peeples | Benham Colored School | Class of 1963

Moreover, they held on to the village pact. A black child was a community asset, and all adults had a part to play in rearing responsible members of society. Parents trusted teachers; teachers trusted parents; and children trusted, feared, and revered their teachers and parents.

> Oh yeah, so much so that our teachers made home visits, okay? Our teachers would visit the parents of each child and rest assured when that teacher showed up at the door that was not and by an appointment that they showed up. They knew what time or day that mama and daddy would be home and mama and daddy was not going to ever turn them away. And they could talk to mama and daddy about any of their children, any of my sisters or my brothers or . . . whomever it was that they wanted to talk [to them] about. And we would pray that they would always be good stories.
>
> —Edgar James Moss | Benham Colored School | Class of 1958

Selecting excerpts for this section was extremely difficult because there are so many examples of the quality and character of education that the children received from their teachers in the black school. This does not mean that these institutions were without problems, as they were surely steeped in intraracial problems similar to those that plague the black community to this day—including colorism and other forms of self-hatred, class bias, and patriarchy.

Living in a single-industry community greatly flattened economic inequality among families. Echoing the statements of many participants, Jeff Turner recalls that "as mountain boys and girls we were such big families . . . and everybody's daddy had the same job. It had a class structure; you were no better than I was, your daddy worked in the coal mines just like mine, they made the same amount, [and] your mama didn't work." However, class distinctions still emerged. Small variations, such as number of children in a household or visibility and participation within social institutions, made all the difference in determining a family's class standing within the community. Those households with fewer children (less than ten in this case); those with members who held leadership roles, such as deacons, ushers, or trustees of one of the black churches; and those who were light skinned tended to hold a higher status among their peers.

> Then there were those that were the gamblers, the heavy drinkers, and the drunks; they were considered more so low class. And I think that category of people were [treated that way by] teachers. If your family were on the poor side then you were treated somewhat that way. If your family was more

involved with the P.T.A. and/or other school activities then you were treated a little bit different than most *(Sam Howard Jr.)*.

Richard Brown, the tenth of fourteen children, remembers being on the receiving end of such treatment:

Everybody used to talk about how great the teachers were, but I didn't have that experience. They weren't good to me. Because if you weren't light-skinned, you weren't smart, you were under privileged—and when I say under privileged, you didn't have that much clothes or no status—they treated you that way. . . . Mm-mm, not for me, they were not that great. Mr. Coleman would never even speak to us, he lived next to us—we could shake hands, that is how close we were.

—Richard Brown | Lynch High School | Class of 1964 |
  Integrated in 10th grade

Skin color was another marker of class distinction, especially for girls.

Well there was one teacher that I felt was partial to the lighter skinned students. She was a brown skinned woman herself. And I felt that she gave them more favors and she was more lenient with them. And [another teacher,] Miss Jackson would call you black, "You look like black Sambo." Yes, she did, Miss Jackson did that *(Clara Smith)*.

Lighter-skinned girls were more likely to get chosen for coveted spots on the cheerleading team or lead roles in school performances, and as Clara Smith points out, this perceived favoritism sometimes spilled over to the classroom itself.

As these examples illuminate, segregated black communities were no racial utopia. White supremacist ideology permeated the consciousness of all people. As chapter 4 demonstrated, the psychosocial effects of double consciousness—the sensation of seeing oneself through the eyes of the Other—shaped black children's subjective understandings of themselves. These thoughts, ideas, and mind-sets did not sustain themselves merely by floating around in individual's heads; rather, they were materialized and reproduced through institutions, laws, and practices. School was one such institution where racist ideologies were affirmed and reproduced. Yet there was something qualitatively distinct about the black pedagogies that were emblematic of the colored school. Black teachers were committed to building high self-esteem, morals, and ethics in the souls of their black students in spite of what Jim Crow dictated about them. This peering into the interior of the colored schools of Benham and Lynch exposes the dualities and tensions of the veil of the color line. These racially segregated institutions were certainly sites of black cultural expression, institutions that inculcated the social order within the black community and served as a wellspring of pride. At the same time, the colored school served its purpose as a racial project, as it allocated resources unequally along racial lines and reinforced negative racial stereotypes and ideologies. These seemingly antithetical truths coexisted. And in the midst of this tug of war between institutionalized subjugation and inequality and pride and self-making, the plate glass of the veil always laid in wait to remind the black coal miners' children of the limits to their freedom.

Encounters with the Veil

As children, their seven-mile, three-town area was all they knew. Born into a segregated society, with parents and grandparents who ventured to Kentucky from Alabama, these children inherited Jim Crow, a structure they took for granted. However, school was one of the main sites where the message was inculcated in black children that they were different from white children. The remainder of this chapter provides memories of schooling in order to examine the ways in which these segregated institutions cultivated a racialized habitus among black children. Stated plainly, we will look at how the colored school reinforced the taken-for-grantedness of physical, social, and psychological segregation through its everyday habits and practices.

In the context of school, difference materialized through relative deprivation. Although the colored schools in Benham and Lynch were considered to be the finest in the region, relative to the fourteen black public schools in eastern Kentucky, they paled in comparison to the normative white schools that stood not a mile away in each community. For example, although the Lynch Colored Public School was considered the premier black school in eastern Kentucky in terms of facilities and resources, it was originally constructed with a budget of $80,000 in 1924, while construction for Lynch High School (the white school) was budgeted at $160,000 that same year. These material inequalities were experienced as a "sensation," as Du Bois would have said it. Vivid memories of the *feeling* of "separate and unequal" often came to the fore throughout the oral history interviews:

> That's one of the examples. I don't remember receiving new books. I remember receiving the hand-downs that'd come from the white school. And there

were other differences as well. For example, a graduated class athlete from Lynch High School would get jackets. They got jackets as a reflection of their athletic prowess. We fought to get sweaters, and I mean literally, sweaters. I remember when we first got the sweaters and how thrilled we were, because before then we could only just look in envy and disappointment at our counterparts at the white schools who were graduating and able to show what they had done. So you had absolute disparity in terms of resources and application of resources and allocation of resources and so forth. You also had differences with curriculum. And this didn't resonate with me until I actually got in college. Yes, we did not have; for example, this is just one case in point. We did not have labs, laboratories.

—Jerome Ratchford | Lynch Colored Public School | Class of 1960

But we practiced every day, five days a week, on the same field. The white team, the Tigers at the east end field just as you were coming to the gate, and the black team, we were at the far end of [the] field after you've come into the gate. But we never played against one another. So that was a negative. Many of the books that we used in the black school were used books from the white school. Now, Professor Matthews would send five or six boys to the white school to get books, used textbooks to be brought back to our school to be used again. And many times the books were all torn and tattered and had pen and pencil marks all through them. There were times that we would, we just—we made the best of what we had.

—Edgar James Moss | Benham Colored School | Class of 1958

When we started buying books they were new books, that was from the 9th grade on that you had to buy your own books. But up to the 8th grade we would get books, but they were secondhand books that came from the White school. It pisses me off every time I think about it. Because the white kids were all sponsored by the same company as us, but we were the ones that got the damn secondhand books.

—Willie French | Lynch Colored Public School | Class of 1960

Now, this is what happened with that; if your parents could not afford to buy you books—sometimes you got books that were handed down from the White school and you would find all kind of names like nigger and all that kind of stuff written in the books.

—Jacquelyn Garner | Lynch Colored Public School | Class of 1963

It is these "little things," the internalized, unarticulated but nonetheless symbolically violent microaggressions within the broader structure of oppression that conditioned a particular racial consciousness. What we can gather from these statements is that the encounter with the used or absent object engendered feelings of desire and shame—from Jerome Ratchford's experience of looking on with "envy and disappointment" to Moss's bringing of the "torn and tattered" books from the white school to the black school to Garner greeted with the word "nigger" when she opened her math book on the first day of school.

As chapter 4 demonstrated, racial segregation is one of the key mechanisms at work in perpetuating and reinforcing cognitive fissures between black and white social worlds. This rings especially true in the context of de jure segregation of blacks and whites in the American South, an era when the uneven hand of Jim Crow loomed large in the everyday lives of all human beings. Jim Crow codes were explicitly embedded into State laws—ordering segregation of schools, railcars, and public recreational spaces, among other contexts—but these laws also pressed a particular set of mores upon black and white bodies, reifying ideologies of racial inferiority and superiority. Once internalized, racial ideologies dimmed the possibility to, as philosopher Immanuel Levinas says, "see the face of the Other,"[24] and instead created the conditions for affective segregation. Under these conditions, Du Bois tells us that "there is almost no community of intellectual life or point of transference where the thoughts and feelings of one race can come into direct contact and sympathy with the thoughts and feelings of the other."[25] This certainly rang true for the black and white communities in Benham, Lynch, and Cumberland.

Schools played a central role in inculcating the Jim Crow ideology in the hearts and minds of all individuals: children and parents, black and white. It is the very everydayness of the school, the machination of going in, day in and day out, along with all the other kids in your community, being split into classrooms by age, playing or cheering by gender, or walking a route determined by race that makes it the ideal breeding ground for making difference real.

Praxis

As a non-company town, Cumberland had no incentive to provide educational services to its black population and instead opted to bus them to Benham. A former Cumberland resident put it squarely:

You will have to recall that segregation prevailed and Cumberland had a white school; it did not have a colored school. So there was an agreement that the colored kids in Cumberland would attend the school in Benham. So the kids in Cumberland were transported by bus to Benham School, and that's where we went to school.

—John Steward | Benham Colored School | Class of 1960

Every day, on their way walking, driving, or busing to school, most blacks had to pass Benham High School, Lynch High School, or Cumberland High School—normatively named for the normal "American" children—before they reached their marked "colored" school. This mundane quotidian practice contributed to the formation of a racialized version of what sociologist Pierre Bourdieu termed *habitus*—"systems of durable, transposable dispositions, structured structures predisposed to function as structuring structures, that is, as principles which generate and organize practices and representations that can be objectively adapted to their outcomes without presupposing a conscious aiming at ends or an express mastery of the operations necessary in order to attain them."[26] Most participants distill their reflections on attending racially segregated schools down to a very simple yet loaded phrase: "That's just the way it was." The "structuring structures" of school segregation normalized practices and behaviors to the extent that they went largely unquestioned. When asked if they ever wondered why they attended separate schools, two participants elaborated:

No, I never did. We went to our high school and they went to their school, and we liked our school as well as anybody ever could. I guess we thought our high school was the only school there was. I mean, we didn't think about them and their school. We never thought about that being a school. I mean, school was where we went to school.

—Willie French | Lynch Colored Public School | Class of 1960

Yeah, we passed them. And there was this little white girl we would used to say, "She better not come on our side!"; but it was not like we started anything. It's like they knew their side and we knew our side. We would pass by them every day, going back and forth, because they are coming up our way and we are going down their way; although we should have all gone to the school that was closest by.

—Patricia Liggins | Lynch Colored Public School | Class of 1963

As these excerpts illustrate, this unquestioning was not bereft of a subjective understanding of their racial positioning. As sociologist Robin Wagner-Pacifici argues, demonstratives not only situate the nature of events but also "become particularly charged in historical transitions in which identities change or in which the identity differences are being highlighted or elided."[27] This is apparent in the consistent deployment of the demonstrative terms "we," "our," "they," "theirs," and "them" to delineate one social group from the other.

The Eve of an Era

The school constructed a particular type of subjectivity for all actors in the black community.[28] Children were conditioned through relentless discipline, surveillance, and an expectation among teachers and parents to be obedient to all adults in the community. However, this obedience did not come without a deep sense of trust. Parents trusted that teachers, and other adult community members, had their children's best interest at hand. Therefore, all black adults were deputized with the authority to discipline a child as they saw fit. Each child was the community's responsibility, and the adults lived the old African proverb "it takes a village to raise a child."

However, this context of community-wide discipline and punishment is not unmoored from history or memory. Escaping the Deep South, coming off the plantations of Alabama, black mothers and fathers understood all too well the repercussions of one member of the community forgetting his or her place. Unlikely was the possibility of an individual being held accountable for his or her own behavior, for to whites, in the event of a misunderstanding, a nigger was *any* and *all* them niggers. Therefore, the consequences of one transgression could easily bear down on the entire community.[29] In this sense, intraracial conformity was very much a strategy for survival. This was also steeped in the black political ideology of a "linked fate," which was based on the belief that each individual person represented the entire black race.[30]

Jerome Ratchford's experience with his high school teacher, Mrs. Hatch, embodies these sentiments of care, community involvement, and trust, as well as the notion of representing one's race. I met Dr. Ratchford in his office at Kennesaw State University to conduct his oral history interview, where we had a lively conversation about a range of topics, including his upbringing in Lynch, Kentucky. When I shared the photo of the teachers at the Lynch Colored Public School with him, he immediately began affectionately identifying the people he saw in the photo. I asked him if he could share a story about one or two of his teachers that had left an indelible mark on his life:

Yes. And for me it was—she's not amongst those on that photograph. But I literally owe everything that I have accomplished to her. And her name, the last name is Hatch. Mrs. Hatch. She, like many of them, migrated from Central Kentucky; in her case I think it was Ohio, very near central Kentucky and so forth. And she came more than capable to Lynch; more than capable as a teacher. And she taught history and she taught—well, history, social studies, and so forth. And she wanted to expand our knowledge and awareness; I particularly remember her adding current events to her teaching curriculum. But the thing that stands out with me with her is that when I started at the South East Center, which is the extension of [the] University of Kentucky, and my classmates, we constituted the first cohort going there.

It was the first desegregated opportunity—certainly in that community, but I daresay in southeastern Kentucky. Our desegregation ironically occurred at the higher education level. It didn't occur like it occurred throughout the country, typically high school and then sometimes even earlier than that. Well, after one year, she knew it was very, very important for me to stay at the extension center in southeastern Kentucky for lots of reasons. She probably understood that we needed successes, she understood what it meant for me personally; probably a lot of things and so forth. But I was poised not to be able to continue to go to school there, because my father had been downsized, as we say today; laid off then.

And so that mere tuition amount of only less than $100, we actually didn't have that amount of money. And so there was a probability that after one year I would stop. And I don't know how she found out about it, but she came to my house and told my parents that she didn't want to be intrusive but she was willing to give me, my family, the tuition money; and gave it to my family, okay; for me to stay in school.

And so I'm ever—and I was filled with tears in my eyes as well—I'm ever indebted. Obviously, I was able to pay her the money back. But more important than paying the money back is passing on the legacy. So when I go back and I think about why I have been facilitative, certainly of black kids having opportunity to higher education but any child having an education. That's the foundation for it. If there's anything that I can do to catapult or influence someone else achieving his or her goals academically, particularly in higher education, I will do that. The foundation for that was Mrs. Hatch, for me. Yes.

—Jerome Ratchford | Born 1940 in Lynch, Ky. | Resides in Atlanta, Ga.

・・・・・・

Opened in 1960, the South East Center was one of nearly a dozen satellite branches of the University of Kentucky, established in an attempt for the university system to diversify its regional intrastate student population. The center gave young people from the otherwise foreign Appalachian region of Kentucky access to the state higher education system by offering an associate degree program in Cumberland. It was also a direct pipeline to the University of Kentucky's main campus in Lexington, where those who demonstrated the merit and fortitude to continue their education went on to attain their bachelor's degree at the flagship campus. Jerome Ratchford was one such person. In fact, he went on to attain a PhD in education from Bowling Green State University and has subsequently maintained a career in academia until recently, when he retired from a deanship at Kennesaw State University in Atlanta, Georgia.

However, as his story illuminates, his college pursuits were tenuous from the start. U.S. Steel had begun to close the mine, and his father was one of the many men who were laid off in the process. At the same time, the urban centers in the Midwest and Northeast were experiencing an industrial boom. So while Dr. Ratchford's peers were migrating to the city, attaining factory jobs and making "big money" or volunteering to serve in the military to travel the world, he was one of six black students who were identified by the teachers as the "talented tenth" and selected to join the first cohort of the satellite system. Reflecting on his feelings at that time, Dr. Ratchford felt that he was left behind by staying in college because his peers were out "doing" something. College did not present itself as a clear pathway to mobility at the time. And even if it did, there was no cultural resource to model.[31] Therefore, beyond his own personal well-being, Mrs. Hatch understood, as Dr. Ratchford put it, that "we needed successes." Coming to his home to see his parents and offering to pay Jerome's tuition at a time when the family was going through a difficult and perhaps shameful time required a deep level of trust, care, and intimacy between Mrs. Hatch and the Ratchford family.

Underlying this act of generosity was Mrs. Hatch's understanding of what was at stake. She knew what most other teachers and adults knew: a change was coming to the tri-city area, one for which the black children must be prepared. Southeast Community College was the first integrated educational institution in southeastern Kentucky, and it foreshadowed the desegregation of the public education system in the region. Jerome Ratchford and his five black counterparts were a signal to the community that black students could perform and thrive in an integrated society.

Southeast Community College foreshadowed the change that was soon to come to the eastern Kentucky public school system. It was 1960, six years after the landmark *Brown v. Board of Education* Supreme Court decision. Although the white administrators on the local board of education were successful in staving off the implementation of the federal mandate, legal segregation would not last. The black teachers at the colored schools in Benham and Lynch sensed the tides changing well in advance of the rest of the community. It was the eve of an era. While they understood that they very well might become obsolete through the transition, this generation of black teachers prepared their students to "go up to the white school." Chapter 6 examines *Brown v. Board of Education* and the subsequent desegregation of the school systems in Benham, Cumberland, and Lynch as what sociologist William Sewell terms an "eventful temporality," which refers to those events that change the course of history and thought.[32] Throughout the chapter, I will center the experiences of this generation of black coal miners' kids to illuminate the ways in which this legal transformation also transformed African American subjectivity and collective identity.

Segregation of white and colored children in public schools has a detrimental effect upon the colored children. The impact is greater when it has the sanction of the law, for the policy of separating the races is usually interpreted as denoting the inferiority of the Negro group. A sense of inferiority affects the motivation of a child to learn. Segregation with the sanction of law, therefore, has a tendency to [retard] the educational and mental development of Negro children and to deprive them of some of the benefits they would receive in a racially integrated school system.

—Chief Justice Warren, *Brown v. Board of Education*

If you look up there right there today in concrete it says Lynch Colored School. . . . It's right there today—the blacks call it West Main High you know. But it's written out there: Lynch Colored School. See because we went through a transformation as to who we were—we went from Colored, to Negroes, to African-Americans . . . and Black. We went through all of those.

—Albert Harris | Born 1950 in Benham, Ky. |
   Integrated in 8th grade

6 A Change Gone Come

. . . .

The U.S. Supreme Court had made its ruling: the nation's public school system was to desegregate. Now that the battle for civil rights on this front had been fought and won by the nation's civil rights leaders, who would be the ones to go in and use their bodies to actually break the barriers and begin the process of integrating our trenchantly segregated society? It would not be the movement leaders or the black intelligentsia who fought so valiantly in the courts, in the press, and on the streets. Nor would it be the black teachers who dedicated their careers and much of their private lives to racial uplift. No, both the inheritance and the risks of desegregation would befall everyday black children. Whether by volunteer or conscription, they would be the historical change agents for dismantling the "separate but equal" doctrine upheld for over half a century by *Plessy v. Ferguson*. What was that experience like? And what did it mean to them? Further, what ever happened to the hundreds of colored schools that once peppered the South?

One of the main purposes of schools in any modern society is to create "good" citizens. During the time of de jure segregation, it was clear that blacks and whites were citizens of different degrees. Therefore, at the core of the institutional logic of the colored school system are complicated questions of African American and American identity, belonging, and citizenship. If the colored school produced a certain type of black identity—one that was both fashioned by the state and self-proclaimed through the agency of black teachers, parents, and students—then what are the ways in which the event of school desegregation transformed the meaning of being black in America? The 1954 decision pierced the broader American imagination, sanctioning the possibility for black people to recalibrate their perceived place within the national citizenry. Through *Brown v. Board of Education*, the "children of integration" *became* African American. We will read this process of becoming through the shared experiences of the black communities in the tri-city area of Harlan County. However, before returning to the small towns in the hills of Kentucky, let us first zoom out and unpack the national political landscape on which the legal mandate for school desegregation emerged.

Brown v. Board of Education: The Battleground for Citizenship

By the early 1950s, blacks throughout the southern and border states were still living under the overtly racist mandates of the Jim Crow caste system, while those in the North were experiencing a more veiled yet equally oppressive form of de facto racism. However, by this time—two to three generations removed from slavery—a black professional middle class had emerged in America. While the majority of the black population still held working-class positions as laborers on the lowest rung of the segmented labor economy, black communities were being established with their own doctors and dentists, real estate agents, teachers and professors, attorneys, nurses, and all manner of professions. Together, blacks were mobilizing more than ever to demand that America, as Martin Luther King Jr. would later say, "cash its promissory note" to grant all her people the guarantee of the "unalienable right" to "Life, Liberty, and the Pursuit of Happiness."[1]

At the top of the agenda was the systematic dismantling of Jim Crow, and civil rights leaders, especially those in the NAACP, identified the school as the ideal battleground to fight for equal rights for the Negro in America.[2] The NAACP filed a series of civil rights lawsuits from the 1920s onward demanding that an individual black plaintiff be admitted into graduate or professional schools at specific U.S. public universities, namely *State of Missouri v. Gaines* (1938), *Sweatt v. Painter* (1950), and *McLaurin v. Oklahoma State Regents for Higher Education* (1950). Many of these suits resulted in victories. For example, in 1946, Herman Sweatt was denied admission to the Law School at the University of Texas because as a segregated institution of higher learning, there was no place for young black Herman. Although the NAACP lost the case in state court, it appealed to the U.S. Supreme Court and won. In 1950, the court ordered the University of Texas to integrate its Law School and its Graduate School. In the *Sweatt* case and those like it, NAACP lawyers argued that there was no equivalent alternative institution for their plaintiffs to attend in their state, thus making the "equal" in "separate but equal" impossible to access. All of these early cases worked within the framework of the separate but equal doctrine affirmed over fifty years earlier, in 1896, with *Plessy v. Ferguson*.

However, in 1952, the NAACP filed a set of class action suits in five states—Delaware, South Carolina, Virginia, Kansas, and Washington, D.C.—that culminated in the landmark *Brown v. Board of Education* decision of 1954. Unlike the previous cases, which argued for equal educational access in the absence of separate and equal institutions, the attorneys in *Brown* argued that the very existence of a racially segregated educational institution was in fact unequal. The previous cases provided legal precedence to support their arguments. Legal scholar Charles Ogletree Jr. asserts that "the Court had supported the "equalization" strategy, but Brown asked it to switch horses in midcourse and revisit *Plessy* as a whole."[3] Also unlike the previous cases, the battleground for *Brown* was not the sphere of higher education but the entire U.S. public school system.

The Case

The case was originally argued before the Supreme Court on December 9 and 10, 1952. John W. Davis represented the appellees—the various boards of education—and Thurgood Marshall the appellants—the black children represented in the class action suit, who symbolically represented all black children in America. Different from his approach in previous cases, Marshall argued on the basis of the inherent inequality of racial segregation of schools. As Marshall explained to Chief Justice Vinson, "At the time, counsel for the appellants, however, made the position clear that the attack was not being made on the 'separate but equal' basis as to physical facilities, but the position we were taking was that these statutes were unconstitutional in their enforcement because they not only produced these inevitable inequalities in physical facilities, but that evidence would be produced by expert witnesses to show that the governmentally imposed racial segregation in and of itself was also a denial of equality." Marshall and his team drove their point home through the expert witness testimony of Drs. Kenneth and Mamie Clark, two African American psychologists at City College of New York (CUNY), who presented findings from their experimental research on children's attitudes toward race—the famous "doll experiments." Similar to Virginia Taylor-Ward's response in chapter 4, where she threw the white doll she received as a Christmas gift across the room in disgust, children in the Clarks' study—black and white—associated the black doll with "bad" and "ugly" and the white doll with "good" and "beautiful." Most damning for the opposing team was that although the black children projected negative associations onto the black doll, they claimed that those were the dolls with which they most closely identified. This gave Marshall the evidence he needed to argue that segregation had not only negative economic effects but also equally negative *psychological* effects on children. With this scientific ammunition, Marshall argued:

Witnesses testified that segregation deterred the development of the personalities of these children. Two witnesses testified that it deprives them of equal status in the school community, that it destroys their self-respect. Two other witnesses testified that it denies them full opportunity for democratic social development. Another witness said that it stamps him with a badge of inferiority. The summation of that testimony is that the Negro children have road blocks put up in their minds as a result of this segregation, so that the amount of education that they take in is much less than other students take in.[4]

In defense of the status quo, Davis and his legal team relied on three logics to support their argument to maintain state-imposed segregation of public schools: original intent, white intolerance, and fear. The court had used original intent to support legal racial subjugation since the years following the ratification of the U.S. Constitution. The premise of the argument requires the court to interpret the original intent of the framers at the time of the Constitution's drafting, asking, "Did the framers intend for these rights to be extended to the non-white population?" In this case, "Are the Negroes citizens or subjects of the United States of America?" Davis began his argument speaking of the Fourteenth Amendment: "The effort in which I am now engaged is to show how those who submitted this Amendment and those who adopted it conceded it to be, and what their conduct by way of interpretation has been since its ratification in 1868." Confused, Associate Justice Frankfurter pressed Davis:

> *Justice Frankfurter:* What you are saying is, that as a matter of history, history puts a gloss upon "equal" which does not permit elimination or admixture of white and colored in this aspect to be introduced.
> *John Davis, Esq.:* I am saying that.
> *Justice Frankfurter:* That is what you are saying?

Moving on from this awkward moment, Davis then proceeded to his other two arguments, ones that he believed attended more directly to the contemporary moment—that Negroes are a biologically inferior race. His second argument hinged on the rationale that irrespective of the constitutionality of separate but equal, whites simply did not want to mix with blacks, and this reality was enough not to proceed. To support this argument, he misappropriated quotes taken from papers and speeches delivered by a host of scholars, including leading sociologists Howard W. Odum and W. E. B. Du Bois. In his analysis of this moment, Ogletree explains that "those representing the states forced to integrate after *Brown* argued that the Court's ruling could do irreparable harm; there would be sustained hostility by whites, withdrawal of while children from integrated schools, racial tensions, violence, and loss of jobs for black teachers. Some opponents of integration went to extremes, arguing that integration could bring blacks with lower IQs into the schools, that many black children were retarded, and that tuberculosis and venereal disease would spread, as would the enrollment of illegitimate children. Their point was that integration would destroy their way of life."[5] Relying on this latent sentiment of fear and supremacy, Davis avers, "Is it not the height of wisdom that the manner in which that shall be conducted should be left to those most immediately affected by it, and that the wishes of the parents, both white and colored, should be ascertained before their children are forced into what may be an unwelcome contact?" After hearing Davis's arguments, Marshall, in his rebuttal the next day, went for the jugular. "So far as the appellants are concerned in this case, at this point it seems to me that the significant factor running through all these arguments up to this point is that for some reason, which is still unexplained, Negroes are taken out of the main stream of American life in these states. There is nothing involved in this case other than race and color, and I do not need to go to the background of the statutes or anything else. I just read the statutes, and they say, 'white and colored.'"

Marshall's observational rebuttal made plain that Davis's arguments were solely based on racism, not the legal statutes to which they were bound. With the arguments presented over the course of this two-day Supreme Court case, Thurgood Marshall and his team, as Stuart Hall would say, *rearticulated* the American citizen.

The Decision

On that day of May 17, 1954, those of the "colored" race—the Negroes—*became* African American, and John Davis and his legal team found themselves on the wrong side of history. Although it took an unprecedented sixteen months, the Supreme Court returned with a unanimous decision. Authored by newly appointed Chief Justice Warren,[6] the court's opinion opens with this statement: "Segregation of white and Negro children in the public schools of a State solely on the basis of race, pursuant to state laws permitting or requiring such segregation, denies Negro children the equal protection of the laws guaranteed by the Fourteenth Amendment—even though the physical facilities and other 'tangible' factors of white and Negro schools may be equal." With a deft legerdemain, Chief Justice Warren affirms Marshall's original argument and disparages Davis's, for not two sentences later he states: "The question presented in these cases must be determined not on the basis of conditions existing when the Fourteenth Amendment was adopted, but in the light of the full development of public education and its present place in American life throughout the Nation." Relying not on the precedent of "separate but equal," affirmed by *Plessy v. Ferguson* in 1896—the Supreme Court decision that had determined the outcome of the half dozen education-based NAACP cases that preceded *Brown*—Warren and his fellow justices relied on the new testimony introduced by the Clark experiments.

> To separate them from others of similar age and qualifications solely because of their race generates a feeling of inferiority as to their status in the community that may affect their hearts and minds in a way unlikely ever to be undone. . . . A sense of inferiority affects the motivation of a child to learn. Segregation with the sanction of law, therefore, has a tendency to retard the educational and mental development of Negro children and to deprive them of some of the benefits they would receive in a racially integrated school system. Whatever may have been the extent of psychological knowledge at the time of *Plessy v. Ferguson*, this finding is amply supported by modern authority. Any language in *Plessy v. Ferguson* contrary to this finding is rejected.

A victory no doubt, this landmark decision came with one string attached: that local communities enforce the desegregation of public schools with "all deliberate speed." These three words compromised the decision from the outset, "as the 'all deliberate speed' language was code for 'slow.'" Using the same logic as gradual emancipation legislation, school desegregation was to happen "in due time" in order to appease white fear and anger about the idea of their children mixing with the colored race. Ogletree rightly observed that this meant that "resisters were allowed to end segregation on their own timetable."[7] In Harlan County, Kentucky, "all deliberate speed" meant 1963, nearly ten years after the Supreme Court ruling.[8]

Negro Discourses on Negro Education

The question of the future of black education in America was also of grave concern to the black community. The debate of the day among the black intelligentsia concerning education was whether or not black children needed integrated schools in order to compete in American society.[9] By the end of Reconstruction, nearly all colored schools in the South were being taught by black faculty, and although under the jurisdiction of white superintendent boards, the day-to-day administration of these schools was left to black principals and teachers. In light of these circumstances, there was a question as to whether black students would and could thrive in an integrated society if left to the institutional and interpersonal prejudices of a white supremacist society.

In his simply titled article "Does the Negro Need Separate Schools?," W. E. B. Du Bois carefully weaves an argument that asserts that an integrated school system would surely be ideal, as it would foster a richer cultural experience and greater self-confidence for both black and white students. However, he de-romanticizes the notion of such an environment through a sober warning: "What [the Negro] must remember is that there is no magic, either in mixed schools or in segregated schools. A mixed school with poor and unsympathetic teachers with hostile public opinion, and no teaching of truth concerning Black folk, is bad. A segregated school with ignorant placeholders, inadequate equipment, poor salaries, and wretched housing, is equally bad."[10] Du Bois's conclusion articulates the paradox of the day. For the black community, the question of the possibility of true "integration" was one of mutual recognition and equality. The material act of school integration would be rendered inconsequential, or even harmful, without it. This uncertainty loomed large in the moments leading up to and immediately following the *Brown v. Board of Education* decision and lingered on up until school desegregation was finally enforced throughout the local public school districts—which in some cases took a full two decades to come to fruition.[11] This situation caused a great deal of anxiety and irresolution within the black community.

For example, anthropologist and public intellectual Zora Neale Hurston, who was on the outs with much of the high society black community at the time, although knowingly way left of the argument vis-à-vis her peers, just could not hold her tongue on the matter. In a letter to the *Orlando Sentinel* in 1955, just one year after the *Brown* decision came down from the Supreme

Court, Hurston opens by resigning herself to the ridicule she will certainly receive for her trenchant critique. She writes, "I was not going to part my lips concerning the U.S. Supreme Court decision on ending segregation in public schools of the South. But since a lot of time has passed and no one seems to touch on what to me appears to be the most important point in the hassle, I break my silence just this once. Consider me as just thinking out loud. The whole matter revolves around the self-respect of my people. How much satisfaction can I get from a court order for somebody to associate with me who does not wish me near them?"[12] In line with Davis's argument in *Brown*, Hurston sees this as an issue of will and desire. To that extent, she argues that she would much prefer what she called "ethical and cultural desegregation" to the forced desegregation of black and white bodies. She also had faith in the possibilities of the colored school system. Through concerted equalization efforts, she believed that black children could receive an education equal to whites, sans the emotional cost evidenced by the Clark findings upon which the *Brown* ruling hinged. "If there are not adequate Negro schools in Florida, and there is some residual, some inherent and unchangeable quality in white schools, impossible to duplicate anywhere else, then I am the first to insist that Negro Children of Florida be allowed to share this boon. But if there are adequate Negro schools and prepared instructors and instruction, then there is nothing different except the presence of white people. For this reason, I regard the ruling of the U.S. Supreme Court as insulting rather than honoring my race."[13]

The integration question loomed large within the black community, and the discourse was certainly not limited to the black elite class. Black principals and teachers on the ground had strong views about the best course of action for the next generation of the young, gifted, and black.[14] They also had to wonder about what desegregation would mean to their careers: Would integrated schools leave the black teacher as an obsolete artifact? Parents and children worried too: Would black children be able to keep up with their white counterparts? For hundreds of years blacks had been told by society that they were inferior to whites; an integrated school presented itself as the site where some of our worst fears could materialize.

Anticipating Integration in Harlan County, Kentucky

The years between 1952—the inception of the *Brown v. Board* arguments—and 1963—the year that the school system in the tri-city area desegregated—marked the twilight of the era of Jim Crow segregation in Harlan County.

This window in time was chock-full of anxiety and anticipation. In the years leading up to desegregation, teachers augured the inevitable change to students and parents. Although they may not have been privy to the exact year that the school system would consolidate, they knew that it was only a matter of time before the educational structures would be transformed in their community. One graduate of the class of 1961 recalls that although he did not integrate, his teachers constantly braced him for the possibility:

> I remember the two things they hammered in my head.... You get an education—you're not going to be able to get no job in no coal mine so you better get your education so you'd be able to get something to do. Second was you better learn something, learn how to compete in an integrated society because segregation is going to end. From the 1st grade all the way through high school I heard that, I don't know how many times.
>
> —Victor Prinkleton | Born 1943 in Lynch, Ky. |
> Graduated Lynch Colored Public School in 1961

The black teachers strove to prepare their students not only to coexist but to *compete* in an integrated society. In their framing, the underlying logic of their desire to compete was still grounded in the us–them binary that was embedded in the epistemological structure of Jim Crow society. For them, instilling a strong sense of self-confidence and capability in their black students before integration was a prime responsibility. It was just as important that their students believed they were prepared as it was for it to actually be so:

> They took an interest in what you were doing education-wise, and they saw to it that you were prepared—you know when I came down [to] University of Kentucky I was not afraid that I could not compete or anything like that. I mean that just was not in my nature. And so I can do the same thing you're doing. And that's the way they prepared us: to be as good, better than anybody else.
>
> —Lee Arthur Jackson | Born 1950 in Lynch, Ky. |
> Graduated Lynch High School in 1968

The feeling that one has to work twice as hard or be twice as good to accomplish his or her goals in mainstream society is a common sentiment across ethnically and racially marginalized communities. Many teachers at the Lynch Colored Public School balanced this pressure to outperform with unwavering encouragement that their natural abilities were more than sufficient and that they were not coming from a fundamental position of lack.

However, not all teachers truly embraced the idea of integration, and some did not bother to hide their contempt. One interviewee remembers her fifth grade teacher, Ms. Jackson, one of the original teachers hired on to the Lynch faculty in 1924, discouraging the class the year before integration:

> And I can remember her saying, "You're going to be like a lost ball on the highways of Georgia next year when you go over to the other school." And I always felt like, you know, *if we are it's your fault. You're not preparing us to go to be integrated,* but that's what she would tell us. She was just really mean.
>
> —Brenda Combs | Graduated Lynch High School in 1972 |
> Integrated in 6th grade

The promise of school desegregation affected the entire African American community. Teachers were tasked with preparing their students mentally and emotionally for the coming transition, even though they themselves did not know exactly what to expect. Few teachers had firsthand experience with integrated academic environments, as the majority of them had been educated in the colored school system and later on at historically black colleges. They also had to deal with the uncertainty of their own futures. Integrating the school systems meant that there would be redundancies in human resources at almost every level, from administrators and faculty down on to the janitors. Parents did their best to instill a sense of pride and confidence in their children, reinforcing the nurturing and structure that they received from their teachers. However, the only ones who would actually come to fully experience the transition were the coal miners' kids; these were the children of integration.

The First Three

The colored schools in Benham and Lynch graduated their last classes in the spring of 1963. The school board in Lynch decided that it was best to adopt a model of gradual desegregation, in which tenth, eleventh, and twelfth graders would participate in the first phase of integration, with the remaining student body following suit over the course of a few years. Mr. Coleman, the principal of the Lynch Colored Public School at the time, held a community meeting in the gym to break the news to students and parents about the coming transition. The students in those grades, who would go on to become the classes of 1964, 1965, and 1966—the first three— were about to encounter something with which most adults in the community had no experience: competing in an integrated social environment. When I asked participants to "take us back to 1964, when you first integrated," members of those classes shared vivid, emotional memories of their initial encounters with school desegregation:

> You know sometimes I try to go back to that, and I'm not sure if I can remember, and that may be one of those kinds of things that you try to put out of your mind . . . because it was something that I didn't want to happen. All the way through high school you look forward to the day when you're the big one, that you're the senior. And they took that away from us, just flat took it away from us. I looked through one of the yearbooks and I looked at a lot of the awards in different groups, they have different things. They were all white kids in our senior year, and I think most of that probably was already done; it was already decided before we went up there. The only thing that we really fully integrated into was sports, football and basketball.
>
> —Porter G. Peeples | Born 1945 | Class of 1964 | Integrated in 12th grade

> When Professor Coleman announced in the gym that that would be our last year, it felt like something stabbed me in my heart because I didn't want to leave.
>
> —Cheryl Baskin-Brack | Born 1947 | Class of 1965 | Integrated in 11th grade

> The original experience going to the integration aspect to me was just a using process. What I mean in a using process is that they didn't want us there. White society really didn't want us there, but they had no choice in it. I really didn't even want to be there; I really didn't. I didn't want to be there because I knew it was just a using aspect to try to get the best black athletes. And it was just a using experience. They still went their way, and we still went our way. We just went to school with them, but you still were not given the props to which you demanded. You could excel in a great many things, but you still were not going to get recognized for it.
>
> —Jack French | Born 1945 | Class of 1964 | Integrated in 12th grade

Although school desegregation affected the entire African American community, the members of those first three classes by far express the strongest sense of trauma, loss, and melancholy over school desegregation. Even now in their late sixties, going back to that time often brought them to tears. The previous three excerpts are representative of the overall sentiment conveyed by the majority of participants; for them, school desegregation was an abrupt encounter with erasure: one that negated the value that they placed on their institution, rendering them invisible with the exception of their athletic prowess. The experience with school desegregation reverberated throughout the student body, even with respondents who "went up to the white school" as early as third grade. One consideration that was clearly overlooked at the time is that in spite of the apparent structural inequality, African Americans *valued* their institutions. As I demonstrated in chapter 5, the colored school was central to the black community, as it was an institution that contributed greatly to the formation of a distinctly black identity.

Although *Brown v. Board of Education* was decided in 1954, no public school in Harlan County made any immediate effort to desegregate the school system. Southeast Community College, established as an integrated institution, was a glaring signal to the community that times were changing. And in March 1963, the *Tri-City News* announced that the Lynch Independent School District would desegregate the following year. The same went for the schools in the rest of the county. According to Elkins Payne, the chairman of the school board, the three main factors leading to the decision were (1) declining enrollment due to persistent decline in the labor force, (2) compliance with state law (Payne notes that the "Lynch and Harlan County School System were without integration plans"), and (3) the fact that West Main would have to be put on an emergency rating basis due to the precipitous decline.[15] Interestingly, in Harlan County, the decision to desegregate was largely motivated by the effects of labor retrenchment and out-migration as opposed to the pressure from the federal mandate of *Brown*.

Although the motivations were singular to the community, the impact on its black children resonated with the experiences of so many others across the country. Therefore, I ask, what was the underlying injury that created this unhealed wound among this generation of newly minted African Americans?[16]

The "Hidden Injuries" of School Desegregation

The mandate to integrate two competing institutional logics, cultures, and classes of citizens was a daunting challenge for communities across the South. What we will see is that in Benham, Cumberland, and Lynch—like hundreds of other communities—school integration never truly took place. Herein lies the crux of the injury for the *children of integration*. At the heart of the matter was an issue of distrust, fear, and misrecognition.[17] Could the enforcement of *Brown v. Board of Education* transform the "us" and "them" that hundreds of years of slavery, Jim Crow, and racial violence had crystalized in the minds of American citizens into a "we"? And does achieving "we-ness" require assimilating into one (the *unum*), or can many parts of a civil body come together as a whole? Participants frame their experience in going through this process of transformation in terms of loss, care, and transforming epistemologies.

Loss of Community

When the schools desegregated in 1964, the black students who formerly attended the colored schools were made to attend the normative school system in their respective community, or as the participants often put it, "We had to go up to the white school." For them, the abrupt closure of their schools was a source of trauma, as it represented the negation of their cultural identity:

> I think it hurt us in a lot of ways, maybe I'm wrong. They just moved us up there and we had nothing left you know, as far as having something left from our school. We had to go and step in their house, that's what I'm talking about—I sleep in their house, they took whatever they had, we didn't have anything left.
>
> —Clara Smith | Born 1940 | Class of 1958 | Never integrated

One man who integrated in the ninth grade remembers he and his friends responding to this feeling of negation by reasserting their attachment to the former colored school:

> And for us, we were mad because they closed our school down and we had the newer building, and they closed our school down. So we were forced to go to their building and stuff, you know. So that part angered us too. All the stuff, it just got thrown away. I remember I was with some of my boys and we went and broke into the old colored school and we took some of the trophies and the basketball warm-up pants. There were four of us and we stole those and we would sport them [the pants] around and wear them. But yeah, they just—they just did away with our stuff. So that was our anger in that.
>
> —Albert Harris | Born 1950 | Class of 1968 | Integrated in 9th grade

The feeling of loss extended to the community level. When pressed about the perceived cost of desegregation, participants consistently cited the loss of their teachers. The same respondent who reclaimed the basketball paraphernalia went on to link his sense of loss to the teachers:

FIGURE 13 Lynch Colored Public School basketball team | circa 1950. Lynch (Kentucky) Colored School/West Main Alumni Assoc. Collection, Southern Historical Collection, Louis Round Wilson Special Collections Library, University of North Carolina at Chapel Hill.

You got to realize that we had our own school, so you had—from principal, assistant principal, math, biology, science, all the way down to the janitors. So the majority of them lost their jobs and it was the same way in Lynch, it was just a few teachers that maintained their jobs. So the rest of them had to leave the area.

—Albert Harris | Born 1950 | Class of 1968 | Integrated in 9th grade

The elimination of the black faculty was by far the most cited perceived loss to the African American community. Living in a segregated community, isolated in the hollows of the Appalachian Mountains, the teachers were intimately embedded into structures of the black community. Yes, they were the children's esteemed educators, but they were also neighbors, family friends, Sunday School teachers, and community organizers. Once desegregation was enforced, the black teachers were a redundant resource to the school system and were, for the most part, let go. Harriet Callaway-

Hill, a 1959 graduate of Benham Colored School, recalled the shock of coming home to Benham after graduating college to find that her role models were no longer there. "The teachers that I had all my life. They no longer had a job there."

These participants' statements shed light on the hidden injury: it was not the actual *act* of integration that generated negative feelings but the *procedure* in which the process was carried out. For them, it was not integration but the fact that they were being called on to move their black bodies from a place where they had constructed a social world to one where they had no familiarity, advocacy, or say in shaping the environment. Although desegregation was challenging to everyone, no white children were put upon to uproot their surroundings and enter into another fully formed environment. Instead, the blacks were mandated, in short order, to leave "their school" and all that came with it and adapt to a new surrounding. John Steward, a 1958 graduate of Benham Colored School, sums up the feeling of such a process: "The thing about integration is an acknowledgment that yours is better than mine, that I am inferior to you."

Care by Teaching Staff

The significance of the loss of the teachers cannot be underscored enough. Born one or two generations out of slavery, few black parents in Harlan County had more than an eighth grade education. They therefore depended on the teachers to elevate their children into full citizenry through education. To that end, parents ascribed a tremendous level of trust, legitimacy, and esteem to the college-educated teachers who were employed at the colored schools in Lynch and Benham, Kentucky, and the teachers, for the most part, accepted the mandate of racial uplift.

Thematically, interviewees' rich memories of their experience in the colored schools are framed in terms of strict disciplinary environments—laced with anecdotes of high teacher expectations in terms of academic performance, behavioral comportment, and physical hygiene—coupled with a strong feeling of care, intimacy, and trust.

> They're the definition of tough love with all of the positive trappings. While it would have been convenient and easy for them to say you can't do it and the world is unfair and say all those things, and then let us sort of bask in mediocrity—they went the other route. They were not going to let us do less than what our abilities would have us do. And so to earn a mark and having

those kinds of expectations and projections in confidence were very, very influential in the successes, and there are many, many successes that have come out of that community. But they were the catalysts for that, along with our parents.

—Jerome Ratchford | Born 1942 | Class of 1960 | Never integrated

Everything was close and the teachers cared—truly cared—about your education, and they made sure that you concentrated on your education. Dot the I's, cross all the T's, and all that kind of stuff. And they constantly prepared you and they followed up with you; they had home visits to your parents, to let parents know how you were doing in school, if you're doing bad or good and what you need to do.

—Chuck Rodgers | Born 1957 in Lynch, Ky. | Class of 1974 |
  Integrated in 2nd grade

However, that social contract between the teachers, parents, and children was breached with school desegregation. When asked to reflect on their memories about "going up to the white school," participants overwhelmingly pointed to a sense of loss of care. The short response that first came to mind for many respondents was that "I didn't want to be there, and they didn't want us there." When pushed to unpack what that meant, participants framed their responses in terms of teacher apathy:

Their teachers didn't seem to care about us like our own did. To me, it was sort of, "If you didn't get it you didn't get it." It was not like they were going to spend that one on one with you.

—Belinda Napier | Born 1951 | Class of 1969 | Integrated in 7th grade

Their mentality was that "these black kids are here, we got to accept the fact that they are here, but I am not going out of my way to give them any extra help if they need it. I am just going to deal with it to the extent to which it is beneficial to the school." To me, that was their mentality. And I watched and observed a great deal of the teachers, because when I came in, it was nothing but all white teachers; that's all.

—Jack French | Born 1945 | Class of 1964 | Integrated in 12th grade

To me, when we integrated it seemed like the teachers, the white teachers, they didn't care whether we learned or not. They were just there, and that was it.

—Cheryl Baskin-Brack | Born 1947 | Class of 1965 | Integrated in 11th grade

Their perception was that they were invisible to the teachers in the integrated school system. They responded to their experience of misrecognition and unwantedness in kind: "I didn't want to be there, and they didn't want us there." In the colored school, black students received affirmative responses to their being; however, the mutual recognition necessary to generate a positive form of what Cooley called "self-feeling" was absent upon integration.[18]

Transforming Racial Epistemologies

Du Bois points to the "thousand and one little actions" that he characterizes as both "elusive" and "essential" for the construction of social worlds.[19] For him, the most detrimental outcome of Jim Crow was the psychological fissure between the white and black social world that thwarted the possibility for mutual recognition. For many children, the integrated school was the first and only public sphere in which black and white children had the opportunity to share any meaningful social exchange. Therefore, previous conceptions of each other were based primarily on myth as opposed to experience. The physical and social separation conditioned by Jim Crow engendered assumptions of white superiority and difference. However, for many, these notions of inherent difference were demystified with time and interaction.

> We had a background from the black school, I honestly say this with all my heart; they gave us a foundation that learning was everything. So it didn't matter if I was in school with white people talking about me, I didn't care. But I wanted to know, [pause] and I wanted to know what they meant. What made them so different to everybody else? . . . We all thought white people were all well to do. All better off than we were. Well as time went on, we started running into people that didn't mind telling you how poor they were and the different things they had to deal with and their environment. And I began to see a different class of people among themselves—white people—especially freshmen in high school. There were people in there that didn't have it like the rest of the white people, and they seemed to be attracted to the black people for some reason. But that was eye-opening moment for me because before, I wondered why white people didn't want to play with us [pause] because they thought they were better.

—Raven Whitt | Born 1955 | Class of 1973 | Integrated in 6th grade

And I tell you the funny thing about that, when we integrated, I was kind of afraid because, see, we always got the books that they had. They had sent us the leftovers . . . and when we integrated I was kind of nervous because I thought that we were not going to be prepared like the whites, but when I got out there it was totally different. I was surprised, we knew more than some of them!

—Cheryl Baskin-Brack | Born 1946 | Class of 1965 | Integrated in 11th grade

The integrated environment occasioned the black students to question otherwise taken-for-granted notions of racial inferiority. While the segregated school system presupposed racial difference between blacks and whites, the integrated system pierced their racial consciousness, allowing for the possibility to think otherwise. Put differently, the possibility for the students in the integrated system to recognize themselves as children, instead of *black* children and *white* children, was a transformation in American imagination. In time, black and white children began to form friendships, particularly young school-age children who were not yet fully aware of the intangible veil of the color line. However, the social forces of racial prejudice were constantly at work to reinforce understandings of racial order. Raven Whitt shared a painful example of how a subtle act of bigotry awakened his racial consciousness at a young age:

Because the same kids we saw at school, their parents wouldn't let them run to us. We played at school, but then when we would see them at the store, we would see their parents hold them back as they were running towards us. Because what do kids do when they see each other?

In this moment, both children were the victims of the white parents' racism. Through that subtle encounter, and many others like it, the black child lost the privilege of just recognizing himself as a human, a child. Instead, he came to understand that he was a black child, which meant that he was a different type of person than his white schoolmate. As for the white child, he or she was unfortunately on the receiving end of an intergenerational transmission of white supremacist ideology. In a Du Boisian formulation, this is an example of the awakening of "second-sight." As, Du Bois lays out in *The Souls of Black Folk*, although second-sight allows the racialized subject to see social forces of the veil at work, it provides no solution for eradicating the problem. In this same way the little Raven, although conscious of the parents' motivation behind the restraint, could only internalize the reality of his social condition. While this awakening was not necessarily a source of trauma to the African American *children of integration*, it was a meaningful transformation that accompanied the process of desegregation.

Fear of Miscegenation

Lastly, and very briefly, there was also a perception that the teachers and administrators had a strong, yet unstated, fear of miscegenation. The following anecdote shared by the first black homecoming queen best describes this perception:

> *Cheryl:* And then, okay, we were supposed to have a parade. At first the principal and all of them said that they were not going to have a parade, so basically the team was made up of almost all of the black athletes. So they decided that if they were not going to treat me the same way that they had treated the previous queens, then they were not going to play. So that was what you call where we were "united," and I was the first. It was an experience.
>
> *Me:* Did they have the parade?
>
> *Cheryl:* They had the parade . . . and they could not find the floats, so my uncle went all the way to Middleborough, Kentucky, to get a float for me to ride on, and it was a convertible car. And during the coronation, usually the football captain kissed the Queen. Well, because the football captain was white they had the chairman of the school board to crown me. And that still makes me mad to this day.

The newly integrated black children at Lynch High School chose the selection of the homecoming queen as the first battleground for incorporation into the social fabric of their new environment. They threatened to revoke the one thing that they felt their white counterparts valued about them. Not their presence, their minds, their fashion, or other forms of cultural expression. No. They threatened to take away the black male body from the athletic sphere. Although typically constructed as something to be feared within the American white imaginary—the brute, stealthily lurching through the streets, looking to and fro for the next white woman to rape; a threat; the oaf; the bogeyman; the criminal—within the context of the desegregated school, young black men were not feared but loved and adored: because they were star athletes! Nearing the end of the basketball season in 1965, when Lynch stood to win a state championship, the mere threat of the black athletes not playing was enough to make a queen out of Cheryl Baskin-Brack.

The Costs and Benefits of School Desegregation

I asked my participants to reflect, sixty years after *Brown v. Board of Education*, on the perceived costs and benefits of school desegregation. Responses varied by generation and by level of abstraction. While acknowledging the benefits of desegregation, they all expressed some form of injury, a loss of community and African American identity. In addition to conducting oral history interviews with the generation who "went up to the white school" as students, I also had the opportunity to interview some of the former black teachers from the colored schools in Benham and Lynch. Four of the eight living teachers identified were willing and able to participate. Their reflections thoughtfully articulate the tension between the perceived benefits and costs of school desegregation:

> When they were talking about integration there were many people who were excited about it; our children can get a better education. Like, I remember this vividly, they can take chemistry so they can be nurses and doctors, and when they got an opportunity to take chemistry I went down there [and] took chemistry voluntarily. But we lost—teachers [who] had interest in children, they were black teachers. They wanted you to learn, they helped you, they worked closely with the home.
>
> And when the children got into the white system, they were on their own. Not all teachers were like that, now; there were some that pushed. But there were some who didn't. And the children just felt it and cried . . . and a lot of our ex-school activities that we had, we didn't have those anymore. And to me most emphasis was put on athletics—can that boy run, shoot that ball. They didn't remember those bright kids that came up there.
>
> —Clara Clements, Graduate of Lynch Colored Public School, Class of 1955 | Former teacher at Jenkins Colored School and Lynch High School (Integrated)

> I know in Lynch we got hand-me-down books. The white school used the books and then we got them and we paid for all of our supplies; the teachers paid for them. When we integrated we got new books and we got—I got all the paper I wanted for typing—you know the reams of paper you print your

exams and things on. Everything was paid for. . . . But I think really that in the black school, black teachers understood the black kids, and I think that made a difference with the black kids. When they integrated, some of those white teachers didn't know anything about the life and livelihood of black people. And I don't think they were as patient with them as the black teachers were.

—Vergie Mason | Former teacher at Lynch Colored Public School and
   Lynch High School (integrated)

We lost and we gained . . . this is how we gained. I think that some of our children thought that they were inferior to whites and they found out that they knew more than a lot of them did. And then some of the whites thought that we were inferior and they found out that we knew more than what a lot of them did.

—Rose Ivery Pettygrue | Former teacher at Lynch Colored Public School

The cost I think was the community. . . . It dissolved and there was sort of an acclimation to people and we sort of lost our identity. The benefits were, I think, more psychological than anything. We learned that we were as good as and better than.

—Charles Price | Former teacher and last principal at
   Benham Colored School

Black parents and teachers alike recognized that school desegregation would broaden the horizon of opportunities for their children, opening up pathways that were previously blocked within the segregated system. And the black teachers attest to the ways in which the integrated school system evened the playing field for black children to thrive in an integrated society. Consistent with the infamous black doll–white doll study presented by Drs. Kenneth and Mamie Clark during the *Brown v. Board of Education* case, the teachers also noticed how the integrated setting helped attenuate black students' latent feelings of racial inferiority.

However, the opportunity and access that school desegregation afforded came at a price. Few black teachers were hired into the integrated system, and black students found themselves in a culturally precarious environment, where racial assumptions, fears, and anxieties played out in their everyday interactions with their white teachers. While these encounters with misrecognition surely occurred in both directions, the power dynamic entangled with the teacher-student, white-black, adult-child relationship gave the white teachers the privilege to determine the nature of their interactions with students.

As with any process of social integration, those who experienced the transition at a younger age, in this case before high school, had an easier time acculturating into the new system. It was the high-school-aged generation, those who integrated between the ninth and twelfth grades, who shared the most visceral, negative responses to questions related to desegregation. At that age, their social selves were developed and their identities formed. They were also much more self-aware of their status as second-class citizens and the material realities of racism. For them, school desegregation was wholly traumatic. The responses from the participants who never integrated, representing half of the interview sample, had mixed reviews about whether or not they would have liked the opportunity to attend an integrated school. Overall, almost all participants responded that they are glad that school desegregation happened; some just wish that it hadn't happened to them.

A *Lieu de Mémoire*

The Lynch Colored Public School, built on the most western parcel of land in the city, closed its doors in 1963, after city officials reluctantly made the decision to desegregate the school system. Although it graduated its last class over fifty years ago, the building still stands—with the "Colored" wording reverently etched in stone. Rarely will you see a colored school building stand in its original form anywhere in the United States, for shortly after *Brown* they stood only as shameful reminders of an ugly piece of our history. Nevertheless, the Lynch Colored Public School building stands today as a reminder of the way it was.

In 1972, the Eastern Kentucky Social Club—a social organization made up of African American migrants from the coal towns of southeastern Kentucky—purchased the building, and it is currently used to host social functions for its members. The African Americans who matriculated through the colored schools in this region ensured that the Lynch Colored Public School building continues to stand as what social theorist Pierre Nora terms a *"lieu de mémoire,"* or a site of memory.[20] It is a striking commemoration of their shared history as both African Americans and the children of coal miners.

Painted on the front and back doors are signs that say "EKSC: Lynch Chapter" and "Property of the EKSC: Members Only." Standing metal plaques commemorating their teachers adorn all corners of the building, and the side street leading to the building's parking lot has been renamed

FIGURE 14 Lynch Colored Public School building | 2014.
Karida Brown personal photograph.

John V. Coleman Way, in honor of the last sitting principal. Individuals purchase bricks inscribed with the names of loved ones who have passed on to be inlaid onto the western corner of the building. And to bring the space alive, the African American migrants who grew up in this community return to Benham and Lynch every Memorial Day weekend to commemorate their heritage. The annual social gathering is always held in "their school."

As Nora argues, "*Lieux de mémoire* are created by a play of memory and history."[21] Far from a random occurrence, related groups intentionally construct *lieux de mémoire* because they have a will to remember that site, moment, or experience.

It is too limiting to frame desegregation as an institutional transfer or a mere opportunity for blacks to enter "mainstream" society. It was a transformation in African American subjectivity and, in this context, an injury that left an indelible mark on the collective identity of the black community. Albert Harris summed it up best when he stated:

> If you look up there, right there, today in concrete it says Lynch Colored School. . . . It's right there today. It's written out there: Lynch Colored School. See because we went through a transformation as to who we were. We went

from Colored, to Negroes, to African Americans . . . and Black. We went through all of those.

—Albert Harris | Born 1950 in Benham, Ky. | Graduated Cumberland
   High School in 1968

Surely on both sides, this event brought to the fore feelings of inferiority and superiority, difference, curiosity, and discomfort on the part of students and parents in these communities. However, the African Americans faced material dislocations in their cultural and economic structures due to the abrupt closing of their schools and the subsequent job loss of their beloved teachers. This event had lasting effects on their perception of their identity and sense of belonging. The collective purchase of this building by the black community is an eternal testament that *We were here*: a quotidian yet powerful assertion of being in the face of erasure.

In the end, most of the interviewees expressed that the benefits of desegregation were undeniable. They are glad that it occurred. However, Clara Clements, one of the few living teachers from the Lynch Colored Public School, most eloquently stated, "We gained what we wanted but we lost what we had."

Home Going

They could feel it in the air. Monumental change was coming to the tri-city area. As this chapter revealed, in 1963, after a forty-year run, the colored schools closed their doors, initiating the end of the era of legal segregation in Harlan County. Integration, however, was not the only transformation underway in Benham, Cumberland, and Lynch. The coal mining industry itself was transforming; it was transitioning from a labor-intensive industry to one that was mechanized. Thus, no longer were International Harvester and U.S. Steel in demand of endless bodies to work the mines. Machines could now do the work that a thousand laborers could, and they could do so without the extra expense of housing, health benefits, insurance, and the like. The mechanization of the industry resulted in mass layoffs of the workforce in Benham and Lynch; and without miners, there would soon be no families, and without families, no community. While the coal mining industry was experiencing a precipitous decline in its labor demand, the United States was having a similar feeling about its desire for coal, for, by this time, oil was emerging as the fuel of choice. In response to the mechanization of the industry and the sharp decrease in national demand, International Harvester and U.S. Steel began the slow process of putting to rest the coal towns they had established nearly fifty years before.

These three concomitant transformations—the desegregation of public schools, the mechanization of industry, and the nation's change in taste in energy resources—had detrimental effects on Harlan County's population. By 1981, Lynch High School had closed; soon after, Benham High School closed, and, in a domino effect, the one in Cumberland soon followed. In some parts of town, entire streets were bulldozed, while in others, entire camps. To most inhabitants of Benham, Lynch, and Cumberland, the writing was on the wall—the coal mining industry was in decline, and job opportunities would be few for the next generation, let alone the current one. This chapter illustrated the ways in which teachers and parents conveyed to school-aged children that they had to be prepared to compete in an integrated world—and a world beyond Harlan County. Victor Prinkleton's recollection of his teachers' constant warnings illuminate the level of awareness that people had of what was on the horizon: "You're not going to be able to get no job in no coal mine, so you better get your education so you'd be able to get something to do."

Yet no one could really imagine that the communities would literally be gone, much like the housing bubble that preceded the 2008 financial crisis. At that time, there was a level of awareness among the general public that the market's good fortune was not sustainable and that the housing market would not continue to rise ad infinitum. As we know, bubbles burst; however, few anticipated the extent or reach of the devastation that would result from the crash. U.S. Steel and International Harvester could not hide the fact that the industry was in decline, as the layoffs, school closures, and vacated company-owned properties were laid bare for all to see. Still, it was difficult for anyone to fathom that their entire social world—the places and people and ways of life upon which their collective memory and sense of self was built—could unravel so quickly, as though it never existed. However, this is exactly what happened to the black communities in Benham, Lynch, and Cumberland.

This process of ruination occurred unequally along racial lines, and as we will uncover in chapter 7, the African Americans from Harlan County were to undergo yet another major transformation. Their hometowns were on a steep slope of industrial decline, and yet the second wave of the African American Great Migration was in full speed. The black coal miners' kids from Harlan County, Kentucky, were primed to become what economist Michael Piore termed "birds of passage"[22]—they were getting ready to fly in order to join the other five million African Americans in the massive journey to the big cities in the North, Midwest, and West. For the most part, their parents would stay behind in the mountains. Those black coal mining daddies and homemaking mamas lived out their lives in the houses that remained in the aftermath of the companies' sudden exodus, and eventually their children's relationship to Appalachia would become one of loss and memory.

In chapter 7, we will peer into these subjects' collective experience with industrial decline. They were simultaneously pushed out by an industry that didn't want them anymore and pulled away by the bright futures that seemed to lie ahead in the big cities up North. Not quite forced to go but with little option to stay, they had to leave the only place they ever knew as home. But in reality, the place was also leaving them. Their home would soon be gone.

Come on y'all, it's time . . .

If you're born in Kentucky you've got three choices:
coal mine, moonshine or move it on down the line.

—Lee Dollarhide | (in the movie) *Coal Miner's Daughter*

And there is a bond, there is a bond that ties us all together to that little coal-mining town in Lynch, Kentucky, and we feel like we are one and the same. No one was better than the other, so it's like a little piece of heaven.

—Katie Sue Reynolds Parks | (a real) coal miner's daughter |
   Born in Lynch, Ky.

7 Gone Home

. . . .

They had been preparing for this their entire lives. Lynch was home. Benham was home. Cumberland was home. Deep down, however, they knew it was never really theirs. Those black children who grew up in those Kentucky mountains—home to centuries of lives and generations and peoples and cultures and tongues and feuds and spilled blood—were a mere sheet of parchment in the thick palimpsest that is this land. From the indigenous peoples who girded their loins as they bore witness to their own genocide, refusing to leave their land, dead or alive; to their perpetrators, the Scotch-Irish frontiersmen who began settling in the Cumberland Plateau beginning in the seventeenth century; to King Coal, the paternalistic industry that brought in its own population of European immigrants and southern black refugees, transforming that same "native" white frontiersman into the invisible and culturally extinct hillbilly; to nature, which is now reclaiming the land that was always her own: in this way, Appalachia belongs to no one.

By the mid-1940s, coal mining had begun to transition from a labor-intensive to a machine-intensive industry. International Harvester Corporation and U.S. Steel no longer invested in bodies but rather in machinery and technology. The companies adopted new strategies to control their labor population, including systematic layoffs, hiring freezes, and imposing certification requirements on certain jobs to create "areas of expertise." Through this process of mechanization, the black population stood witness to its own erasure.[1] Laborers were expelled from Harlan County in the same way that they were recruited: by a judicious mixture of race and ethnicity. It is no surprise that the black body was the most expendable to the company. Suddenly cut out of the labor economy, black working-age adults found themselves with no job opportunities in sight. Earl Turner worked in the mines in Lynch for fifty-five years before retiring. One of the first black mine foremen in Harlan County and a veteran member of the United Mine Workers of America, Turner braced his children to dream of another world. His son Jeff was a young child when the industry transitioned:

Absolutely we saw it because our fathers were telling us what was going to happen and what my father said was going to happen has happened, because nobody black got jobs any longer. . . . Before the mechanization of the industry, coal mining was definitely in your blood, it was in your blood. What the mechanization of the industry did was it eliminated jobs. It eliminated jobs because mechanization increased tonnage . . . but when they brought in those big machines to Lynch . . . I will never forget that as a little boy when they brought the machines in.

Where the pick and shovel symbolized the miner in all his necessity, the machine symbolized his superfluity. As a community they braced themselves, albeit unconsciously, for the ruination to begin. Black teachers warned their students that they needed to get an education because there would be no jobs in the mines for them when they came of age, fathers eschewed the idea of their children even thinking about following in their footsteps, mothers told their children that "you better get you an education." No matter what, it would not be an option for this generation to stay in the place that they called home.

Concomitantly, at the macro level, the demographic landscape of the United States was changing dramatically. The period between 1940 and 1970 marked the second wave of the African American Great Migration. Whereas a little less than two million blacks migrated from the South to the North during the three decades prior, another five million migrants poured out of the South during the second wave. Although the geographic thruways were very similar to those established during the first wave of the Great Migration—migrating from states in the Deep South such as Mississippi, Georgia, and Alabama to resettle in Chicago, Detroit, Philadelphia, Cleveland, Los Angeles, and New York—the second iteration of this outpour took place on a very different social, political, and economic landscape.

First, unlike the earlier migrants, the second wavers had access to information and support from established migrant networks; they were more likely to know family, friends, or fellow home folks in potential urban destinations. As a result, second-generation migrants had a virtual blueprint on which to map their own migratory pathways. Second, the racial political landscape was in flux by the 1940s and would undergo a transformation over the course of the decades to follow. By this time, blacks across the country—in the South and in the North—had established an assemblage of cultural centers, institutions, media channels, organizations, rhetoric, and practices that supported the needs and interests of black people in America. The NAACP, the black church, the black Freemasons, and the Eastern Stars are all examples of black social organizations that had flourished in the early twentieth century and thrived through the decades. In addition, information about the conditions of black life throughout the country circulated at a much greater force due to black newspapers such as the *Crisis* and the *Defender*. The emergence of this interconnected system of personal and institutional networks created the infrastructure for what would later become the civil rights movement.[2] This network was also the vehicle that mobilized the black migration out of Harlan County, Kentucky.

In a single generation, these black coal miners' children engaged in a community-level ritual in which, within a few days of graduating from high school, they received a one-way ticket out of town and resettled in a new destination in an urban location outside Appalachia. This out-migration took place over the course of a thirty-year period, beginning shortly after World War II, and was facilitated by a well-oiled migratory network system. Older siblings came home on high school graduation day to pick up their younger siblings and bring them along with them to Cleveland, New York, Chicago, or Detroit to help them get on their feet. The Air Force and Marines was a conduit for young men to make it out West, and once they completed their military duties, many of them settled throughout California and Texas. In an entrepreneurial moment, one former community member went so far as to set up a boardinghouse in Milwaukee, Wisconsin, solely for the purpose of renting rooms to newly arriving Harlan County kinfolk for a few months, until they could establish a place of their own in their new city. By 1970, Harlan County had lost 70 percent of its African American population.

Country Cosmopolitan

The black community groomed them for this migration from childhood. Although they were geographically isolated, light-years away from the pace and culture of the urban city, living in the hollows of the Appalachian Mountains—insular communities with one-lane roads, one radio station, four television channels, and movie theaters that trafficked in out-of-date B westerns—they were incredibly networked people. This is because they were forerunners of the African American Great Migration. The men and women who originally journeyed to eastern Kentucky from Alabama were among the first wave of the Great Migration. When they escaped Alabama, they often went alone, leaving behind their family and community in search of a better life. However, as decades passed, many of the siblings, cousins, and friends who had initially remained in the Deep South also partook in the mass exodus to the North. While some of them had remained up until that point by choice, many had stayed due to other factors, such as fear, coercion, economic constraints, and family responsibilities. With the Great Migration in full force by the 1950s, the pathways to the major metropolises of the United States were clear. Therefore, these family members and friends, who had initially stayed behind in Alabama, tended to migrate directly to the cities in the North, as opposed to layover destinations, such as the coalfields of central Appalachia. Because black families in Harlan County now had such expansive networks—both in the South and the North—parents made sure that their children traveled and were exposed to the world that awaited them.[3]

· · · · · ·

Even though we were isolated in this little one-horse town in Lynch, Kentucky, in the middle of nowhere, most of everybody had somebody that had previously migrated. And so over spring break and summer, you went and visited those siblings or whoever. And we brought back all the fashion of that time, from the Detroits, the Clevelands, the Chicagos *(Jerome Ratchford)*. No, because I had been exposed to the big city. New York, Chicago—so I didn't want to stay there. So when I left, I went to Chicago with my aunt *(Betty Williams)*. And we got our exposure to the city, how we got to these cities was through our siblings living [in] the mountains before us. And since I'm the youngest of eight, I have seven brothers and sisters who left the mountains before I did. I attribute that to how I got out of the mountains and got an education because I followed my brother's footsteps *(Jeff Turner)*. And they were the underground railroad to get us on our feet. Verla and Norma went first, and Dad took us into Cincinnati for vacation, and Auntie Ruth lived in Cleveland, and then in Detroit there was Uncle Charlie and Auntie Lou. So we had our family connection all the way up *(Arnita Davis-Brown)*. Yes, I went to Long Island when I was a sophomore in high school. I wanted to go there and work in the summer, so that I could buy myself some clothes for school. We were all getting ready to go to high school, you want to at least have three or four changes of clothes. But my parents could not afford to buy all those clothes. So I would work, and that is how I went there. I went there in the sophomore year, junior year, and in the senior year *(Richard Brown)*. It was a desire on the part of our parents, and I applaud them for having a vision—

that they wanted us to know about the world outside of the confines of the big Black Mountain.... And we had older brothers and sisters, many of us. Our uncles and aunts who were in Philadelphia, Detroit, Cleveland, and Chicago; you would go and they would open their house, and you would live with them that summer with the understanding that you were going to get a job, you were going to work, you were going to save money *(Porter G. Peeples)*.

· · · · · ·

Participating in these rituals of visiting extended family in the big cites and witnessing siblings and friends "move it on down the line" instilled a tacit understanding within these children that they too would migrate. Not only did their early experiences in these urban environments shape their individual worldviews, but they also affected the larger community back home in the hills. After a summer of working and vacationing, kids would bring back urban culture—the dances, the slang, the fashion, as well as the dreams and aspirations for something more.

That's how come we loved dancing so much because once I got to Cleveland they taught us how to hand-dance. My boy cousins would take us to those parties. And the Cleveland hand-dance was different from anybody else's— you're pushing and holding hands. I still know how to do the Cleveland dance because of my cousin Wayne [who] used to take us to parties.... What we did during the summers, even if it was two or three events you had so much fun, you had to come back home and share that with the country people in Lynch because you had something new to bring back. And then they go and buy us all this [sic] little new outfits for the first couple of weeks of school. So yes, going away to your older sisters and brothers and coming back was more than rewarding.

—Arnita Davis-Brown | Born 1954 in Lynch, Ky. | Resides in Atlanta, Ga.

Through this process of exposure and cultural transmission, these mountain kids became *country cosmopolitan*. Although the tri-city area might have been behind the times in terms of popular culture and some forms of modern living, the black community downloaded new iterations of black cultural expression from the cities and incorporated them into their own way of being back home. It also affected the way in which they imagined their futures; instead of dreaming of reproducing their parents' lives, this next generation's aspirations lay in the as-yet possibilities of the city.

Move It on Down the Line . . .

Home transformed into a reference point in the life course the day after high school graduation. Between the combination of local push factors—fathers forbidding their children from aspiring to become miners, teachers warning pupils that there wouldn't be anything there for them in Harlan County, the mechanization of the coal mining industry, and the subsequent forced attenuation of the labor force—and the broader socioeconomic pull factors—extended family and community networks, the call of the military, new industrial booms in big cities, cultural transmission and exposure to the city, and of course the momentum from the social force that was the African American Great Migration. With all this in the mix, the notion that they were people on the move was a given.

> From my standpoint, graduating in 1964, it was not even talked about. It was like a creed in other societies—you left home when you got eighteen and finished high school. It was never said; it was never told to you. It was an expectation, like a kid in a tribe when you reach sixteen you become a man, like a bird leaving a nest. When you finished high school, it was time to fly.
>
> —Melvin Duncan | Born 1946 in Lynch, Ky. | Resides in Charlotte, N.C.

> I never had a second thought. I never thought about staying. Why?! There was nothing there for me as a woman unless I chose to marry another coal miner. Women were not allowed in the mines. But as I recall, you automatically knew that at high school graduation . . . you were leaving. Did mother and father ever say that you were leaving? No! But you just knew. It was automatic. On graduation day the sisters and brothers that had already left and were in Ohio, or wherever they were, they came back on graduation day. And. We. Left. With. Them. Maybe even the next day! You were in the car and you were riding to Cleveland with an aunt or an older sister or brother and you were gone.
>
> —Wanda Davis | Born 1957 in Lynch, Ky. | Resides in Cleveland, Ohio

> Well, you know that was never a decision. It was pretty much understood in Kentucky that when you graduate—as a child your parents' and the community's responsibility is to get you to adulthood and adulthood was expressed by your graduating from high school. When you graduated from high school, you were expected to not be in town the following Monday. If you were in town the following Monday, then resources had been wasted to train and develop you, because you were supposed to be gone out to establish yourself

and get a job and to become a contributing member of society and hopefully send something back home. But no, I don't think that was ever an expectation that you would graduate from high school and stay.

—John Steward | Born 1942 in Benham, Ky. | Resides in Alisa Viejo, Calif.

Chain, Chain, Chain . . .

High school graduation was the defining moment of transition in every student's life. It was not a question of whether or not they would stay or go; it was more so a matter of where would they go and what they would do.[4] All the classical mechanisms of mass migration were at play to facilitate this out-migration. At the family level, chain migration was the primary way in which individuals accomplished their first move. Chain migration is a process through which family and friends from one's community of origin assist with migration and resettlement, usually in the form of indirect support, such as housing, food, job referrals, and information.

Leona and Major Brown reared sixteen children in Lynch, Kentucky. Like most parents, they were adamant that their children leave home after high school graduation. The Brown family profile is an exemplar of how the chain migration process unfolded for many black families in Harlan County. Richard, the tenth of Leona and Major's children, recalls how he and his siblings ended up resettling in Long Island, New York.

> Well, it started with my sister Johnetta. I think Johnetta was the first to go to do domestic work, and right after my sister Vickie came. She did the same thing with the domestic work. And then my sister Shirley came. And then my sister Charlene came. And then we all—me and my sisters—had rented this house. First off my sister Johnetta lived in this room in the house, and there were a few rooms available. So my sisters came and each one of them rented the room. So my brother came and he lived in there in the house with them. He got a job at a factory and a couple of years after that, my brother, who lived in Cleveland, came to New York and he got a job in the same factory as my brother, and then after that, he got a job at the Patterson nursing home where my sisters were working. And it just went on, and then after my brother came, my sister Mary came to live there for a while. So, then after that me and my sister Charlene came to live there permanently. And we all stayed in the same house and we rented the house and it had four bedrooms in the house, plus the kitchen and living room.

—Richard Brown | Born 1947 in Lynch, Ky. | Resides in Atlanta, Ga.

One by one the Brown siblings visited New York from Lynch and eventually relocated to Long Island until fourteen of the sixteen siblings had resettled there. One of the youngest Brown siblings, Linda Faye, resisted the idea of moving, and secretly planned to stay home after graduation. However, Leona and Major were not having it. She remembers her mother intervening:

> She had my bags packed, had two garbage bags full of my clothes, a bucket of food. I said, "I am not going." I cried and I cried and she said, "Yes, you are!" I got up that morning [and] Daddy said, "You're going." I didn't want to go. I am grown now, think about it, I am grown. And next thing you know I am at Eastern Kentucky University—they drove me to school. She had planned everything; she did it all for me.
>
> —Linda Faye Brown | Born 1953 in Lynch, Ky. | Resides in Lynch, Ky.

Although Linda Faye eventually ended up returning to Lynch, she did attend college for a few years before making that decision. What the Brown family illuminates is the way in which chain migration worked at the family level. Siblings supported one another not only with housing and material support but also with making connections in their new environment—including facilitating relationships with employers, religious institutions, and new friends. They also demonstrate the urgency and durability of these family networks in facilitating a way out of Harlan County—one that was sustainable and without the economic and social shocks that can come with starting anew.

Paths More and More Traveled

Institutions had an important impact on the geographic diversity of the migration. While chain migration was by far the most common migration mechanism, thus overly determining intrafamily migration patterns, the military, higher education, and marriage created alternative pathways for Kentucky's coal camp blacks.

In 1948, President Harry Truman integrated the U.S. military through Executive Order 9981. Although blacks were always in the military, volunteering to join in an integrated context symbolized a new type of citizenship.[5] In this pre-*Brown*, pre–civil rights movement era, the military was one of the only public spheres that was expressly principled—in word at least—on racial equality, signaling the possibility of attaining the status of "American citizen" as opposed to the stateless "Negro." However, the specter of Jim Crow still haunted the hearts and minds of military officials, so much so that not even orders from the president of the United States could break the mental stronghold of racial prejudice. Odell Moss remembers joining the Air Force shortly after the order had been issued: "President Truman had just signed the bill to integrate the military. It was integrated alright, but segregation was still being practiced" *(Odell Moss | Benham)*. Blacks continued to be excluded from the full range of military ranks and positions, still had to eat separately from their white counterparts, and, as always, were subject to the caprice of racism from any white person who felt like exerting it at any given moment.

One way that they could loose themselves from the tight grip of the color line was through sports, as the trope of the athletic Negro provided some sense of sanctuary. The black male body was well received as a source of entertainment, and young men were happy to offer it in exchange for being sent to the front lines of war. Both Korean War veterans, Odell Moss and Gean Austin took advantage of this path. Moss recalls, "I was shipped overseas to the Far East, and in the process I went out for the track team overseas—and I was rather fast, I admit that, and I went to the Far East Air Force track team in a place called Nagoya, Japan." While Moss tried out for the Air Force track team, Austin was recruited to the military solely for his athletic abilities. He said that the "[Korean] war broke out and they were trying to get volunteers to go serve. So we came up there and you know, one day we were playing basketball somewhere and some soldiers come around looking at us. The marine said, "You look like a good athlete," you know, he said, "So how would you like to go in the military and play basketball with us?" I said, "Huh, you heard well." He said that he'd get me to serve and play basketball, so I volunteered right there *(Gean Austin | Lynch)*.

Through the 1940s and 1950s, there were two gendered pathways for working-age blacks to take—women could migrate to a city with a sibling or family member and find employment, or do so with a husband to start a family. My own mother chose the latter option. While nine of her ten siblings migrated from Lynch to resettle in Cleveland, Ohio, she chose a different path. Reflecting on her decision process, she revealed that her reason for breaking the chain was "marriage, being in love, wanting a family, having education, and being able to get more opportunities. . . . It was the commitment to a man that I loved. So that really is the primary reason I was in New York." Men, on the other hand, had the choice of following the pre-carved path of a chain migration, joining the military voluntarily, or being drafted.

However, Southeast Community College presented a "cultural disruption," what Trondman, Taha, and Lund describe as "a piercing of consciousness" that allows otherwise subordinated or marginalized groups to "believe or aspire to new possibilities."[6] It was not that higher education was not an option for black high school graduates all along, as their teachers were examples of black people with such degrees; but the pathway to college was unclear to these black youth, as there were no examples among their peers. However, when the local community college opened in 1960—the first integrated educational institution in Harlan County—its first class consisted of seventeen students, ten white and seven black. One of the members of that first class, Jerome Ratchford, reflects on this watershed moment:

> We didn't have choices when we graduated from high school. So it was either try to find a job or go to the military. So I was so hell bent on going to the military, but thankfully, being young, being sixteen, my parents vetoed that. So I went sort of as an alternative to the university—but it only took me about one semester to say, "I like this, this is a good fit for me." So once that took place we were able to symbolize possibilities for those who followed, and like I said, the rest is history.
>
> —Jerome Ratchford | Born 1942 in Lynch, Ky. | Resides in Atlanta, Ga.

Quoting Trondman, Taha, and Lund again, these seven students became "cultural resources"—that is, "figures who become an example to what others can do and show the pathway to incorporation" to the many that would come after them. Witnessing Jerome and his fellow black classmates succeed at attaining an associate's degree from Southeast Community College and then to see some of those students move on to the elite, formally all-white flagship institution—the University of Kentucky—exposed a whole new world of dreams to which younger cohorts would aspire. Speaking of the impact of having a local college in the eastern Kentucky region, Ratchford asserts:

> It gave choices from a lifestyle perspective. You could entertain, along with getting a job, going to the military; you could entertain going to higher education. And you could do it at a reasonable cost. You also had the opportunity to impact the lifestyle that you wanted for yourself. As the successes occurred amongst my colleagues and myself,

people realized that they could choose to emulate what we did from a major perspective, from a career perspective, or they could deviate from it. So they had more choices in terms of the types of lifestyles, career lifestyles that they wanted to embark on and so forth. It opened up opportunities, career opportunities and prosperity that we never could have imagined. So it was a very, very important institution.

Those students from the class of 1960 broke a symbolic barrier, and as a result, the choices for black high school graduates expanded from two to three. College became an aspiration for many and a no-brainer for some.

Well, I was not going to stay there. Years before then I knew I was going to leave, and I knew I was going to go to school someplace but I didn't know exactly where.

—Virginia Taylor-Ward | Born 1949 in Cumberland, Ky. | Graduated Cumberland High School in 1967 | Resides in Dayton, Ohio

Well, you had three choices, as my daddy said. Get a job, go in the army, or go to college. When you reach eighteen and you're in the town of Lynch, Kentucky, there was not many choices. By age eighteen I had the privilege personally to visit multiple cities because I have lots of brothers and sisters ahead of me. I had been to the University of Notre Dame to watch my brother Tony. I have been to the University of Notre Dame just to visit my brother Bill. I have been to Fisk University to visit my brother Karl. I have been to Vassar University to watch his wife graduate.

—Jeff Turner | Born 1959 in Lynch, Ky. | Graduated Lynch High School in 1977 | Resides in Indianapolis, Ind.

I knew I was going to college, okay. Because my dad and my parents always told me, "Boy, you aren't working in the coal mine, you're going to school." So I knew that I was going to school somewhere. So I started out at Southeast and then transferred to the University of Kentucky because I knew I was going to school somewhere.

—Lee Arthur Jackson | Born 1950 in Lynch, Ky. | Graduated Lynch High School in 1968 | Resides in Lexington, Ky.

The dual influence that the local institution and early black successes had on the black community's posture toward pursuing a college education cannot be underscored enough. Porter G. Peeples was in ninth grade at the time when Jerome Ratchford and his fellow classmates went up to Southeast

Community College. He remembers looking up to the older guys in his neighborhood and attributes his own decision to attend college, as he would be the first in his family to do so, to watching Jerome and other role models in his neighborhood:

> Some of the guys who I knew who went there before me, one of the main ones who went there was Jerome Ratchford, now Dr. Jerome Ratchford, and he is in Georgia running a college. Another guy from my street who didn't go to Southeast but went to Kentucky State on a football scholarship was Willie French. You know I looked up to these guys . . . they were role models, very positive role models. And we started saying "Yes we can." That's what they said to me, "Yes we can." And you know I guess watching some of that was what made me get myself back on track, you know back to tenth or eleventh grade and say "Ooh, wait, I want to do what they're doing."

Porter followed in Jerome's footsteps, attending Southeast Community College to attain his associate's degree and then transferring to the University of Kentucky to attain his bachelor's. After graduating from college, Porter decided to take root in Lexington and to devote his life to serving his community and his state of Kentucky. He is the president/CEO of the Urban League of Fayette County in Lexington, a position he has held since 1968, and serves on the board of trustees for all the community colleges—including Southeast—in the Commonwealth of Kentucky.

Dispersion

They moved everywhere: Newington, Connecticut; Cleveland, Ohio; San Jose and Los Angeles, California; Indianapolis, Indiana; Chicago, Illinois; and Long Island, New York. There are few cities in America where you cannot find a black coal miner's child from Bloody Harlan County. It was a perfect storm of micro- and macrolevel processes and assemblages that caused this particular out-migration to articulate itself in this way.

The moves from Harlan County map almost perfectly onto the major destination cities of the African American Great Migration—with the most concentrated destinations being once-booming industrial cities in the Midwest and North; later pathways in the West, which largely became a possibility because of the opportunities created by the pseudo-integrated Marines and the Air Force; and finally a wave of return to the South, by migrants who resettled there after retiring from careers in the North. However, theirs was not just a mass migration but a diaspora, characterized by the collective feeling of loss, mourning, and homesickness that accompanies the experience of abrupt displacement and dispersion. In this way, diaspora is a consciousness.

Ruination

Today, the once bustling mining towns of Benham, Cumberland, and Lynch resemble old western ghost towns. International Harvester and U.S. Steel began mass layoffs shortly after the end of World War II, as they stealthily prepared to close up shop and leave town. As the population dwindled, the companies maneuvered to relinquish their responsibility for the model communities they had created. The company home—the quintessential feature of any company-owned town—would soon be no more. Blocks at a time, mothers and fathers, or sometimes children, would return home to a pink notice on their door: the family would have ninety days to find another home, or worse yet, the company would soon be vacating their entire street. Some families resigned themselves to the obvious and chose to leave town at that point, while others were able to find available housing on other streets or in camps.

In 1963, in a last-ditch effort to divest from their housing inventory, U.S. Steel put out a notice that they were offering all their employees the opportunity to partake in the American dream of homeownership. This no doubt came as a surprise, given that the word *ownership* had never been associated with anything in those parts since the company town was established. So many families jumped at the opportunity and did whatever they could to scrape up enough money to claim a stake in the bounty that the company was offering. These folks did not see the writing on the wall.

> I remember my dad and mom when we moved into that house, they purchased that house through acquiring money from relatives. My mom's sisters and brothers, family members, I don't know the exact ones but I remember my parents calling on them to help send maybe $100 toward the $1,000 it was going to cost to purchase that home. And they received that, and they were able to buy that house at 422 First Street. It was a real sharp memory because I remember that amount of money was very tough for them to acquire, but you know family came to the rescue.

> —Arnita Davis-Brown | Born 1953 in Lynch, Ky. | Resides in Atlanta, Ga.

The houses sold for random amounts—$500, $800, $1,000, $1,500, really whatever the company could shake down from one family to the next. However, by this time the slow rot of ruination was already in motion. Entire camps were evacuated and eventually erased, as though they never existed. Dwayne, the eighth and youngest child of Cleo and Sylvester Baskin, slowly became aware of what was happening to his community.

> Unfortunately when I grew up there were only a couple of camps actually. It was just Number One, Number Two, and then Number Five. So obviously the other coal camps had ceased to exist, but I just recall hearing the countless stories of Number Three, Number Four, the bathhouse, and those types of things; to the point where I could sometimes visualize them because the physical structures were still there in a lot of cases. . . . It was not until probably I became a young man or adolescent when I started recognizing that the class sizes were getting smaller and actually the school system itself became less and less and less. But I never thought that it wouldn't be there. That goes to the point of how much it was instilled in us that home is always going to be there, and I never ever gave it any thought that it would dissolve to what it is now, to the point where literally very few people [reside] in Lynch as we speak.
>
> —Dwayne Baskin | Born 1962 in Lynch, Ky. | Graduated Lynch High School in 1980 | Resides in Indianapolis, Ind.

Families had little choice in the matter. More and more fathers found themselves laid off or underemployed, with a wife and eight or ten kids to feed. In these cases, they had to move to survive, and with such large families, they could not always stay together. Brenda Thornton was only eleven years old when her bucolic life changed forever.

> Well, I remember that I was eleven years old and I was in the 6th grade and I remember saying to God—we had to do plays, we did plays from every grade, grades 1–12 did a play. And the play that we were doing at this time was in the 6th grade, I was in the 6th grade and Ms. Jones was the teacher. And I remember that I had to practice with Anne Marie Coleman and Lois Mitchell, we were going to be singing a song together. And because I was so afraid that I could not hold the tune I was saying to God, "Can you get me out of this?"
>
> And I guess my prayers were answered, I went home and my father said, "We're going to have to take you kids to West Virginia to stay with your grandmother because I'm no longer going to have a job in the coal mine." I said, "God, I didn't ask for you to move me, I just asked for you to get me out of the play!" This was just before Christmas of 1960. We didn't know when but

it would be soon. So I was not even too sure if I was going to have a Christmas in Kentucky ... there was no warning as far as exactly when. I didn't even really have time to say good-bye. I never said good-bye to my classmates.

—Brenda Thornton | Born 1950 in Lynch, Ky. | Resides in White Plains, N.Y.

Brenda and her siblings did get to spend that one last Christmas in Lynch, and she even got to perform in the play. However, by the next month, her parents had packed her and her siblings in a car and sent them to live with their grandmother in West Virginia until her father could find stable employment elsewhere. They left over the winter break, so she did not have the chance to announce her pending departure to her classmates. They just disappeared. Reflecting on how she felt during that car ride in 1961, Brenda says, "I think I was in denial. I thought it was temporary and we would be staying with Grandma maybe just a short time, and then we would come back home. I never thought it was permanent; I always thought it was temporary."

But it wasn't. That was the last time Brenda would live in Kentucky. These were the moments when parents and children alike became aware of how disposable they were to U.S. Steel: just as the company giveth, the company taketh away.

I think I realized it the day we left in 1961. I realized that whatever we had was controlled by U.S. Steel and that my life would change because U.S. Steel no longer had a position for my father. And that's when I realized that they controlled everything, that they controlled my destiny at that time. And it was very heartbreaking to realize that I wouldn't grow up with my friends and possibly never see them again.

—Brenda Thornton | Born 1950 in Lynch, Ky. | Resides in White Plains, N.Y.

Brenda's experience with root shock was not unique.[7] There are several stories of children unexpectedly "going for a ride" and not coming back.

Well, my granddaddy and grandmother said we were moving—we had no choice; we had no say in it. I'll never forget it. It was May 24, 1959, we were walking home from school—Kenneth, Eddy, Brenda, and Cynthia—we all walked home from school; my grandmother had a car parked in front of the house and said, "Get in." We had to go. We left that day; we didn't get a chance to say good-bye to our friends because we didn't even know we were leaving.

—Curtis Mason | Born 1948 in Lynch, Ky. | Resides in Chicago, Ill.

The Devolution of a Community

The colored schools in Benham and Lynch closed their doors in 1963, in part because of pressure by the governor and in larger part because of the precipitating population. The black children in Lynch integrated into Lynch High School, while all children in Benham were bused to attend Cumberland High School, as the Benham School System had closed in its entirety. By 1981, Lynch High School had also closed its doors. Over a series of school closures and consolidations over the years, there is presently only one public high school in Harlan County, Harlan High School, which is mandated to serve all children throughout the hills and hollows of those mountains. Children who reside in Benham, Cumberland, and Lynch travel twenty-one miles each way to attend school, while the remnants of the old schools in their communities stand tall, in ruin.

Both International Harvester and U.S. Steel began razing entire sections of town, especially in the black neighborhoods. Eventually, the homes from which families were evicted—empty artifacts of life and love—were bulldozed and left for nature to reclaim. Over time, the people who had built their memories in those spaces began to wonder if they ever existed.

> No longer there, there's nothing there anymore. In fact, when you go you can barely see the roads when you're walking because it's so overgrown now with weeds and trees, and sometimes when we go home we try to find the graveyard. Because at the end of our very street, on 4th Street, there was a graveyard there, and so it's like we could not find the graveyard, it's still overgrown with weeds and stuff, yeah, but—I can look at the mountains and still see pictures of that mountain that I saw as a little girl you know even though the houses are gone or just, I don't know. . . . It's strange but that will always be my home place.
>
> —Sally Pettygrue Davis | Born 1941 in Lynch, Ky. | Resides in Covington, Ky.

> So we drove down to Cumberland, to Sawmill Hollow, and we drove to where my uncle's house was supposed to be . . . and there's nothing there. . . . At some point my uncle had tore down the porch and filled it in with rocks and dirt and made a concrete porch, okay. So you got this long porch that's concrete and you got a block wall in the front that comes up about two feet and then poles to hold the roof. That was all that was left. And the rest has been bulldozed up into a pile of rubble. . . . We had taken pictures until we got out of the car not realizing it. . . . When we got there the whole trip psychologically ended. We never took another picture . . . you don't want that memory, you

FIGURE 15 Church Hill Row, Benham, Kentucky | 2016.
Karida Brown personal photograph.

know. You want the memory of the little house where you grew up as a kid
that is not there anymore, so we're not taking pictures.

—John Steward | Born 1942 in Cincinnati, Ohio; reared in Benham, Ky. |
Resides in Alisa Viejo, Calif.

When Brenda Thornton returned to Lynch decades after being sent off to
West Virginia to live with her grandmother in 1961, she was heartbroken to
see that the home that she knew and loved was gone.

And when I saw that, it hurt. It was like I never lived there. There were no
houses there, there was no community up there, it was just a mountain, and
I could not believe that, there was not even a street going up there. And what
hurts me more is that I have not been able to fill that gap in my mind. I don't
know when they tore it down and I have no idea if anybody ever took a picture of it before it was torn down.

—Brenda Thornton | Born 1950 in Lynch, Ky. | Resides in White Plains, N.Y.

Most devastatingly, the people were gone—the "misters" and "misses" that
they had to say hello to every time they saw them on the street; the children
playing homemade games outdoors, picking wild apples and blackberries

for their mothers to can, and catching lightning bugs; the black teachers who whooped their behinds, expected the best, and loved them like their own—they were all long gone. The four-room homes that they grew up in watching their mothers cooking in the kitchen and their fathers chewing tobacco and staring at the daily paper, the homes where six or eight siblings shared two or three beds without wishing it was any other way. Eventually they witnessed a generation of fathers—their own fathers who did not talk—give their bodies back to the Black Mountain with which they had made a deal so long ago.

Thirty or forty years prior, these men well understood that the same coal mine that bought them their freedom would also issue their death sentence. Going into the mouth of a mountain so dark and damp, digging a labyrinth of rock mineral under the earth, picking, exploding, and roof bolting; breathing in that coal dust eight to ten hours a day, five days a week, year in and year out over three to four decades—black lung was inevitable. It is one thing to witness the death of a parent—your mother, your father, or the person who raised you—it is quite another to witness everyone's father die the same slow death, from the same disease, within a month or a year or two of your own.

These are the ties that bind. It is through this shared experience with community and culture, struggle and striving, pride and joy, landscape and environment, the sudden unraveling of the very social fabric that defined who they were, and the ongoing ruination of the built environment that their diasporic consciousness emerged. As I mentioned earlier, diaspora is not constituted solely through mass migration and dispersion; it is a consciousness, a practice, a stance—diaspora is a condition of subjectivity.[8] Home did not pass away with distance or time for this generation of African American migrants; instead, it transcended from a physical entity to a symbolic one. Over time, home was a symbol of death and memorial instead of a symbol of life and expression.

> So Christmas was an identifier, it was a symbol of the progress for black people from that community . . . and you saw fewer people coming home for Christmas, you knew that they were the roots, that having kin in that community was no longer present. In other words, you had nobody that you could come and stay with or visit. So as families had to move out and you didn't have root families—nuclear families—to welcome their offspring and so forth; you could see a decline in the people coming back for the major holiday for Christmas.

And then you actually saw literally a juxtaposition later on, when more people were coming back to visit the deceased than they were to affiliate with their living relatives. So we went from Christmas being indicative of progress and prosperity and so forth to Memorial Day.... So I absolutely remember coming home and wondering why more people were not at home. And you sort of, over a period of time, you gradually saw that that phenomenon was going out of existence.

—Jerome Ratchford | Born 1940 in Lynch, Ky. | Resides in Atlanta, Ga.

Through decades of going and returning, remembering and storytelling, performing and presenting, they have rescued home from erasure. Although African Americans are largely overlooked in the national narrative of Appalachia, these black people have reinscribed their being into this place. Through these practices, they remind themselves that "we were here."

· · · · · ·

So we still go home, and when I go home it gives me an opportunity to fill my tank up. Sometimes in the city your tank gets so empty and you have to re-fuel. So when I go back home to rejuvenate the mountain spirit, it's all through the concept of home. Because at home you don't have to impress nobody, you can just be yourself, it is home. Also we're seeing home before our eyes, we're seeing the mountains die, we're seeing the streets being swallowed up with the trees, we're seeing death which is imminent to all of us. Where I'm the youngest of eight in my family, we've now lost two siblings.

I must say that when I go home there's nobody living in our home any longer, but we still keep a homestead, we still have electricity on in our home, we still got the water on in the home, but nobody lives in the home any longer. But home is where Mama and Daddy raised us in that little house. So I sort of call it our condo in the mountains. Another thing is, the mountain has a way of defining who you are, your character, you have something that's symbolic that you have to hang on to.

—Jeff Turner | Born 1959 in Lynch, Ky. | Resides in Indianapolis, Ind.

Memorial Day Weekend

Every Memorial Day weekend, hundreds of black migrants from the tri-city area of Harlan County return home. They come in from all over the country, from Springfield, Massachusetts, to Los Angeles, California, and everywhere in between. During this long holiday weekend, the communities resurrect as though nothing has changed. The few families that still own their family homes return to the homestead, with two, sometimes three, generations piled into one little house. Home folks go from house to house visiting each other, participating in community festivities, eating each other's barbecue, and socializing at "the club"—formerly known as the Lynch Colored Public School.

Memorial Day, from all my life I can remember, that was the week that everybody that ever lived in Lynch came back home. And I can remember it was just like a reunion; we went to the cemetery to put flowers on the graves. You just see so many people, and it was just the way we did things, you know. Back then there were a lot of people in Lynch; you know when I told you I lived in Number Three, now it seems Number Three doesn't even exist.

—Brenda Clark Combs | Born 1954 in Lynch, Ky. | Resides in Lexington, Ky.

I do not know how it started, but I know it started [a] long time ago, before I even started coming back. Now, to show you the importance to me, I would come all the way from here just for the weekend. . . . I would come back that weekend just to be with my friends that I grew up [with] and have known all of my life. You know where First Street is? You'd have twenty-five cars lined up, and nobody would be blowing their horn for you to move, can you believe that? . . . So, I can remember coming home and starting at my mama's house and working my way all the way down the street, and then up Second Street, speaking to everybody on those two streets, First and Second Street. . . . [It would take you] the whole day! You had to speak to everybody. A lot of them want you to come in and have a drink or come in and get something to eat. Maybe you would get a piece of chicken on your way out. . . . Everybody would be outside their car, standing up; and you would walk from your car all the way down to that car; that is how it was on Memorial Day. I do not know how the tradition started but I love it. I love it.

—William Jackson | Born 1944 in Lynch, Ky. | Resides in Los Angeles, Calif.

The dénouement of the weekend is the church service at Greater Mt. Sinai Baptist Church on Sunday morning, followed by a trip to the cemetery to dress the tombstones of family, friends, and loved ones. By Monday morning, everyone is gone.

The meanings laden in the ritual of "coming home" for Memorial Day are laden with dualities, as it is both sacred and profane, about life as much as it is about death, and about presence and absence.

> Yeah, Memorial Day is a sacred day. It is a memory of the ones gone and it became the tradition of our community of Lynch to just seek some refuge in that quietness of being home in that little town leading up to the church service on Sunday for the memorial of whomever's parents or loved ones had deceased and visiting the grave site down there. The whole weekend is centered around that memory, and as our parents became the deceased ones we became even more driven to just go back and pay that respect to the ones that are gone, like when we go to church [it] would just spiritually uplift you. You know they don't live here anymore, you know they could not sing a song that didn't touch you, and it makes you think about your parents. [Speaking of her in-laws and her own parents] I remember when Mr. Major first passed, when Miss Leona passed, when my parents passed. So it just always brought us together just to, you know, share a little communion away from the busyness of, you know, city life and the stresses that you endured. I don't know. It's just something sacred I would say about Memorial Day and that weekend.
>
> —Arnita Davis-Brown | Born 1953 in Lynch, Ky. | Resides in Atlanta, Ga.

The meaning of the tradition oscillates between extended community-level experiences with loss and direct personal experiences, as the loss of one parent or family member resonates deeply as a blow to the entire community. It is a place of mutual recognition, where everyone understands the history, context, and meaning of the simultaneous sense of peace and sorrow that home conjures in their spirits. The weekend is not only a time to remember those who have passed on but also a time to reconnect and rejoice with the living.

> That's what happened in Lynch during Memorial Day, everybody would drive home nice, fine cars, and their kids and spouses and what have you, and it was common for 1st Street to be blocked—full of traffic. And you just understood that if you could come home for Memorial Day that there's just going to be a traffic jam up and down that street and you're just going on and park your car, you're not going to be able to move forward. And you reconnected, exchanged pleasantries, hugged, kissed, and just reacquainted yourself out of joy in a lot of cases.... It was that spirit of just coming back together, fellowship and just enjoy seeing each other, everything else just stopped. And

it's hard to describe it, and I get a little choked up right now just thinking about it—a lot of my classmates are no longer with me. And to remember a lot of the folks that would come back for this Memorial Day festivity and it still continues on a lesser scale because I don't have any blood relatives still in Lynch but this is still home, that's my place of birth and that's where my father is buried and my mother is buried in San Jose.

—Jeffrey Ratchford | Born 1956 in Lynch, Ky. | Resides in Atlanta, Ga.

Returning to Kentucky for Memorial Day is one way in which they claim their roots by situating their memories in place. It is an "invented tradition" that restores some sense of materiality to their collective memory and serves as a referent for the narrative they construct as to who they are.[9] However, their performance of home extends well beyond the physical borders of Harlan County. They have also adopted traditions that honor the physicality of home but that also perform the homelessness of it all—an expression of their roots and routes.

The Eastern Kentucky Social Club

In 1969, seven Benham migrants living in Cleveland, Ohio, decided to host a reunion to reconnect with other friends and community members who had also partaken in this intergenerational journey through the hills of Kentucky. One year later, after much discussion and planning, they hosted their first reunion at a bar on the east side of the city. The organizers spread invitations by word of mouth through family and community networks. Without a clear estimation of the turnout, the organizers found themselves hosting a reunion that drew in over three hundred home folks from cities across the country.

This inaugural event sparked the establishment of the Eastern Kentucky Social Club (EKSC). Chapters of the organization sprang up in over fifteen cities across the country, each passing the other the baton of responsibility for hosting the following year's reunion. The club expanded to include members from other nearby coal mining communities in eastern Kentucky, and at its height, the EKSC drew over three thousand African American migrants to the event.[10] These reunions have continued without interruption each year for nearly fifty consecutive years, existing for the sole purpose of creating a space for African Americans who share roots in the coal towns of eastern Kentucky to reunite.

Through that thing of the Kentucky social club we keep networking, you know, we keep that connection. And you know I try to explain to people as well, everybody came out of the little town and all of the United States, and they formed the Eastern Kentucky Social Club in their particular city. And it goes from one city to another; you got the Kentucky Social Club in New York, Chicago, Cleveland, Atlanta, you know. Each one gets a time to host and all the other social clubs come to that one.

—Albert Harris | Born 1950 in Benham, Ky. | Resides in Sunrise, Fla.

Both Memorial Day and the EKSC reunion are sustained through the collective memories of these migrants and are full of rituals and practices that perform "home." These traditions are the connective tissue that binds their pasts with the present, and allows home to exist in the realm of the symbolic. Brenda Thornton knows this all too well. During a serendipitous encounter in Detroit, Michigan, she bumped into a fellow eastern Kentuckian who told her about the EKSC reunions. She was an adult by then—it had been over twenty years since that day she left Lynch in the middle of her sixth grade year. She attended that year's reunion and almost every one since. She explained why she attends:

Because that was the most important part of my life. That was my home, that was where I was born at. I never wanted to leave Lynch, Kentucky; I always wanted to go back, and the only way I could go back was through the Eastern Kentucky reunions. I went back twice after I left when I was 11 years old, and each time I went back it was like a tease. Lynch, Kentucky, was like no other part in the whole United States; there were people there that you could count on, you were in the class with these kids from the time you were years old, you formed bonds with them, they knew you more than anybody.

Now that the population is in their seventies, eighties, and nineties, attendance has been greatly affected by illness, disability, and passing on. However, the reunions are still active and draw migrants by the busload to partake in the tradition. This year's (2018) reunion will be in St. Louis, Missouri.

Race and Roots through Appalachia

Yeah, but home, Lynch will always be home to me. Always. People that are from the city think that we are from the Appalachian Mountains and we are just a bunch of hillbillies. But we're not hillbillies, honey! And I am proud to be from that mountain. I am proud of my learning, my teaching, my training, and everything that I learned from up there.... And we had it good, we had beautiful homes and everything... and U.S. Steel saw to that. And we had beautiful churches and what have you. And I tell you that there was so much love there, and I will never forget it. Lynch is home for the kids that were raised there. And you could not find a better place. And one day I went to the city and one of the ladies asked me, "Where you from?" and I said from the Appalachian Mountain, Lynch, Kentucky, and she told me that I was telling her [a] lie.

—Lena Margaret Jones | Born 1938 in Lynch, Ky. | Resides in Louisville, Ky.

• • • • • •

In my heart, Lynch is home, and it never will be nowhere but there *(Chuck Rodgers | Lexington, Ky.)*. Home will always be 469 First Street *(Dwayne Baskin | Indianapolis, Ind.)*. And I tell anybody we are from Kentucky; we're from Lynch—"Where is it at?" "Well, do you know Harlan County?" and I try to explain it to them, then I go to naming people that came out of those hills, and they say, "You're kidding!" I say, "No, they came out of those hills" *(Curtis Mason | Chicago, Ill.)*. Harlan County; Benham, Kentucky! *(Odell Moss | Lexington, Ky.)*. Lynch will always be my home. I don't care where I go; Kentucky is my home. I mean, you can't take that away; that is where I got my beginning, and that is where I learned to love people *(Barbara Haury | Chicago, Ill.)*. Lynch. Lynch is home. I live in Lexington, but Lynch is home, yes *(Brenda Clark Combs)*. Home is always in Kentucky, Lynch. You know, even now when somebody asks me where I'm from, when I'm away, I will say, "Well, I live in Waterbury, Connecticut, but originally I'm from Lynch, Kentucky" *(Humes Perry | Waterbury, Conn.)*. I still have a very, very sensitive, compassionate feeling for home. I love Lynch, I love home. I love the people *(Joyce Hall)*. Benham. This is my roots. This is my roots. This is home here. There is no place like it. There is no group of black people that are growing up in [the] United States that equally *(Albert Harris | Sunrise, Fla.)*. Lynch—I live in Lexington, that's what I tell people when I am traveling and they ask, "Where are you from?"... "Well, I live in Lexington but I am from Lynch, Kentucky. And Lynch is a small town in Harlan County and you know in Southeast, Kentucky." You got to explain all that to them but that's home—Lynch is home *(Lee Arthur Jackson | Lexington, Ky.)*. Lynch will always be my home *(Porter G. Peeples | Lexington, Ky.)*. Lynch! Oh, Lynch will always be my home. I have been here forty-four years, but Lynch is my home. I just moved out to California, but when you say "home"—I am a Kentuckian. Born and bred right there in Lynch, Kentucky *(William Jackson | Los Angeles, Calif.)*. You know what, Lynch is still home for me. In spite of all the boarded houses and torn down houses, there is no place like home. When I go there you would think that place was still filled with people. It's the feeling that when you hit that street and you are in Lynch—that is my home, that is my home *(Sally Pettygrue Davis | Covington, Ky.)*.

· · · · · ·

Why? Because I was born and raised there, all my family was born and raised there. And before my people passed away their home was there. And when people began to pass away that's where they are buried, right at Benham; now I have an older brother who was not buried there, but the rest of them they were buried right there in Benham. And my baby sister, she was buried there because she was cremated, but we buried, at least I did, buried her right down between Mom and Daddy, you see. And you know, because my oldest brother was the only one who was not buried there. I've already prepared things for myself to be buried there, everything is already set and lined up and everything.

—Odell Moss | Born 1932 in Benham, Ky. | Resides in Lexington, Ky.

Well, it's important to me because we all started on the same playing field more or less. And I like it because I think we really have a rich heritage because sometimes I just sit down and think and remember all of the people that I know, the families that I know that had lots of kids or didn't have lots of kids. Like almost everybody from up in our hollow that I know. The ones that stayed down there, that lived down there, graduated high school. I came to Milwaukee when I was fifteen, and I didn't graduate high school. But all of the children that I went to grade school with down there all graduated high school and went on to college. I like that. And I have my *being* down there—I wish that I could have stayed down there up until high school. But I love all of them people. And I go just to keep a little piece of that alive—every year. I've missed a couple of years, but I try to go so I can have a little memory. And I love it.

—Roselyn Baker | Born 1944 in Jenkins, Ky. | Resides in Milwaukee, Wis.

Because of the way I was raised. The culture, the love that I still feel for the people that I grew up with and the love I have for Lynch, that is why I say it is home, because it is just in me. Everything that I believe in or obtained—caring for people when you were having that respect that came from Lynch, because of the way I was raised, and that never left me and that is just home for me.

—Richard Brown | Born 1947 in Lynch, Ky. | Resides in Atlanta, Ga.

Well, if I could do that, I could probably explain to you why the salmon goes back and does its thing—it's just a part of you. I mean, this is home. I love it; it's home.

—Leslie Lee | Born 1948 in Lynch, Ky. | Resides in Harlan, Ky.

I think because it's close-knit, it's a small town. I think it's mainly to do with our school, our teachers, our church, our neighborhood. We didn't have much. That was our world. Imagine yourself—it was a valley, a community surrounded by mountains, and we were just all in that little community. So that's all we knew, so we became close, families became close. So I basically think that's why we're connected. And I hope that's why we're connected because of our upbringing.

—Cynthia Brown-Harrington | Born 1954 in Lynch, Ky. |
Resides in Greensboro, N.C.

Over the course of the last six decades, this black diaspora has invented a repertoire of practices, rituals, and traditions to archive home—the place from which they came, if only for one generation, through the long durée of black migration in America. The changing same of dispossession and dislocation is inherent to mass movement of the black body in this country in all its various iterations, from the forced migration that was the transAtlantic slave trade, to the great escape of the first wave of the Great Migration, to the subsequent outpouring of blacks from the South to the rest of the nation that ultimately shaped the composition and character of the American city. In this way, for almost all African American people, home is always an elusive concept. The natal alienation from a physical place of origin—for we are no more African than we are American, but all the time African and American—stirs in our souls a will of autopoiesis—an internal, eternal drive for self-making. This is the improvisation of blackness.

Acknowledgments

Every aspect of the making of this book was a labor of love. From the three-year cross-country road trip conducting oral history interviews, to establishing the EKAAMP archive, to curating exhibitions, to theorizing and analyzing the data, to the writing of the thing—I have loved it. That doesn't mean that this journey did not come with setbacks or disappointments—it certainly did. However, at the end of the day, there was never anything else I would have rather been doing. I sought to write a book about African American subjectivity and the transformation of the self. However, in the process of carrying out this research, I myself was transformed by the sheer generosity and love that so many people showed me along the way. Through this research, I cultivated in my own self a sense of purpose and collective responsibility. For that, I am grateful.

I am deeply indebted to and forever thankful for Jose Itzigsohn for seeing potential in this project—and in me—from the first day I mentioned this quirky story of Kentucky's coal camp blacks. Your commitment to supporting scholarship that is both rigorous and meaningful, and offering that support to such a motley crew of "unusual suspects" who attempt to produce it, is truly sublime. I also owe so much to Michael Kennedy, Paget Henry, Anthony Bogues, Françoise Hamlin, and William Ferris. They all went above and beyond in apprenticing me to become the scholar that I am today. They selflessly offered hours—and I mean dozens of hours—discussing the trajectory of the project, reading and rereading drafts of the manuscript, providing critical feedback, and challenging me to think through the big ideas. Each of you has left an indelible mark on my intellectuality. I also offer my sincere gratitude to my wonderful colleagues and friends who so generously read chapters of this manuscript, offered thoughtful feedback, and encouraged me to push forward in this endeavor: Kimberley Kay Hoang, Robert Vargas, Marcus Hunter, Ashanté Reese, Stefan Timmermans, Roger Waldinger, Marjorie Faulstich Orellana, Christopher Muller, Anthony Jack, Cecilia Menjivar, Claudio Benzecry, Leisy Abrego, Saida Grundy, Hiroshi Motomura, Steven P. Wallace, Gail Kligman, Malinda Maynor Lowery, Josh Whitford, Isaac Reed, and Aldon Morris. I am also deeply grateful to Stewart E. Tolnay and David Cunningham, both for setting an early example for me, a junior scholar, as to what amazing historical sociological research looks like, and for their most insightful, expansive, and rigorous comments on several drafts of this manuscript.

Collecting the data for this research required extensive travel across the country and access to professional-grade audio and visual equipment. I am thankful for the generous material support from the various foundations, centers, and individual donors that made this possible. Namely, many thanks to the Kentucky Historical

Society, the Southern Historical Collection at UNC Chapel Hill, the California Chapter of the Eastern Kentucky Social Club, John Powell, the Kenan Foundation, the Andrew W. Mellon Foundation, and the African American Success Foundation. I am also most grateful for the full-year fellowships at the Population Studies and Training Center and the Cogut Center for the Humanities at Brown University, and to the Department of Sociology at UNC Chapel Hill. Those opportunities provided the unfettered time that was necessary for me to conduct the fieldwork for this research and to complete the writing of this book. UNC Press has backed this project from its inception. I am truly grateful to my editor extraordinaire, Lucas Church, and to the entire editorial team at the Press for believing in the project and going above and beyond to give careful consideration to every detail regarding the content, placement, and aesthetic quality of *Gone Home*.

Through countless visits to archives for this research, I discovered that archivists are magical people. I am thankful for the tremendous resources at the Southern Historical Collection at UNC Chapel Hill and the Southeast Appalachian Archives at Southeast Community and Technical College. However, beyond the historical resources that these institutions hold, I came to love and appreciate so many of the wonderful people who so diligently steward these archives to ensure that researchers can access their collections. A special thank-you in this regard to Biff Hollingsworth (my brother from another mother), Theresa Osborne, Phyllis Sizemore, Barrye Brown, Bernetiae Reed, Ashlyn Velte, Shauna Collier, Holly Smith, Chaitra Powell, Bryan Giemza, Matt Turi, Lydia Neuroth, Susanne Erb, Josephine McRobbie, Brenna Edwards, and Eileen Lewis. All of you, in so many ways, have contributed to the production of *Gone Home* and to EKAAMP. I thank you from the bottom of my heart.

I journeyed through two academic homes through the production of this project—Brown University and UCLA. The people and experiences at both institutions have shaped me as a scholar and as a friend. Thank you to all the people who made up my community at Brown—you all are my village: Virginia Thomas, Tina Park, Ricarda Hammer, Orly Clerge, Weeam Hammoudeh, Erica Jade Mullen, Trina Vithayathil, Michael Rodriguez-Muniz, Michael Warren Murphy, Diana Graizbord, Marcelo Bohrt, Suzanne Enzerink, Felicia Bevel, Kenneth Berger, Amanda Boston, Michael Sawyer, Aisalkyn Boteva, Yashas Vaidya, Meg Caven, Jennifer Bouek, Heather Randell, Kelley Alison Smith, Meghan McBride, Apollonya Porcelli, Johnnie Lotesta, Juyoung Lee, Shane Martin, Amanda Figgins, Joan Picard, Susan Short, Mary Fennell, Suzanne Stewart-Steinberg, and Ariella Azoulay. You all supported the early ideas for this book and inspired me to feel empowered in my attempt to pull it off.

While my journey "going home" began at Brown, I was fortunate to have completed this manuscript in the good company of my institutional family at UCLA. I could not have landed on more fertile ground, and I am so grateful for all of the support from my colleagues in the Departments of Sociology and African American Studies at UCLA. A special thanks to Darnell Hunt, Gail Kligman, Marcus Anthony Hunter, Dant'e Taylor, Abigail Saguy, Aliza Luft, Kevan Harris, Jeff Guhin, Lauren Duquette-Rury, Jacob Foster, Min Zhou, Rogers Brubaker, Cesar Ayala, Rubén Hernández León, Ka-Yuet Lui, Ed Walker, Gabriel Rossman, Aaron Panofsky, Jemima

Pierre, Peter Hudson, Walter Allan, Patricia Turner, Muriel McClendon, and Robin "to the" D. G. Kelly.

I would be remiss if I did not also thank the various circles of friends who fiercely encouraged and supported me every step of the way, both in and outside the academy. A special thanks to Crew: Kara Pierre, Vanessa Hunter, Chantal Spencer, and Nicole Gray; to the Undercommons: Patricia Lott, Lara Stein Pardo, and Kimberly Juanita Brown; to my amazing circle of free black women: Zandria F. Robinson, Courtney Patterson-Faye, and Ashanté Reese; and to my dear friends Alicia and Kola Jegede, Zigi Makhombothi, the Rwayitare family, Tabatha Pirtle, Larry and Ivanna Wade, and Charly Palmer.

Last but certainly not least, to my family. To my parents, Richard Brown and Arnita Davis-Brown. Your unconditional love, support, and wisdom gave me the strength and courage to see this project through. Not only were you there in word, but you both rolled up your sleeves without asking and joined my research team. Daddy, thank you for driving me literally thousands of miles across the country to make it to the interviews for this project, for carefully documenting the process through your skillful photography, and for running a phone bank—setting up appointments, verifying identities, and making introductions. Mom, thank you for keeping me organized and on point through establishing the algorithm of my personal library, transcribing documents, and serving as my research assistant in the archives. To my one and only brother, Richard "Charu" Brown; my sister-in-law, Latobia Smith Brown; and my wonderful nieces and nephew, Chania, Sy'rai, Chazz, and Eisele—y'all truly are my inspiration. To my Godmother, Charlene Brown Hicks, thank you for being my confidant, my support system, and my role model for what it means to embody all that is good in the world. A big shout out to all of my many (and I have many!) aunts, uncles, and cousins from the Brown and Davis families—I know that Leona, Mamie, Major, and Thornton are so proud of us for the fact that we stuck together throughout the generations and love one another so. Lastly, to the hundreds of eastern Kentucky home folks—you coal miners' kids—who so generously contributed your stories, your time, and your hearts to *Gone Home*. I am forever grateful to each and every one of you and the legacy that you have bestowed upon my life.

[Sociological interpretation] should aim to study those finer manifestations of social life which history can but mention and which statistics can not count, such as the expression of Negro life as found in their hundred newspapers, their considerable literature, their music and folklore and their germ of esthetic life— in fine in all the movements and customs among them that manifest the existence of a distinct social mind.

—W. E. B. Du Bois, *The Study of Negro Problems*

For th[e sociological] imagination is the capacity to shift from one perspective to another—from the political to the psychological; from examination of a single family to comparative assessment of the national budgets of the world; from the theological school to the military establishment; from considerations of an oil industry to the military establishment; from considerations of an oil industry to the studies of contemporary poetry. It is the capacity to range from the most impersonal and remote transformations to the most intimate features of the human self—and to see the relations between the two.

—C. Wright Mills, *The Sociological Imagination*

Research Appendix

Our America has transformed itself many times over. From its founding in 1776 to the present moment, our quest to live up to the ideals upon which this country was founded—by incorporating them into our daily lives and practices, and outwardly projecting them as a collective demonstration of who "we" are as citizens and as a people—has been a work in progress. The first three-quarters of the twentieth century marked a time of rapid and contentious structural transformation of America's racial landscape. Not only did a series of hard-fought battles for racial justice take place, but the revolution was televised. Unlike the century before, the struggle of our country's black citizens for Life, Liberty, and Happiness was on stage for the world to bear witness. This study provides a cultural sociological analysis of the emergence and transformation of African American subjectivity in the context of massive social transformation. As my case, I used a group of historical change agents—a population of African Americans who partook in an intergenerational stepwise migration through the coalfields of eastern Kentucky. Across the generational arc of this study, these people suffered through the various iterations of racial violence that was Jim Crow, but they were also active participants in dismantling this legal caste system. This group also partook in both waves of the African American Great Migration. Whether or not they took part in pickets or protests, the African Americans represented in this study were all active participants in reshaping the demographic, political, and cultural landscape of the United States. Yet through all the struggle, striving, and ostensible progress toward realizing our ideals, America's latent disposition still flares and reminds us of the *changing same*.

This book offers an analysis of race, racialization, and racism that is both structural and phenomenological and one that is just as much about American society as it is about African American subjectivity. Our ideologies, conceptions, and notions of "race" are reified and inculcated by material structures—policies, institutions, regionalisms, spatial configurations, and the like. However, it is not just the material structures themselves but the power and inequality with which they are endowed. Further, the distribution and presentation of this power and inequality is a site of continual contestation in society, making the process of racialization and the forms of racism ongoing and dynamic, as opposed to something that is held constant in place and time. There is also a very real phenomenological dimension to race, a dimension that throughout this book I term "racialized subjectivity." Preceding identity—the outward projection and reception to and from the world of who you are—subjectivity refers to the interior process of self-making and subjective understanding. Its focus is on the lifelong philosophical question: How do you come to know yourself as a self? The community biography of black migrants presented in *Gone Home* examines the dialectics of these structural and phenomenological dimensions of race, racialization, and racism in all their robustness, fluidity, and nuance.

The first generation of black folks who escaped from Alabama to the coalfields of eastern Kentucky tell the story of African American struggle and striving. Even while living under the oppressive conditions of post-Reconstruction Alabama, our country's unintended citizens still managed to dream of an America that included them—one where their thread could be woven into the social fabric of "we the people." In the act of leaving, those early movers risked their lives in their endeavor for a place where their humanity would be taken for granted and recognized—a place where they could live with dignity as women and men, as mothers and fathers, and as full citizens. We can be sure that not all of those first-wavers who made an attempt at the Great ~~Migration~~ Escape made it safely to their final destinations. However, for those who did, the decision to migrate did not come without sacrifice. Those people uprooted themselves from their homes—from daily interactions with their families and communities, country landscapes, familiar faces and smells, the red dirt of the Deep South, and their memories—to advance their quest for what they believed could be a promised land. A clean slate: this is the inheritance that the first generation hoped to bestow upon their children.

Born in the margins of the margins—black in Appalachia—the progeny of the first-generation migrants grew up in what seemed to be a very different racial landscape from that of their parents. Under the blanket of the company town, there was no racial contract that allowed for the local white men to "come see about" a black man's wife, no convict labor or chain gang, no open Ku Klux Klan activity, no sharecropping agreements, and no lynching. Their generation, these coal miners' daughters and sons, were a symbol of racial progress. They lived through the civil rights movement and helped dismantle Jim Crow, and they were on the front lines of desegregating our country's public school system—they were a generation of "firsts." To Albert Harris once again: they were the ones who, all in one generation, went from "Colored, to Negroes, to African-Americans . . . and Black."

However, as my analysis revealed in chapter 4, what seemed like a promised land in the company-owned towns of eastern Kentucky was in fact a new genre of the same racial project of the Old South. What America called racial progress was a move toward a postracial society, which really meant a society where individuals no longer had to bear the responsibility for maintaining the racial order through force or overt violence.[1] This was a transformation in the history of U.S. race relations in that institutions, systems, and racial ideology now did much of the work that hate groups, statesmen, mobs, and individuals once did. Under this new system, American society began to prefer their racism under the veneer of politeness.[2] At the same time, African Americans' rights and access to the nation's institutions and economies were expanding broadly as a result of the civil rights movement.

I attempted to trace the ways in which African Americans navigated this new "landscape of meaning,"[3] articulated by ersatz postracialism and broadened horizons of possibility. I used the body of the 153 oral history interviews I conducted with this population in an attempt to "grasp history and biography and the relations between the two," what W. E. B. Du Bois and C. Wright Mills inspired me to believe was the "task and the promise of the sociological imagination."[4] What I found was that African Americans continued striving in their quest toward full incorporation into American society in spite of their acute awareness of the unequal realities and challenges of racial subjugation. However, as the landscape transformed, so too did their subjective understanding of who they were and who they aspired to be. In true pragmatist fashion, they recalibrated their aspirations, their practices, and the way they moved through the world as it expanded, yet they always held on to the ideal of full American citizenship. In that way, one of the broad findings of this study is that the twentieth-century African American project was largely one of incorporation.

Incorporation, however, is not the same as assimilation. All of the chapters show that there is and always has been a rich and uniquely black culture that thrives within the black community and pours out into mainstream society. This incorporative project is the impetus for the twoness that Du Bois articulated in *The Souls of Black Folk*: the desire to be both Negro and American without one negating the other. Why should we choose? Nowhere in the book is this more apparent than in chapter 7, "Gone Home," in which I discuss the emergence of my participants' diasporic consciousness and their love for home. Their shared experience with the displacement, dispossession, and loss resulting from industrial decline and ruination conditioned a homeland attachment that is analogous to what is typically observed in transnational mass migrations.[5] Through their invented traditions, practices, and rituals, they articulate and refashion their collective identities, and they reinscribe themselves in the regional narrative of Appalachia in spite of their apparent erasure. Hence the subtitle of this book: although their roots may no longer be planted *in* Appalachia, they surely run deep *through* there.

One immediate contribution that I hope this book will make to the sociological canon is to present an empirical analysis of the veil, originally theorized by W. E. B. Du Bois,[6] with special attention to the tensions, nuances, and dualities inherent in this concept. The sociological literature on African American community and culture is dominated by research focusing on the social ills of the black urban environment.[7] While studies like these shed light on aspects of the African American experience by illustrating structural effects of racialization and hyper-segregation, as a body of literature these studies can easily translate into a culture of poverty argument that pathologizes blackness as abject and criminal.[8] However, another effect of, or response to, the veil is a remarkable resistance, culture, improvisation, and artistic expression, which is also characteristic of African American communities.[9] The latter response is a testament to the fact that black life has always mattered a great deal to black people. This study is one example of the ways in which that self-appreciation takes place in spite of and behind the veil of the color line.

The Making of the Study

I decided to pursue this research project over Memorial Day weekend 2012, while I was sitting on a lawn chair on my grandparents' front porch on First Street in Lynch.

I hadn't been up to the mountains in twelve years, and at my parents' behest, I "came home": they, from Atlanta, Georgia, and I, from Providence, Rhode Island, where I was finishing my first year of graduate school at Brown University. The visit was so familiar. It was as though no time had passed. Every person that I greeted while walking the streets knew exactly who I belonged to: "There goes a Brown!" or "You must be a Davis; Nita's girl, right?" That's just how intimate and close-knit the community is there, even in the forty-year aftermath of mass out-migration.

Typical of Memorial Day weekend, Benham, Lynch, and Cumberland were bursting at the seams with black people. They were all over the place—walking in the streets, sitting on the porches of the few standing family homes, kids playing in the ballpark that separates Benham and Lynch, barbecuing in the back or on the side of the house, in church, and decorating their loved one's graves on the "colored" side of the cemetery in Cumberland. It brought back so many happy memories from my childhood visits when my grandparents were still living.

However, the state of the place itself was jarring. The built environment of the towns looked half the size of what I remembered from a little over a decade ago. So many homes were torn down or rotting in ruins. And although there were plenty of people there for the weekend, it was markedly fewer than how it used to be. Returning to the hollows of eastern Kentucky as a budding sociologist, I understood that I was looking at the effects of a particularly racialized industrial decline, mass migration, morbidity, mortality, and corporate and commercial disinvestment. I had found my case.

I drew on three classical works of sociology to develop the research design for this study: *The Souls of Black Folk*, *The Philadelphia Negro*, and *Black Reconstruction*. Du Bois's self-stated aim in *Souls* was to reveal "the strange meaning of being black here at the dawn of the twentieth century"—an inquiry of great import because, as he is oft quoted, "the problem of the color line is the problem of the twentieth century." My research question for this book is very much an extension of Du Bois's in *Souls*. I was interested in the phenomenological questions of racialized subjectivity, specifically for that of African Americans. However, Du Bois asked this question of the meaning of being black in America in 1903, at the dawn of the twentieth century. This was a time in which 90 percent of America's black population still resided in the South. Given the mass exodus of black Americans out of the strictures of the Jim Crow South, I thought the question begged investigating once again—this time within the context of the flux, fluidity, contestation, and heterogeneity of the African American Great Migration and the civil rights movement. Empirically, I wanted to pursue a rich population study that was deeply rooted in history—hence my use of *The Philadelphia Negro* and *Black Reconstruction* as models.

In essence, *Gone Home* is a Du Boisian sociological study. In it, I combined his analytical approach to urban and community studies with his theoretical framework for the study of the phenomenology of racialized subjectivity. Du Bois's analytical approach to urban community studies was based on three elements: (1) a strong focus on the forms and possibilities of agency; (2) centering the color line as a historical structural element affecting the lives of and opportunities for racialized people, thus conditioning the limits and possibilities of agency; and (3) a multimethod strategy of data collection, which privileges historical analysis and the historical contextualization of sociological research and findings.[10] Drawing heavily from Du Bois's canonical empirical studies and foundational theories of racialized subjectivity, I developed the research design for this study. What follows is my research process for the production of this study.

Preliminary Research: The Ethnosurvey

Before conducting the oral history interviews that would be my primary source of data, I conducted preliminary demographic research on this population of African American migrants. This preliminary data allowed me to identify the demographic patterns and events that were significant and unique to their migration story. Between January and May of 2013, I conducted ninety-eight ethnosurveys on a subsample of African Americans who had once lived in eastern Kentucky and who migrated to Chicago, Cleveland, or Detroit sometime between 1940 and 1980. The ethnosurvey I designed for this population drew heavily on the survey instruments used by the long-standing Mexico Migration Project, founded by Douglas Massey and Jorge Durand.[11]

The ethnosurvey was especially valuable for this study because it captures not only demographic data but also discrete events over time. For example, the interview schedule on migration and mobility captured every interstate migration and every intracity move that my participants made over the life course. Given that their median age at the time of the interviews was sixty-nine years old, this survey generated rich demographic data that was dynamic and historical. The ethnosurvey, for example, is how I discovered through one seemingly simple question how common the experience of displacement due to eminent domain was to black people in urban cities in the mid-twentieth century:

> *Karida:* Mrs. So and So, please tell me all of the addresses that you have
> resided in since you moved to Chicago, starting with your first move in
> 1958.
> *Mrs. So and So:* Well, I first moved to XYZ Halsted St., then we moved from
> there when we bought our first house at, well, I can't really explain it to you
> because that place doesn't exist anymore . . .
> *Karida:* Doesn't exist?
> *Mrs. So and So:* You know, the eminent domain thing. It's the highway now.
> *Karida:* ???

Through the data I collected from the survey's series of questions on the topics of migration, residential mobility, occupational mobility, educational attainment, marriage pattern, and family structure, I was able to sketch the structure of their demographic profile over time. Conducting these preliminary descriptive analyses provided keen sociological insight into the population, and I believe it helped me ask more nuanced questions in the oral history interviews than I would have asked without it. It also taught me an indelible lesson about "knowing." What I knew, or what I wanted to know more about for the purposes of my budding sociological study, was sometimes different from what my participants knew or believed was interesting and important. In this way, conducting the ethnosurvey interviews challenged me to think carefully about listening, epistemology, and considerations of power—she who holds the pen. My early experiences with conducting preliminary survey research factored heavily into my decision to transition to oral history interview-based research to carry out this study, not only in deciding what methods would best get at my object of analysis but also in my ethical considerations of what my relationship to my research participants was in the process of producing scholarly knowledge.

The Sample: Oral History Interview-Based Research

I began conducting the oral history interviews with this population in June 2013, a project that is still ongoing. I used the first 153 interviews, conducted through August 2016, in my analysis for this study. The sample includes a cohort of African Americans who migrated out of the coal mining communities of Harlan and, to a much lesser extent, Letcher County, Kentucky, between 1940 and 1980. The sample also includes a subset of "stayers"—those who never migrated out of the region or those who migrated but later resettled in the region.

I employed snowball sampling techniques to enroll participants in the project; recognizing that members of a "special population"—defined as small subgroups of a population that are considered rare and not commonly visible—will be aware of other members in that population.[12] Given their strong family and institutional ties, participants were most inclined to personally refer family members, such as siblings and cousins, as well as members of their high school graduating class. The majority of the participants in this research are retirement-age African Americans who were born and raised in eastern Kentucky, and who migrated out of the region shortly after high school graduation. Table 2 represents the descriptive statistics of the sample of 153 participants at the time of their oral history interview.

Participants' median age at the time of the interview was sixty-nine years old, with ages ranging from thirty-eight to ninety-four years old. Half of the individuals in the sample attended the segregated colored schools in eastern Kentucky for their entire K–12 education, while the other half experienced school desegregation at some point in their childhood. This delineation is important, because as I argue in chapter 6, the event of school desegregation was a watershed moment in African American subjectivity and identity formation. In an attempt to trace the paths most traveled throughout this massive out-migration while staying attentive to less popular "routes to rootlessness" that articulate this black diaspora,[13] I made an effort to identify participants all over the country and visit them in their homes to conduct their oral history interviews. In total, this study represents black eastern Kentuckians who currently reside in thirty-one cities across fourteen states.

I cannot make claims to the representativeness of this study, as I am working with a community *en diaspora*. There is no enumerated list of the population during the time in which they lived in their place of origin, and given the issues of dis-

TABLE 2 Descriptive Statistics: Participant Sample, *n*=153

Age*			
Younger than 65	34%		
Between 65 and 80 years old	41%		
Older than 80 years old	25%		
Sex			
Male	53%		
Female	47%		
Generation			
Never integrated	51%		
Integrated 9th–12th grade	15%		
Integrated 1st–8th grade	23%		
Always integrated	11%		
High School Graduate			
Yes	93%		
No	7%		
Destination Region			
Midwest	49%		
Northeast	5%		
Southeast	16%		
West	7%		
Stayers	23%		
Central Tendencies			
	Median	Minimum	Maximum
Age	69	38	94

*At time of interview

location, morbidity, and mortality, I cannot make speculations in this regard. Those matters are, however, beyond the scope or concern of the project.

However, collected systematically, oral history data has the potential to fill the extant knowledge gaps in the sociological literature on the Great Migration. Demographer Stewart Tolnay urged that "time is quickly running out on our opportunity to gather information from the participants in the Great Migration. Before this valuable repository of information disappears, researchers should consider the potential of well-designed approaches to record the life histories of migrants."[14] In spite of sampling limitations, he argues that "such qualitative evidence may not be generalizable to the entire population of southern migrants, but this limitation is counterbalanced by the richness of the first-hand information that can be obtained from the migrants."[15] Echoing the latter part of Tolnay's argument, I also find oral history to be a fecund data source with which to produce research that attends to cultural sociological questions of meaning, such as subjectivity, identity formation, and the formation of lifeworlds to carry out what Cobb and Hoang call "protagonist-driven" research.[16]

Oral History Methodology

Oral history methodology provided the clearest entry into the interior dimension of the human experience in which I was interested. Oral histories are life stories, however they are slightly different from semi-structured interviews in that they are very much driven by the participant's narration of his or her own life history. In this way, they are the "protagonists of their own history."[17] They are also different from semi-structured interviews in that they are intended to enter the historical record by virtue of being deposited in an institutional archive (more on this later).

Stories are audio-textual representations of "discourse, vehicles of ideology, and elements of collective action frames" that have been used in sociology as a cultural tool for interpreting subjective experience, collective identity, and sense-making.[18] The stories captured in the oral history data are particularly valuable for studying marginalized populations because they bring to the fore "hidden transcripts" that articulate their social world—traces that would otherwise remain undocumented and run the risk of historical erasure.[19]

Each oral history interview for this study covered seven predetermined topics: (1) childhood memories of growing up in their community of origin, (2) family structure in their community of origin, (3) perceptions of race relations, (4) educational experiences, (5) migration, (6) career trajectories, and (7) attachment to place. They are intentionally guided by questions that are broad and open ended, such as, "What was it like growing up as a little boy or girl in Lynch, Kentucky?" or "Take us to school. What was that like?" This loosely structured interview style gave respondents the opportunity to share memories that are most meaningful to them and to cross-reference memories across topics. Allowing participants the time to triangulate their memories across time and topic lends itself to empirically rich interview data that is primed to be cross-referenced with other historical sources. Interview times ranged from forty minutes to three and a half hours, subject to such factors as the complexity of the participant's life history or the level of intersubjective engagement between my research participant and myself.

One obvious limitation of using oral history data for this study is the "messiness" of memory, particularly working with a group of retirement-age individuals. However, following the long tradition of the social thought on collective memory, my central interest is the way in which groups negotiate their collective identity through continual representation of a shared experience.[20] According to sociologist Ron Eyerman, "Collective memory unifies the group through time and over space by providing a narrative frame, a collective story, which locates the individual and his and her biography within it."[21] Thus, the way in which groups presently narrate what happened in the past is of as much sociological import as what "actually" happened.

Taken collectively, the oral history interview offered the optimal data for this study, as it allows for the interpretation of how this generation of African Americans "collectively engage in meaning-making processes" that "structure people's ability to think and to share ideals."[22] One measure to enhance the durability of the frame of the collective memories is the large sample size. In their annual review on the sociology of storytelling, Polletta et al. argue for the possibility that "stronger narratives might be those that were less coherent rather than more coherent, or that groups might be better off with multiple, even inconsistent, narratives that somehow seemed to hang together."[23] This statement rings true with the narratives in this sample. The body of oral history data used for this study captures the tensions between experiences that were particular to this migrant group and those that were general of the twentieth-century African American experience. Reconciling or teasing out the tensions present within the body of oral history data was the task of sociological interpretation.

On Theory, Interpretation, and Form

In this analysis, I sought to take up race—a socially constructed category of analysis—and racialization—the ongoing process of the (trans)formation of the racial subject—toward an interpretation that is both structural and phenomenological. From this perspective, I approached the *racial self* as a refraction projected through the interfaces of the state, public opinion, everyday social interaction, and the interiority of self, addressing the questions that loom large in theoretical considerations of the human condition: *Who am I?* and *Who are We?*—questions that situate the self in relation to society[24]—and for the racialized being, *What am I?*—an ontological question of humanity.[25]

While categories are useful for our own cognition, as they provide concepts and groups of signs and symbols that help us order "words and things," historicizing them and attending to their lumpiness is crucial to this type of sociological analysis. Beyond the external meaning of these categories—Colored, Negro, African American, and Black—what did these various racial identifiers articulate in the souls of the people who were seized by those words? Broken down into a series of questions: How did this generation of black folks internalize the racial categories that were superimposed on them? How did they reappropriate these categories within their own meaning systems? How did these words in turn structure their internal horizon of possibilities: their hopes, aspirations, fears, desires, and so on? And, connecting these smaller questions back to the question of the larger racial epistemic order, how did that series of discursive transformations affect the way in which this generation of black folks understood themselves as racialized subjects within the tabula rasa of the American body politic? These were the questions that motivated this study.

As I stated in the opening of chapter 4, I adopted Sherry Ortner's definition of subjectivity that she put forward in her essay "Subjectivity and Cultural Critique," in which she states, "By subjectivity I mean the ensemble of modes of perception, affect, thought, desire, and fear that animate acting subjects. But I always mean as well the cultural and social formations that shape, organize and provoke those modes of affect thought, and so on."[26] In her formulation, subjectivity is produced, shaped, and transformed through an ongoing process of what Anthony Giddens termed "structuration"—that is, the ongoing dialectic between structure and agency, through which structures create behaviors and subjects' behaviors create structures.[27]

However, the examination of racialized subjectivity requires the social observer to make plain the material conditions under which the social forces of racism, prejudice, and dehumanization manifest themselves in and on the black body, as well as the ways in which the racialized subject *makes* him- or herself within the constraints of racial subjugation. Philosopher Linda Alcoff frames the question of racialized subjectivity as "experienced selfhood" and "the everydayness of racial experience," arguing that "objectivist approaches that define race by invoking metanarratives of historical experience, cultural traditions, or processes of colonization and that take a third-person perspective can be inattentive to the microinteractions in which racialization operates, is reproduced, and is sometimes resignified."[28] For the scholar wishing to engage with the analysis of racialized subjectivity, she urges us to hold on to the notion that "the epistemically relevant point here is that the *source* of racializations, or at least one important source, is in the microprocesses of subjective existence."[29] Du Bois describes this as the "atmosphere of the land, the thought and feeling, the thousand and one little actions which go to make up life."[30] In this essay, "Of Masters and Men," he expounds on human experience in the Jim Crow South:

> It is, in fine, the atmosphere of the land, the thought and feeling, the thousand and one little actions which go to make up life. In any community or nation it is these little things which are most elusive to the grasp and yet most essential to any clear conception of the group life taken as a whole. What is thus true of all communities is peculiarly true of the South, where, outside of written history and outside of printed law, there has been going on for a generation as deep a storm and stress of human souls, as intense a ferment of feeling, as intricate a writhing of spirit, as ever a people experienced.

This is the theoretical frame that guided my analysis for this research.

So what then can be said about those African American citizens who, two, three, and four generations removed from slavery, embarked on one of the most profound social movements in American history? And who did so not only in their mass out-migration from the South to the North but also in their incessant striving for incorporation into national life? This endeavor can largely be read as a collective making and remaking of the self, the ultimate auto-poetic project. We only need to turn to the literary works of Richard Wright, Zora Neale Hurston, and Langston Hughes; the soulful lyrics of Sam Cooke, James Brown, Gladys Knight, Ray Charles, Tina Turner, and Nina Simone; or the art of Aaron Douglas, Jacob Lawrence, and Gordon Parks to sense the inextricable linkages between the Great Migration and the black experience throughout the twentieth century. In *Gone Home*, I examine these linkages along the grain of the African American Great Migration.

In the writing of the text, I was intentional about using form as method. The writing was a constant negotiation between whose voice would take up space on the text: the participants, the theories with which I engaged, and myself, the author.

What I attempted to accomplish with form was writing from within the veil of the color line. What I mean is that I wanted to produce a work of sociology that emerged within the lifeworld of the community studied as opposed to one that relied solely upon the outside gaze for sociological explanation. My approach to accomplishing that goal was to put the experiences and worldviews of my participants in direct conversation with theory, and to lead the analysis with their lived experience as opposed to the other way around. In this way, I believe the analysis grapples with epistemological presuppositions, recalibrates the power dynamic between the subject and the researcher, and allows for a sociology that is relational.

On the Archive

During my early research I was disappointed to learn that there was little to be found about the black experience in Appalachia in formal institutional archives—so disappointed that we—my participants and I—built one. The Appalachian region often escapes the mainstream American imaginary. Even when representations of the region do enter the cultural-historical discourse in academia or in the media, African Americans are rarely inscribed into the social heritage of this region. This erasure can be traced through iconic popular media, such as the Academy Award–winning films *Coal Miner's Daughter* and *Harlan County, USA* and contemporary television series like *Justified* and *Kentucky Justice*.[31] In spite of the region's diversity, depictions of Appalachian culture are primarily constructed through the gaze of outsiders who are in search of the iconic white, poor, toothless, backward hillbilly.[32] Much of what we have come to know about Appalachian culture is based on depictions from nineteenth-century travel diaries, literature, and popular magazines, such as *Harper's* and the *Atlantic Monthly*. Algeo argues that America's internal Other, Appalachia, "serves as a counterpoint to the idea of an increasingly unified and modern United States. Where the nation was progressive and industrial, Appalachia was backward and agricultural."[33] These tropes play a significant role in how people even begin thinking about Appalachia.

And yet as Edward Cabbell squarely put it thirty years ago, "Black people in Appalachia are a neglected minority within a neglected minority," and "their experiences are often so artfully clouded in myth and reality that they remain virtually invisible."[34] Speaking of his frustration, Jack French complained:

> It's always "drinking Mountain Dew. Sisters and brothers sleeping together. Can't read or write." I kind of resented that though because it became a national picture of Appalachia. Only white people. I throw out the rest of the case. When I say that—and I have said to a lot of people that really don't know that I am from Kentucky—and I say the exposés and the things that they portray on Kentucky are all negative, but they never tell you the successful stories and all that. They never mention anything about blacks in Appalachia; the thing with that is they always go to the poor white section of the state.

Therefore, in 2013, I founded the Eastern Kentucky African American Migration Project (EKAAMP), in partnership with the Southern Historical Collection at UNC

Chapel Hill, to provide a space for African Americans who share eastern Kentucky roots to inscribe themselves in the institutional archives, lest they be written out of history.[35]

The Southern Historical Collection and the Formation of EKAAMP

Established on January 14, 1930, the Southern Historical Collection was founded with the mission to document the history and culture of the American South. Inaugurated with a $25,000 endowment from Sarah Graham Kenan, newly minted director J. G. de Roulhac Hamilton began an aggressive collecting campaign to build "a great library of Southern records." Within twenty years of inception, by the time of Hamilton's retirement, "The Southern" held approximately 2.1 million manuscript items. Today, it holds over 15 million individual items assembled in 4,600 collections.[36] The largest university collection on the American South, the Southern Historical Collection is renowned as the gold standard for archival and preservation sciences among peer institutions. The archive maintains extensive collections relating to slavery, the Civil War, the civil rights movement, southern communities, and the antebellum South. Its holdings on Appalachia include materials related to local community histories, settlement, labor, and culture.

However, it remained virtually silent on the African American experience in the region. That changed on June 19, 2013, when I met with staff members about "the stuff."

I brought along samples of materials that my participants had given me to "get the story right"—two 1929 report cards from the Wise County Colored School, some old photographs, a 1951 United States Steel Corporation paycheck, the articles of incorporation for the California Chapter of the Eastern Kentucky Social Club, and an unpublished book assembled by Mr. Sam Howard, one of my participants, about the history of the Lynch Colored Public School titled, "Wanting to Be Remembered." By the end of the meeting, we shook hands and agreed to form a partnership: the Southern Historical Collection would provide a home for the materials relating to the black experience in eastern Kentucky, and I would facilitate its collection. After months of discussion, we agreed to the terms of how EKAAMP would function. The project would exist as a stand-alone collection within the SHC; ultimately, all the materials I acquired would fall under the umbrella of one master finding aid. Because of our relative ignorance about this community, we also agreed not to restrict the content of the donations, meaning that they would consider objects and other nontraditional donations. Lastly, they agreed to my only non-negotiable request: no consignation. This meant that no individual donation (whether from a person, a family, or an organization) would ever be mixed with another. Future users of the archive would encounter it as the participants had originally articulated it.

EKAAMP is one of the five major ongoing community-driven archival projects at the Southern Historical Collection. The donations to the collection are an extension of the stories shared in the oral history interviews, and they only come to the archive if and when a participant chooses to donate them. You can find all the oral history interviews from this study, as well as the documents, photographs, manuscripts, and objects from the EKAAMP collection, at http://finding-aids.lib.unc.edu /05585.

· · · · · ·

Through my experience with conducting interviews for this project, I discovered what a powerful methodological tool oral history presented to sociology. My research participants shared their stories, stated their political philosophies on all manner of issues, decided how they wanted their historical documents managed, and contributed to the research by donating source materials to the EKAAMP archive. I offered them the option to have their interview materials anonymized, fictionalized, or named and made public for future research through the archive at the Southern Historical Collection, and all but two opted for the latter. Beyond their individual interviews, dozens of participants have stayed in contact with me to follow up on my progress on "their" book. Well, here it is. From beginning to end, this has truly been a collaborative research project.

Appendix A

Interviewee Schedule

Last Name	First Name	Birth Year	Birth City	City of Residence
Akal	Derrick	1966	Hempstead (NY)	Lynch
Akal	Katina	1972	Hempstead (NY)	Lynch
Akal	Sherry	1973	Hempstead (NY)	Columbus
Allen	Carla	1960	Cumberland	Cumberland
Andrews	Arletta	1941	East Bernstadt (KY)	Detroit
Atkinson	Clara	1948	Lynch	Lynch
Austin	Gean	1930	Fayette (AL)	Lynch
Austin	Michael	1955	Lynch	Lynch
Austin-Mimes	Teresa	1958	Lynch	Lynch
Baker	Roselyn	1942	McRoberts	Milwaukee
Barnes	Cynthia	1954	Lynch	Greensboro
Baskin	Anne	1950	Benham	Benham
Baskin	Dwayne	1962	Lynch	Indianapolis
Baskin	Jaunita	1943	Lynch	San Jose
Baskin	Milton	1952	Lynch	Dayton
Baskin	Sanford	1948	Lynch	Benham
Baskin	Tony	1951	Lynch	Dayton
Baskin-Brack	Cheryl	1947	Lynch	Lexington
Bickerstaff	Bernard	1943	Benham	Cleveland
Bickerstaff	Joyce	1941	Benham	Cleveland
Brown	Eddify	1925	Selma (AL)	Los Angeles
Brown-Kirkland	Geraldine	1944	Lynch	Danville
Brown	Janice	1953	Benham	Indianapolis
Brown	Linda Faye	1953	Lynch	Lynch
Brown	Patricia	1953	Cumberland	Uniondale
Brown	Richard	1947	Lynch	Atlanta
Brown	Tony	1958	Lynch	Lynch
Brown	Viola	1938	Lynch	Danville
Brown-Harrington	Cynthia	1954	Lynch	Greensboro
Brown-Hicks	Charlene	1948	Lynch	Danville
Callaway-Hill	Harriet	1941	Benham	Detroit
Callaway	Rhonda	1951	Benham	Little Rock
Chapman	Richard	1955	Lynch	Lynch
Clark	Charles	1956	Lynch	Columbus

Last Name	First Name	Birth Year	Birth City	City of Residence
Clark	Lorene	1931	Lynch	Lynch
Clements	Clara	1937	Tuscaloosa (AL)	Lynch
Coleman	Samuel	1957	Lynch	Lynch
(Anonymous)	—	—	—	—
(Anonymous)	—	—	—	—
Combs	Brenda	1954	Lynch	Lexington
Davis	Clarence	1938	Cumberland	Covington
Davis	Jimmy	1936	Cumberland	Lima
Davis	Lisa	1959	Lynch	Cleveland
Davis	Patricia	1944	Lynch	Cleveland
Davis	Sally	1941	Lynch	Covington
Davis	Wanda	1957	Lynch	Cleveland
Davis-Brown	Arnita	1953	Lynch	Atlanta
Ellington	Mike	1958	Lynch	Benham
Ferguson	Mother	1925	Haynesville	Milwaukee
Fielder	Freda	1931	Harlan	Louisville
Fielder	Nathaniel (Tineye)	1927	Greensboro	Louisville
Fikes	Charles	1936	Lofton (AL)	San Jose
Freeman	Charles	1944	Lynch	Dayton
French	Jack	1945	Lynch	Cleveland
French	Willie	1942	Lynch	Lexington
Gardner	Ike	1930	Marion Junction (AL)	Chicago
Gist	Edwin	1942	Lynch	Chicago
Gist	James III	1976	Lynch	Lynch
Grey	Roy	1944	McRoberts	Detroit
Griffen	Barbara	1944	Lynch	Waterbury
Griffen	Tommy Jr.	1949	Lynch	Waterbury
Griffey	Lacey	1928	Benham	Benham
Hall	Joyce	1951	Lynch	Waterbury
Hampton	Deborah	1954	Benham	Lynch
Hampton	Ronnie	1951	Lynch	Lynch
Harris	Albert	1950	Benham	Sunrise
Haskins	Rosie	1940	McRoberts	Milwaukee
Haury	Barbara	1942	Lynch	Chicago
Hauser	Arthur	1954	Lynch	Indianapolis
Hauser	Barney	1956	Lynch	Indianapolis
Howard	Sam	1942	Lynch	Louisville
Hudson	Donald	1931	Jenkins	Detroit
Huston	James	1945	Lynch	Detroit
Jackson	Gerald Wayne	1950	Lynch	Lynch
Jackson	Lee Arthur	1950	Lynch	Lexington

Last Name	First Name	Birth Year	Birth City	City of Residence
Jackson	William (Biscuit)	1944	Lynch	Los Angeles
Jones	Lena	1940	Lynch	Louisville
Kendrick	Sylvester	1949	Lynch	Beavercreek
Ledford	Helen	1932	Lynch	Cumberland
Lee	Lacey	1943	Benham	Atlanta
Lee	Leslie	1948	Lynch	Harlan
Mason	Curtis	1948	Lynch	Chicago
Mason	Delores	1943	Lynch	Lexington
Mason	Mike	1952	Lynch	Columbus
Mason	Terry	1958	Lynch	Columbus
Mason	Vergie	1923	Mount Sterling	Columbus
Massey	Bennie	1949	Lynch	Lynch
Massey	George	1952	Lynch	Lynch
Massey	Teresa	1968	Lynch	Lynch
McBath	Lelia	1926	Lynch	Los Angeles
McCaskill	Yvonne	1946	Fleming	Milwaukee
McDonald	Eddie	1928	Benham	Detroit
Merton	Rutland	1948	Lynch	Lynch
Mitchel	Cynda	1950	Lynch	Lynch
Mitchel	Lois	1953	Lynch	Lynch
Moore	Ervine	1935	McRoberts	Milwaukee
Morris	Beverly	1949	Benham	Los Angeles
Morrow	Dwayne	1952	Lynch	Lynch
Morrow	William	1922	Plantersville (AL)	Lynch
Moss	Armenia	1935	Benham	Cleveland
Moss	Edgar James	1940	Benham	Newington
Moss	Jean	1938	Benham	Bedford Hts
Moss	Odell	1932	Benham	Lexington
Motley	Roland	1934	Benham	Chagrin Falls
Motley	Timothy	1961	Benham	Benham
Mullins	Ryland	1942	Lynch	Columbus
Mullins	Uvella	1937	Lynch	Columbus
Mullins	Vivian	1936	Lynch	Columbus
Napier	Belinda	1951	Syman (VA)	Cumberland
Nolan	Brenda	1958	Cumberland	Dayton
Oden-Williams	Debra	1958	McRoberts	Lexington
Parks	Katie Sue	1948	Lynch	Lorraine
Peavy	Ronnie	1947	Cumberland	Dayton
Peeples	Billy	1948	Lynch	Springfield
Peeples	Porter G.	1945	Lynch	Lexington
Peeples	Vera	1948	Cumberland	Springfield
Perry	Humes	1942	Lynch	Waterbury

Last Name	First Name	Birth Year	Birth City	City of Residence
Perry	James	1940	Lynch	Waterbury
Pettygrue	Ernest	1938	Lynch	Indianapolis
Pettygrue	Rose Ivery	1937	Greensburg	Indianapolis
Pollenitz	Robert	1927	Benham	Chicago
Powell	Betty	1937	Clinton (AL)	Dayton
Price	Charles	1933	Louisville	Indianapolis
Prinkleton	Victor	1944	Lynch	Lexington
Ratchford	Cynthia	1949	Lynch	San Jose
Ratchford	Jacquelyn	1945	Lynch	San Jose
Ratchford	Jeff	1956	Lynch	Atlanta
Ratchford	Jerome	1942	Lynch	Atlanta
Richardson	Ruth	1928	Evarts	Dayton
Robinson	Vera	1937	Lynch	Indianapolis
Rodgers	Chuck	1953	Lynch	Lexington
Rogers	Betty Jewel Watts	1934	Docena (AL)	Cleveland
Rogers	Clarence	Unknown	Birmingham	(AL) Cleveland
Schaffer, Jr.	William (Bo)	1926	Lynch	Chicago
Simmons	Arthur (Three Knots)	1937	Lynch	Chicago
Smith	Clara	1942	Cumberland	Detroit
Smith	George	1932	Butler (AL)	Cleveland
Smith	Herbert	1945	Cumberland	Detroit
Stevens	James	1935	Killbear (AL)	Cleveland
Stevens	Roy	1954	Lynch	Lynch
Steward	John	1942	Cincinnati (OH)	Los Angeles
Taylor	George	1950	Cumberland	Dayton
Taylor-Ward	Virginia	1949	Cumberland	Dayton
Thomas	Ron	1949	Lynch	Indianapolis
Thompson	Norman	1949	Lynch	Cleveland
Thornton	Brenda	1950	Lynch	White Plains
Thrasher	Joyce	1946	Benham	Indianapolis
Turner	Jeff	1959	Lynch	Indianapolis
Turner	Millie	1966	Hazard	Indianapolis
Ward	William	1942	Lynch	Chicago
Watts	Della	unknown	Harlan	Cleveland
Watts	Willie	1936	Docena (AL)	Cleveland
Whitt	Raven	1955	Benham	Cumberland
Williams	Betty	1944	Benham	Indianapolis
Williams	Jimmy	1943	Jenkins	Cleveland
Williams	Vyreda	1947	Lynch	Cleveland
Willis	Jessie	1920	Irvington (GA)	Detroit
Wilson	Ruthie Mae	1949	Lynch	Benham

Appendix B

Consent and Deed of Gift Forms

IRB Consent Form

Ties That Bind: The Impact of Migrant Networks on
Migration, Resettlement, and Integration
Over the Life Course

KARIDA L. BROWN, GRADUATE STUDENT
DEPARTMENT OF SOCIOLOGY | BROWN UNIVERSITY

I, _____, have been invited to provide an oral history interview for this dissertation research. I understand that Karida L. Brown is interviewing African Americans from Harlan, Letcher, and Fletcher Counties, Kentucky, to trace the out-migration to cities throughout the United States. I also understand that she may use material from my interview in her dissertation and possibly in subsequent publications. Unless I indicated otherwise, there will be no restrictions on the use of my interview by either Karida L. Brown or the university archive.

Research Methodology and Interviewee Rights

This audio/video-recorded interview will be conducted in the form of a guided conversation and will last from 45 minutes to an hour. I understand that I will be free to decline to answer any question that I consider to be uncomfortable or inappropriate. Moreover, I will have the right to stop the interview at any time without any negative consequences. There are no foreseeable risks to my participation. While there may be no direct benefit to me, this interview may contribute toward increased public knowledge about my personal experience with the black migration out of southeastern Kentucky for researchers, my descendants, and the general public. There is no cost to my participation in this study, and I will not receive any compensation in exchange for a recording of my interview. I further recognize that there is no assumption of confidentiality unless I specifically request it.

☐ For research purposes keep the interview **entirely confidential**.

☐ For research purposes use a **fictitious name**.

☐ For research purposes use **actual names**.

If you have any questions or concerns about this study or the oral history process, you can contact Karida L. Brown at (401) 500.1662 or Karida_Johnson@brown.edu, or her faculty advisor Jose Itzigsohn at (401) 863.2528 or Jose_Itzigsohn@brown.edu. If you have questions about your rights as a research participant, you may also contact the Brown University Office of Research Integrity at (401) 863.3050.

_____	_____
Interviewee	Karida L. Brown
_____	_____
Date	Date

_____

_____

Mailing Address

Deed of Gift Form

Deed of Gift

I, _____, do herein permanently donate and convey my oral history interview to Karida L. Brown. In making this gift, I understand that I am assigning all right, title, and interest in copyright to Karida L. Brown.

I further understand that she wishes to donate my interview to a university library archive to make the interview available to the public, including researchers, lay-people, and my family and descendants. This interview can be used in any number of ways, such as for academic research, book publications, or documentaries. While there is no direct benefit to me, this donation may add significant value to our current knowledge about African American history and culture. This donation may include the transfer of all interest in copyright that I herein assigned. Karida L. Brown agrees in turn to inform me of the library or archive that will ultimately be the repository of my interview/s and materials.

I choose to:

☐ Keep the interview **entirely confidential**.
Do NOT gift my interview to a university library.

☐ Make the interview publicly available using a **fictitious name**.
Gift my interview to a university library using a fictitious name.

☐ Consent to make the interview publicly available using **actual names**.
Gift my interview to a university library using my actual name.

Questions & Concerns

If you have any questions or concerns about this study or the oral history donation process, you can contact Karida L. Brown at (401) 500.1662 or Karida_Johnson@brown.edu.

_____   _____

Interviewee   Karida L. Brown

_____   _____

Date   Date

Notes

Introduction

1. Du Bois, *Souls of Black Folk*; Woodward, *Origins of the New South*; Wilson, *Black Codes of the South*, 6; Woodward, *Strange Career of Jim Crow*.

2. Hirschman, *Exit, Voice, and Loyalty*.

3. For book-length treatments of these aspects of the African American Great Migration, see Chatelain, *South Side Girls*; Du Bois, *Philadelphia Negro*; Gottlieb, *Making Their Own Way*; Gregory, *Southern Diaspora*; Grossman, *Land of Hope*; Harrison, *Black Exodus*; Lemann, *Promised Land*; Marks, *Farewell—We're Good and Gone*; Martin, *Detroit and the Great Migration*; Painter, *Exodusters*; Trotter, *Great Migration in Historical Perspective*; Wilkerson, *Warmth of Other Suns*; Woodson, *Century of Negro Migration*.

4. Hunter and Robinson, *Chocolate Cities*.

5. Marcus Anthony Hunter, "WEB Du Bois and Black Heterogeneity."

6. Cabbell, "Black Invisibility and Racism in Appalachia"; Turner and Cabbell, *Blacks in Appalachia*.

7. Marks, *Farewell—We're Good and Gone*; Ravenstein, "Laws of Migration"; Alexander, J. Trent, "Great Migration in Comparative Perspective."

8. Trotter, *Coal, Class, and Color*; Lewis, "From Peasant to Proletarian."

9. Banishment is a form of ethnic cleansing widely carried out in the United States in which the white inhabitants of towns and cities forced the entire black population to leave town, often overnight. Those black inhabitants who refused to leave were killed. Banishments occurred primarily in towns outside the South, mainly between 1890 and 1940, and their legacy in terms of the ethnoracial composition of U.S. towns and cities in the Midwest, Northeast, and West persist to this day. For works on this hidden history of American racism, see Loewen, *Sundown Towns*; Marco Williams, *Banished*.

10. Tolnay and Beck, *Festival of Violence*; Bailey and Tolnay, *Lynched*; Wells-Barnett, *On Lynchings*; Tolnay and Beck, "Racial Violence and Black Migration in the American South."

11. Fullilove, *Eminent Domain and African Americans*; Hunt and Ramón, *Black Los Angeles*.

12. Deener, "Decline of a Black Community by the Sea," 81; Wilder, *Covenant with Color*.

13. Here I adopt Ann Laura Stoler's dynamic definition of ruination, where in her edited volume *Imperial Debris* she asserts: "Imperial projects are themselves processes of ongoing ruination, processes that 'bring ruin upon,' exerting material and

social force in the present. By definition, *ruination* is an ambiguous term, being an act of ruining, a condition of being ruined, and a cause of it. Ruination is an *act* perpetrated, a *condition* to which one is subject, and a *cause* of loss." Mah, *Industrial Ruination, Community, and Place*; Gordillo, "Landscapes of Devils"; Stoler, *Imperial Debris*.

14. Wagner, *African American Miners and Migrants*.

15. Du Bois, *Souls of Black Folk*; Itzigsohn and Brown, "Sociology and the Theory of Double Consciousness."

16. W. E. B. Du Bois was one of the disciplinary founders of American sociology; however, his work is seldom included in the sociological canon. This is largely due to the racism and discrimination he faced during his time in the academy, on and off between 1896 and 1934, and because he held a long-term position outside the academy, as the editor of the NAACP's *The Crisis*. For these reasons, many still do not identify Du Bois as a "real" sociologist. For works on the systematic and intentional exclusion of Du Bois from the sociological canon, see Morris, *Scholar Denied*; Morris, "Sociology of Race and W. E. B. Du Bois"; Wright, *First American School of Sociology*; Rabaka, *Against Epistemic Apartheid*.

17. Brown, "On the Participatory Archive"; Eastern Kentucky African American Migration Project (EKAAMP), http://finding-aids.lib.unc.edu/05585/.

18. Schomburg, *Negro Digs Up His Past*.

19. Derrida, *Archive Fever*.

20. EKAAMP, http://finding-aids.lib.unc.edu/05585/.

Chapter One

1. This group of early white settlers is commonly referred to as "mountaineers" or "hillbillies." Their migration into the Appalachian Mountains and their rich cultural identities and worldviews are topics of great importance to the understanding of American social and labor history. For studies on the social mind of the Appalachian mountaineer, see Woodson, "Freedom and Slavery in Appalachian America"; Caudill, *Night Comes to the Cumberlands*; Erikson, *Everything in Its Path*; Harkins, *Hillbilly*; Portelli, *They Say in Harlan County*.

2. Wright, *Racial Violence in Kentucky*.

3. "Autochthony" is a concept referring to identities that are based on being *of* the land. For additional readings on the concept, see Ceuppens and Geschiere, "Autochthony"; Geschiere, *Perils of Belonging*.

4. Corporate absentee landownership was one of many factors leading to the persistent poverty in central Appalachia. Before the coming of the coal industry, it was the mass deforestation of timber and the entry of U.S. railways into the region. Other factors leading to economic atrophy in the region, as identified by Billings and Blee, include "capital markets, state coercion, [and] cultural strategies" that created central Appalachia's "road to poverty." For key readings on the historical factors leading to economic distress in central Appalachia, see Billings and Blee, *Road to Poverty*; Caudill, *Night Comes to the Cumberlands*; Eller, *Miners, Millhands, and Mountaineers*; Lewis, *Transforming the Appalachian Countryside*.

5. Caudill, *Night Comes to the Cumberlands.*

6. Caudill, 92.

7. "Report of the United States Coal Commission."

8. The companies employed an internal settler colonial logic, in which they took interest in the land of the "indigenous" population (in this case, the white Scotch-Irish peoples) but not their labor. For an in-depth reading on this colonial structure, see Veracini, *Settler Colonialism*; Veracini, *Settler Colonial Present*; Wolfe, "Land, Labor, and Difference"; Wolfe, *Settler Colonialism.*

9. This is a riff on Emma Lazarus's infamous poem "The New Colossus," which is imprinted on the pedestal of the Statue of Liberty. The excerpt to which I am referring reads: "Give me your tired, your poor, Your huddled masses yearning to breathe free, The wretched refuse of your teeming shore. Send these, the homeless, tempest-tost to me, I lift my lamp beside the golden door!" For the full poem, see Lazarus, *Emma Lazarus.*

10. Caudill, *Night Comes to the Cumberlands*; Cressey, "Social Disorganization and Reorganization in Harlan County, Kentucky"; Shifflett, *Coal Towns.*

11. Caudill, *Theirs Be the Power.*

12. Caudill, 86.

13. See government report citation in Lewis, *Black Coal Miners in America*, 147.

14. Agamben, *Homo Sacer.*

15. Dunbar, "Labor Matters."

16. Caudill, *Theirs Be the Power.*

17. Caudill, *Night Comes to the Cumberlands*; Caudill, *Theirs Be the Power*; Shifflett, *Coal Towns.*

18. Perkins, "Response to 'Labor Matters.'"

19. Gitelman, *Legacy of the Ludlow Massacre.*

20. Gitelman.

21. Caudill, *Night Comes to the Cumberlands*; Green, *Company Town*; Lewis, *Black Coal Miners in America*; Shifflett, *Coal Towns.*

22. Dunbar, "'Letter from F. B. Dunbar to H. F. Perkins.'"

23. Dunbar, "'Letter from F. B. Dunbar to H. F. Perkins.'"; Caudill, *Theirs Be the Power.*

24. Perkins, "Response to 'Labor Matters.'"

25. Dunbar, "U.S. Coal & Coke Company Developments."

26. Perkins, "Response to Mr. Dunbar Re: Colored School House."

27. Portelli, "Patterns of Paternalism in Harlan County," 152.

28. Portelli, 142.

29. Hirschman and Reed, "Formation Stories and Causality in Sociology."

30. This phenomenon occurred not only in eastern Kentucky but through the hundreds of coal camps established in West Virginia and a small area of Tennessee.

31. There is a vast literature on Appalachia and the coal economy. However, most studies explicitly focus only on the white population. For exceptions, see Lewis, *Black Coal Miners in America*; Turner and Cabbell, *Blacks in Appalachia*; Trotter, *Coal, Class, and Color*; Wagner, *African American Miners and Migrants.*

32. Lewis, "From Peasant to Proletarian."

33. Lewis, 81.

34. Lewis.

35. The term *biopolitics* refers to the governmental techniques and technologies that govern human social and biological processes. In this case, I am referring to the biopolitics of mass migration. For an elaboration of the concept of "biopolitics," see Foucault, Davidson, and Burchell, *Birth of Biopolitics*. For studies on the state's and federal government's interventions in the first wave of the African American Great Migration, see Leavell, Dillard, and Snavely, *Negro Migration in 1916–1917*; Bernstein, "Law and Economics of Post–Civil War Restrictions on Interstate Migration by African-Americans"; Alilunas, "Statutory Means of Impeding Emigration of the Negro."

36. Hernández-León, "Conceptualizing the Migration Industry."

37. News of the "Promised Land" in the North largely traveled through Black newspapers, such as the *Chicago Defender*. Pullman porters who worked the national railways distributed these northern papers widely throughout the South. For more on the national influence of the black newspaper on the black imagination at during the first half of the twentieth century, see Michaeli, *"The Defender."*

38. Postmemory refers to those deep-seated, sometimes unconscious memories that are transmitted through generations in the wake of trauma. The source of collective memories are usually events that caused large-scale and irreparable dislocation, such as mass violence or the dislocation experienced as a result of mass expulsion. What is distinctive about postmemory is that it is the second (or subsequent) generation's memory of the event. According to social theorist Marianne Hirsch, "postmemory describes the relationship of the second generation to powerful, often traumatic, experiences that preceded their births but that were nevertheless transmitted to them so deeply as to seem to constitute memories in their own right." For more on postmemory, see Kim, "Redefining Diaspora through a Phenomenology of Postmemory"; Marianne Hirsch, *Family Frames*; Marianne Hirsch, "Generation of Postmemory."

Chapter Two

1. Blackmon, *Slavery by Another Name*; Caudill, *Night Comes to the Cumberlands*.

2. Blackmon, *Slavery by Another Name*; Lewis, *Black Coal Miners in America*.

3. Bailey and Tolnay, *Lynched*.

4. Althusser, *Ideology and Ideological State Apparatus*.

5. Portes and Böröcz, "Contemporary Immigration."

6. W. E. B. Du Bois, *Souls of Black Folk*; Woodward, *Strange Career of Jim Crow*, 53.

7. Du Bois, *Souls of Black Folk*.

8. The Redemption era refers to the overthrow of Northerners, referred to as "carpetbaggers," who came to the South seeking leadership positions after the American Civil War. See also Woodward, *Strange Career of Jim Crow*.

9. Woodward, *Strange Career of Jim Crow*, 6.

10. Blackmon, *Slavery by Another Name*; Mandle, *Not Slave, Not Free*; Tolnay, *Bottom Rung*; Tolnay and Beck, *Festival of Violence*.

11. Woodward, *Strange Career of Jim Crow*; Wiener, "Social Origins of the New South."

12. Du Bois, "Spawn of Slavery."

13. Tolnay, *Bottom Rung*.

14. Du Bois, "Negroes of Dougherty County, Georgia"; Kelley, *Hammer and Hoe*; Tolnay, *Bottom Rung*.

15. Michelle Alexander, *New Jim Crow*; DuVernay, Averick, and Barish, *13th*.

16. Haley, *No Mercy Here*; Lichtenstein, *Twice the Work of Free Labor*; Mancini, *One Dies, Get Another*; Ida B. Wells, "Convict Lease System"; Blackmon, *Slavery by Another Name*.

17. Douglass, "Convict Leasing," 5.

18. Lewis, *Black Coal Miners in America*.

19. Mancini, *One Dies, Get Another*.

20. Office of the Governor of the State of Alabama, "Governors Announcement to State Convict Board."

21. Office of the Governor of the State of Alabama.

22. Office of the Governor of the State of Alabama.

23. While the entire convict leasing system was cruel, illegitimate, and immoral, Alabama earned a reputation for its especially heinous treatment toward its inmates. This is largely because of the dangerous and physically taxing nature of coal mining.

24. "Letter from Ezekiel Archey and Ambrose Haskins."

25. Lewis, *Black Coal Miners in America*, 30.

26. Douglass, "Convict Leasing," 6.

27. Gordon, *Ghostly Matters*.

28. Blackmon, *Slavery by Another Name*, 287.

29. Tolnay and Beck, *Festival of Violence*.

30. Tolnay and Beck.

31. Wells-Barnett, *On Lynchings*; Wells-Barnett, *Red Record Tabulated Statistics*; Bailey and Tolnay, *Lynched*.

32. Tolnay and Beck, *Festival of Violence*.

33. Allen et al., *Without Sanctuary*.

34. Saxton, *Indispensable Enemy*.

35. Duff, "Class and Gender Roles."

36. Hughes, *I Dream a World*: "I dream a world where man No other man will scorn, Where love will bless the earth And peace its paths adorn. I dream a world where all Will know sweet freedom's way, Where greed no longer saps the soul Nor avarice blights our day. A world I dream where black or white, Whatever race you be, Will share the bounties of the earth And every man is free, Where wretchedness will hang its head And joy, like a pearl, Attends the needs of all mankind—Of such I dream, my world!"

37. Miller, *Errand into the Wilderness*.

38. Bailey, "Judicious Mixture"; Lewis, *Black Coal Miners in America*.

39. Caudill, *Night Comes to the Cumberlands*.

40. Peck, *Reinventing Free Labor*.

41. Peck, "Padrones and Protest."

42. Lewis, *Black Coal Miners in America*.

43. Duff, "Class and Gender Roles."

44. Dunbar, "Letter from F. B. Dunbar to H. F. Perkins."

45. The issue of who counted as "white" in terms of full legal and social citizenship in the United States was not sorted out until the early twentieth century. For readings on this, see Jacobson, *Whiteness of a Different Color*; Glazer, "Is Assimilation Dead?"

46. Lewis, "From Peasant to Proletarian"; Trotter, *Coal, Class, and Color*.

47. Gates and Jarrett, *The New Negro*, 112.

48. Hirschman and Reed, "Formation Stories and Causality in Sociology."

Chapter Three

1. Green, *Company Town*; Caudill, *Theirs Be the Power*; Shifflett, *Coal Towns*.

2. Brown, Murphy, and Porcelli, "Ruin's Progeny."

3. I used to say "born and raised," but the Reverend Edgar James Moss (Interviewee #64) admonished me that you raise corn, cows, and green beans. You can just clear a garden and water them, and they will grow up just fine. Children, on the contrary, are reared.

4. Portelli, "What Makes Oral History Different."

5. Du Bois, "Study of the Negro Problems."

6. Portelli, "Patterns of Paternalism in Harlan County."

7. Portelli.

Chapter Four

1. Raymond Williams, "The Analysis of Culture."

2. Du Bois, *Souls of Black Folk*, 181.

3. This does not excuse the racist practices of the rest of the country, for the United States is at its formation a racial state; however, the post–Redemption era South had a way of dealing with the aftermath of slavery in a way that makes its context singular.

4. Franklin et al., *Young, Gifted and Black*.

5. Du Bois, "Study of the Negro Problems"; Lavelle, *Whitewashing the South*; Thompson-Miller, Feagin, and Picca, *Jim Crow's Legacy*; Woodward, *Strange Career of Jim Crow*.

6. Ortner, "Subjectivity and Cultural Critique."

7. Mead, *Mind, Self and Society*; Du Bois, *Souls of Black Folk*.

8. Mead, *Mind, Self and Society*, 138.

9. Du Bois, *Souls of Black Folk*, 3.

10. Itzigsohn and Brown, "Sociology and the Theory of Double Consciousness."

11. Du Bois, *Souls of Black Folk*, 164.

12. Woodward, *Strange Career of Jim Crow*.

13. Du Bois, *Souls of Black Folk*, 165.

14. Bogues, *Empire of Liberty*.

15. Chafe, *Civilities and Civil Rights*, 8.

16. Chafe, 8.

17. Blee, "Racial Violence in the United States," 610.

18. Blee, 610.

19. Clark and Clark, "Emotional Factors in Racial Identification and Preference in Negro Children"; Clark, "Brown Decision."

20. Hunter, "Persistent Problem of Colorism"; Monk, "The Cost of Color"; Monk, "Skin Tone Stratification among Black Americans."

21. Telles, *Race in Another America*; Monk, "Consequences of 'Race and Color' in Brazil"; Glenn, *Shades of Difference*.

22. Black vernacular for "promiscuous."

23. Jacobson, *Whiteness of a Different Color*, 2.

24. Glazer, "Is Assimilation Dead?"

25. Elijah Anderson, *Cosmopolitan Canopy*.

26. Taylor, "Black Ethnicity and the Persistence of Ethnogenesis."

27. Racial discrimination toward ethnic white groups in the United States was not unique to eastern Kentucky. What differed in the coal towns of Harlan County was that they were loosely segregated, meaning that interethnic contact at work, home, and in commercial spaces was inevitable, even if a great deal of social distance between ethnicities and races persisted. This context was also unique because the coal companies would directly intervene in any social disruption, mediating race relations in the community.

28. Harkins, *Hillbilly*.

29. Lewis, *Black Coal Miners in America*.

30. The year 1492 marks the European encounter with the Americas and the subsequent decision to apply a durable taxonomy on race. Thereafter, "black" was associated with slavery or the candidacy to be enslaved. For deep reading on the relationship between 1492 and the emergence of racial categories, see Wynter, "1492"; Sala-Molins, *Dark Side of the Light*; Charles Wade Mills, *Racial Contract*; Pagden, *European Encounters with the New World*.

31. Du Bois, *Souls of Black Folk*.

32. Itzigsohn and Brown, "Sociology and the Theory of Double Consciousness."

33. Du Bois, *Souls of Black Folk*, 233–34.

34. Du Bois, 182.

35. Du Bois, 2.

Chapter Five

1. Omi and Winant, *Racial Formation in the United States*.

2. Woodward, *Strange Career of Jim Crow*.

3. Omi and Winant, *Racial Formation in the United States*.

4. Gilbert, "Administration and Organization of Secondary Schools."

5. Gilbert.

6. Dunbar, "Letter from F. B. Dunbar to H. F. Perkins."

7. It was part of the African American tradition to address the school principal, usually a male educator, as "Professor." For an in-depth analysis of the role of the black principal in the segregated South, see Vanessa Siddle Walker, *Hello Professor.*

8. The Hampton Model was a form of industrial education adapted specifically for Black and Native American learners. The main premise behind the model was to teach black children how to *do,* not necessarily how to *think.*

9. James D. Anderson, *Education of Blacks in the South;* Fairclough, *Class of Their Own;* Watkins, *White Architects of Black Education.*

10. Fairclough, *Class of Their Own;* Vanessa Siddle Walker, *Their Highest Potential.*

11. Du Bois, *Souls of Black Folk,* 60.

12. Du Bois, 61.

13. See Du Bois, "The Talented Tenth."

14. Anderson, *Education of Blacks in the South;* Fairclough, *Class of Their Own.*

15. Fairclough, *Class of Their Own.*

16. Vanessa Siddle Walker, *Hello Professor;* Walker and Byas, "Architects of Black Schooling in the Segregated South."

17. Vanessa Siddle Walker, *Hello Professor.*

18. Cecelski, *Along Freedom Road;* Shircliffe, "'We Got the Best of That World'"; Stewart, *First Class.*

19. Vanessa Siddle Walker, *Their Highest Potential;* Vanessa Siddle Walker, "Valued Segregated Schools for African American Children in the South."

20. Vanessa Siddle Walker, "Valued Segregated Schools for African American Children in the South."

21. Pattillo-McCoy, "Church Culture as a Strategy of Action in the Black Community"; Corey D. B. Walker, *Noble Fight;* Du Bois, *Souls of Black Folk;* Frazier, *Negro Church in America;* Cecelski, *Along Freedom Road;* Morris, *Origins of the Civil Rights Movement.*

22. Hamlin, *Crossroads at Clarksdale;* Mungo, "Our Own Communities, Our Own Schools"; Shircliffe, "'We Got the Best of That World'"; Stewart, *First Class;* Walker and Tompkins, "Caring in the Past."

23. Shircliffe, "'We Got the Best of That World.'"

24. Levinas and Poller, *Humanism of the Other.*

25. Du Bois, *Souls of Black Folk.*

26. Bourdieu, *Logic of Practice.*

27. Wagner-Pacifici, "Theorizing the Restlessness of Events."

28. The colored school was an "ideological state apparatus," in that it was a state institution that "hailed," or formed, subjects and subjectivities. For an elaboration on this concept, see Althusser, "Ideology and Ideological State Apparatus."

29. For examples of how entire African American communities were destroyed or massacred for one community member's alleged crime, see Hirsch, *Riot and Remembrance;* Allen et al., *Without Sanctuary;* Bailey and Tolnay, *Lynched;* Loewen, *Sundown Towns;* Jones, "Rosewood Massacre and the Women Who Survived It"; Dye, "Rosewood, Florida."

30. Dawson, *Black Visions*; Du Bois, *Dusk of Dawn*; Simien, "Race, Gender, and Linked Fate."

31. A "cultural resource" is a person who is the first to break a barrier in a disadvantaged community. This person is more than a role model, as he or she also expands the horizon of dreams and aspirations for both him- or herself and peers. For an elaboration on this concept, see Trondman, Taha, and Lund, "For Aïsha."

32. Sewell, *Logics of History*.

Chapter Six

1. King, "'I Have a Dream' Speech."

2. Marshall and Tushnet, *Thurgood Marshall*; Ogletree, *All Deliberate Speed*.

3. Ogletree, *All Deliberate Speed*.

4. All excerpts from the *Brown* trial are found in "Brown v. Board of Education Online Archive," University of Michigan Library, accessed April 20, 2018, https://www.lib.umich.edu/brown-versus-board-education/.

5. Ogletree, *All Deliberate Speed*.

6. Chief Justice Vinson had serendipitously died in 1953, eight months before the *Brown* ruling. Legal scholars speculate that had he lived, the *Brown* decision would have gone the other way.

7. Ogletree, *All Deliberate Speed*.

8. This was fast compared to many other southern communities, as many of them were not desegregated until the 1970s, and in some extreme cases, the 1980s.

9. Du Bois, "Does the Negro Need Separate Schools?"; Hurston, "'Court Order Can't Make the Races Mix.'"

10. Du Bois, "Does the Negro Need Separate Schools?"

11. Cecelski, *Along Freedom Road*; Diehl, *Dream Not of Other Worlds*; Hamlin, *Crossroads at Clarksdale*; Wolff, "Segregation in the Schools of Gary, Indiana."

12. Hurston, "'Court Order Can't Make the Races Mix.'"

13. Hurston.

14. Fairclough, *Class of Their Own*.

15. In the early 1950s, the Lynch Colored Public School changed its name to West Main High, and Lynch High School became East Main High. This name change was a common strategy used among white school boards throughout the South. They believed that the "East" and "West" would give the semblance of equality and not raise eyes in the wake of desegregation suits.

16. Similar arguments can be found in studies examining the transition from one lifeworld or status position to another. A classic sociological study that examines the transition of twentieth-century U.S. European immigrants and their children from working-class to middle-class "white" is Sennett, *Hidden Injuries of Class*.

17. These experiences are by no means unique to Harlan County, Kentucky. For key texts examining the experiences of the children of integration in other communities and their lasting effects, see Allen, *Talking to Strangers*; Tieken, *Why Rural Schools Matter*; Morris and Morris, *Price They Paid*; Wells, *Both Sides Now*; Pitts, *Victory of Sorts*; Pratt, *We Shall Not Be Moved*.

18. Cooley, *Human Nature and the Social Order*.

19. Du Bois, *Souls of Black Folk*, 181.

20. Nora, "Between Memory and History."

21. Nora, 19.

22. Piore, "Birds of Passage."

Chapter Seven

1. Lewis, *Black Coal Miners in America*.

2. Gregory, *Southern Diaspora*; Chatelain, "'The Most Interesting Girl of This Country Is the Colored Girl'"; Chatelain, *South Side Girls*; Michaeli, *Defender*; Tolnay, "African American 'Great Migration' and Beyond"; Trotter, *Great Migration in Historical Perspective*; Wilkerson, *Warmth of Other Suns*; Aldon Morris, *Origins of the Civil Rights Movement*; Aldon Morris, "Retrospective on the Civil Rights Movement."

3. Robinson, *This Ain't Chicago*.

4. Like Dr. Seuss said, *Oh, the Places You'll Go!*

5. Yẹmisi and Hamlin, *These Truly Are the Brave*.

6. Trondman, Taha, and Lund, "For Aïsha."

7. Fullilove, *Root Shock*; Fullilove, "Root Shock."

8. Brah, *Cartographies of Diaspora*; Kim, "Redefining Diaspora through a Phenomenology of Postmemory"; Hall, "Cultural Identity and Diaspora"; Sarup, "Home and Identity"; Brubaker, "'Diaspora' Diaspora."

9. Hobsbawm and Ranger, *Invention of Tradition*.

10. Wagner, *African American Miners and Migrants*.

Research Appendix

1. Bonilla-Silva, *Racism without Racists*.

2. Chafe, *Civilities and Civil Rights*.

3. Reed, *Interpretation and Social Knowledge*.

4. Mills, *Sociological Imagination*, 6.

5. Tölölyan, "Rethinking Diaspora(s)"; Tölölyan, "Contemporary Discourse of Diaspora Studies."

6. Du Bois, *Souls of Black Folk*.

7. Anderson, *Place on the Corner*; Goffman, "On the Run"; Goffman, *On the Run*; Venkatesh, *Gang Leader for a Day*.

8. For exceptions, see Lacy, *Blue-Chip Black*; Pattillo-McCoy, *Black Picket Fences*; Young, *Minds of Marginalized Black Men*; Robinson, *This Ain't Chicago*; Hunter, *Black Citymakers*; Hunter and Robinson, *Chocolate Cities*.

9. Moten, *In the Break*; Hunter and Robinson, *Chocolate Cities*; Du Bois, *Negro Church*; Du Bois, *Souls of Black Folk*.

10. Itzigsohn and Brown, *Racialized Modernity*.

11. Massey and Zenteno, "Validation of the Ethnosurvey"; "MMP—Home."

12. Penrod et al., "Discussion of Chain Referral as a Method of Sampling Hard-to-Reach Populations."

13. Hall, "Cultural Identity and Diaspora."

14. Tolnay, "African American 'Great Migration' and Beyond."

15. Tolnay.

16. Cobb and Hoang, "Protagonist-Driven Urban Ethnography."

17. Portelli, "History-Telling and Time."

18. Somers, "Where Is Sociology after the Historic Turn?"; Tilly, *Stories, Identities, and Political Change*; Wilkins, "Becoming Black Women: Intimate Stories and Intersectional Identities"; Polletta, *It Was Like a Fever*; Polletta et al., "Sociology of Storytelling."

19. Scott, *Domination and the Arts of Resistance*.

20. Durkheim, "Elementary Forms of the Religious Life"; Eyerman, "Past in the Present Culture and the Transmission of Memory"; Halbwachs and Coser, *On Collective Memory*; Trouillot, *Silencing the Past*; Davis, *Yearning for Yesterday*.

21. Eyerman, "Past in the Present Culture and the Transmission of Memory."

22. Lamont and Swidler, "Methodological Pluralism and the Possibilities and Limits of Interviewing."

23. Polletta et al., "Sociology of Storytelling."

24. Cooley, *Human Nature and the Social Order*; Descartes, *Discourse on Method*; Mead, *Mind, Self and Society*.

25. Alcoff, "Towards a Phenomenology of Racial Embodiment"; Bogues, "And What about the Human?"; Césaire, *Discourse on Colonialism*; Fanon, *Black Skin, White Masks*.

26. Ortner, "Subjectivity and Cultural Critique."

27. Giddens, *Constitution of Society*.

28. Alcoff, *Visible Identities*, 183.

29. Alcoff, 185.

30. Du Bois, *Souls of Black Folk*, 181.

31. Funny enough, my first cousin Derek Akal is a longtime Harlan County sheriff. He was frequently taped during the filming of *Kentucky Justice*, and just as frequently edited out of the final shots.

32. Algeo, "Locals on Local Color"; Harkins, *Hillbilly*.

33. Algeo.

34. Cabbell, "Black Invisibility and Racism in Appalachia."

35. "EKAAMP Website"; Brown, "On the Participatory Archive."

36. Capell and Kaiser, "Southern Sources: An Exhibition Celebrating Seventy-Five Years of the Southern Historical Collection, 1930–2005."

Bibliography

Agamben, Giorgio. *Homo Sacer: Sovereign Power and Bare Life.* Stanford, Calif.: Stanford University Press, 1998.

Alcoff, Linda Martín. "Towards a Phenomenology of Racial Embodiment." *Radical Philosophy* 95 (1999): 15–26.

———. *Visible Identities: Race, Gender, and the Self.* New York: Oxford University Press, 2005.

Alexander, J. Trent. "The Great Migration in Comparative Perspective." *Social Science History* 22, no. 3 (1998): 349–76.

Alexander, Michelle. *The New Jim Crow: Mass Incarceration in the Age of Colorblindness.* New York: New Press, 2012.

Algeo, Katie. "Locals on Local Color: Imagining Identity in Appalachia." *Southern Cultures* 9, no. 4 (2003): 27–54.

Alilunas, Leo. "Statutory Means of Impeding Emigration of the Negro." *Journal of Negro History* 22, no. 2 (1937): 148–62.

Allen, Danielle S. *Talking to Strangers: Anxieties of Citizenship since* Brown v. Board of Education. Chicago: University of Chicago Press, 2009.

Allen, James, Hilton Als, John Lewis, and Leon F. Litwack. *Without Sanctuary: Lynching Photography in America.* Santa Fe, N.Mex.: Twin Palms, 2000.

Althusser, Louis. "Ideology and Ideological State Apparatus (Notes towards an Investigation)." In *Lenin and Philosophy and Other Essays (Ss. 127–186).* New York: Monthly Review Press, 1971.

Anderson, Elijah. *The Cosmopolitan Canopy: Race and Civility in Everyday Life.* New York: W. W. Norton, 2011.

———. *A Place on the Corner.* Chicago: University of Chicago Press, 2003.

Anderson, James D. *The Education of Blacks in the South, 1860–1935.* Chapel Hill: University of North Carolina Press, 1988.

Bailey, Amy Kate, and Stewart E. Tolnay. *Lynched: The Victims of Southern Mob Violence.* Chapel Hill: University of North Carolina Press, 2015.

Bailey, Kenneth R. "A Judicious Mixture: Negroes and Immigrants in the West Virginia Mines, 1880-1917." *West Virginia History* 34, no. 2 (1973): 141–61.

Bernstein, David. "The Law and Economics of Post-Civil War Restrictions on Interstate Migration by African-Americans." *Texas Law Review* 76 (1998): 781–847.

Billings, Dwight B., and Kathleen M. Blee. *The Road to Poverty: The Making of Wealth and Hardship in Appalachia.* New York: Cambridge University Press, 2000.

Blee, K. M. "Racial Violence in the United States." *Ethnic and Racial Studies* 28, no. 4 (2005): 599–619.

Blackmon, Douglas A. *Slavery by Another Name: The Re-Enslavement of Black Americans from the Civil War to World War II.* New York: Anchor, 2009.

Bogues, Anthony. "And What about the Human? Freedom, Human Emancipation, and the Radical Imagination." *Boundary 2* 39, no. 3 (2012): 29–46.

——. *Empire of Liberty: Power, Desire, and Freedom.* Hanover, N.H.: University Press of New England, 2010.

Bonilla-Silva, Eduardo. *Racism without Racists: Color-Blind Racism and the Persistence of Racial Inequality in the United States.* Lanham, Md.: Rowman & Littlefield, 2003.

Bourdieu, Pierre. *The Logic of Practice.* Translated by Richard Nice. Stanford, Calif.: Stanford University Press, 1990.

Brah, Avtar. *Cartographies of Diaspora: Contesting Identities.* New York: Psychology Press, 1996.

Brown, Karida L. "On the Participatory Archive: The Formation of the Eastern Kentucky African American Migration Project." *Southern Cultures* 22, no. 1 (2016): 113–27.

Brown, Karida L., Michael W. Murphy, and Apollonya M. Porcelli. "Ruin's Progeny: Race, Environment, and Appalachia's Coal Camp Blacks." *Du Bois Review: Social Science Research on Race* 13, no. 2 (2016): 327–44.

Brubaker, Rogers. "The 'Diaspora' Diaspora." *Ethnic and Racial Studies* 28, no. 1 (2005): 1–19.

Cabbell, Edward J. "Black Invisibility and Racism in Appalachia: An Informal Survey." *Appalachian Journal* 8, no. 1 (1980): 48–54.

Capell, Laura, and Nancy Kaiser. *Southern Sources: An Exhibition Celebrating Seventy-Five Years of the Southern Historical Collection, 1930–2005.* Chapel Hill: UNC University Library, 2005.

Caudill, Harry M. *Night Comes to the Cumberlands: A Biography of a Depressed Area.* Boston: Little, Brown, 1962.

——. *Theirs Be the Power: The Moguls of Eastern Kentucky.* Urbana: University of Illinois Press, 1983.

Cecelski, David S. *Along Freedom Road: Hyde County, North Carolina, and the Fate of Black Schools in the South.* Chapel Hill: University of North Carolina Press, 1994.

Césaire, Aimé. *Discourse on Colonialism.* Translated by Joan Pinkham. New York: Monthly Review Press, 2000.

Ceuppens, Bambi, and Peter Geschiere. "Autochthony: Local or Global? New Modes in the Struggle over Citizenship and Belonging in Africa and Europe." *Annual Review of Anthropology* 34 (2005): 385–407.

Chafe, William Henry. *Civilities and Civil Rights: Greensboro, North Carolina, and the Black Struggle for Freedom.* New York: Oxford University Press, 1981.

Chatelain, Marcia. "'The Most Interesting Girl of This Country Is the Colored Girl': Girls and Racial Uplift in Great Migration Chicago, 1899–1950." PhD diss., Brown University, 2008.

——. *South Side Girls: Growing up in the Great Migration*. Durham, N.C.: Duke University Press, 2015.

Clark, Kenneth B. "The Brown Decision: Racism, Education, and Human Values." *Journal of Negro Education* 57, no. 2 (1988): 125–32.

Clark, Kenneth B., and Mamie P. Clark. "Emotional Factors in Racial Identification and Preference in Negro Children." *Journal of Negro Education* 19, no. 3 (1950): 341–50.

Cobb, Jessica Shannon, and Kimberly Kay Hoang. "Protagonist-Driven Urban Ethnography." *City and Community* 14, no. 4 (2015): 348–51.

Cooley, Charles Horton. *Human Nature and the Social Order*. New Brunswick, N.J.: Transaction, 1992.

Cressey, Paul Frederick. "Social Disorganization and Reorganization in Harlan County, Kentucky." *American Sociological Review* 14, no. 3 (1949): 389–94.

Davis, Fred. *Yearning for Yesterday: A Sociology of Nostalgia*. New York: Free Press, 1979.

Dawson, Michael C. *Black Visions: The Roots of Contemporary African-American Political Ideologies*. Chicago: University of Chicago Press, 2003.

Deener, Andrew. "The Decline of a Black Community by the Sea: Demographic and Political Changes in Oakwood." In *Black Los Angeles: American Dreams and Racial Realities*, ed. Darnell Hunt and Ana-Christina Ramón, 81–114. New York: New York University Press, 2010.

Derrida, Jacques. *Archive Fever: A Freudian Impression*. Chicago: University of Chicago Press, 1996.

Descartes, René. *Discourse on Method: And Other Writings*. London: Penguin Books, 1960.

Diehl, Huston. *Dream Not of Other Worlds: Teaching in a Segregated Elementary School, 1970*. Iowa City: University of Iowa Press, 2007.

Douglass, Frederick. "Convict Leasing." Manuscript/Mixed Material, 1893. Frederick Douglass Papers. Library of Congress. https://www.loc.gov/item/mfd.01008/.

Du Bois, W. E. B. "Does the Negro Need Separate Schools?" *Journal of Negro Education* 4, no. 3 (1935): 328–35.

——. *Dusk of Dawn: An Essay toward an Autobiography of a Race Concept: The Oxford WEB Du Bois*. Vol. 8. London: Oxford University Press on Demand, 1940.

——. *The Negro Church: With an Introduction by Alton B. Pollard III*. Eugene, Ore.: Wipf and Stock, 2011.

——. "The Negroes of Dougherty County, Georgia." In *On Sociology and the Black Community*, edited by Dan S. Green and Edwin D. Driver, 154–64. Chicago: University of Chicago Press, 1978.

——. *The Philadelphia Negro: A Social Study*. Philadelphia: University of Pennsylvania Press, 1899.

——. *The Souls of Black Folk*. Chicago: A. C. McClurg, 1903.

——. "The Spawn of Slavery: The Convict Lease System in the South." *Missionary Review of the World* 14 (1901): 737–45.

——. "The Study of the Negro Problems." *Annals of the American Academy of Political and Social Science*, January 1898, 1–23.

——. "The Talented Tenth." In *The Problem of the Color Line at the Turn of the Twentieth Century: The Essential Early Essays*, edited by Nahum D. Chandler, 209–42. New York: Fordham University Press, 2015.

Duff, Betty Parker. "Class and Gender Roles in the Company Towns of Millinocket and East Millinocket, Maine, and Benham and Lynch, Kentucky, 1901–2004: A Comparative History." PhD diss., University of Maine, 2004.

Dunbar, F. B. "Labor Matters," August 6, 1917. Appalachian Archives. Southeast Community and Technical College.

——. "Letter from F. B. Dunbar to H. F. Perkins," September 27, 1917. Wisconsin Steel Corporation Correspondence. Southeast Community and Technical College.

——. "Letter to President Perkins regarding U.S. Steel coal tipple," September 4, 1917. Wisconsin Steel Corporation Correspondence. Southeast Community and Technical College.

——. "U.S. Coal & Coke Company Developments," September 21, 1917. Wisconsin Steel Corporation Correspondence. Southeast Community and Technical College.

Durkheim, Emile. *The Elementary Forms of the Religious Life.* London: George Allen & Unwin, 1915.

DuVernay, Ava, Spencer Averick, and Howard Barish. *13th.* Directed by Ava DuVernay. October 2016. 1:40. www.netflix.com.

Dye, R. Thomas. "Rosewood, Florida: The Destruction of an African American Community." *Historian* 58, no. 3 (1996): 605–22.

Eastern Kentucky African American Migration Project (EKAAMP). Accessed December 1, 2017. http://ekaamp.web.unc.edu/.

Eller, Ronald D. *Miners, Millhands, and Mountaineers: Industrialization of the Appalachian South, 1880–1930.* Knoxville: University of Tennessee Press, 1982.

Erikson, Kai T. *Everything in Its Path.* New York: Simon and Schuster, 1976.

Eyerman, Ron. "The Past in the Present Culture and the Transmission of Memory." *Acta Sociologica* 47, no. 2 (2004): 159–69.

Fairclough, Adam. *A Class of Their Own: Black Teachers in the Segregated South.* Cambridge, Mass.: Harvard University Press, 2009.

Fanon, Frantz. *Black Skin, White Masks.* New York: Grove, 1967.

Foucault, Michel, Arnold I. Davidson, and Graham Burchell. *The Birth of Biopolitics: Lectures at the Collège de France, 1978–79.* Basingstoke: Palgrave, 2008.

Franklin, Aretha, Jerry Wexler, Arif Mardin, Tom Dowd, Nina Simone, Kenny Gamble, Jerry Butler, Burt Bacharach, Otis Redding, and William Hart. *Young, Gifted and Black.* Atlantic, 1972.

Frazier, Edward Franklin. *The Negro Church in America.* New York: Schocken, 1974.

Fullilove, Mindy Thompson. *Eminent Domain and African Americans: What Is the Price of the Commons?* Perspectives on Eminent Domain Abuse, vol. 1.

Arlington, Va.: Institute for Justice, 2007. http://ij.org/wp-content/uploads /2015/03/Perspectives-Fullilove.pdf.

——. *Root Shock: How Tearing Up City Neighborhoods Hurts America, and What We Can Do about It.* New York and Canada: One World/Ballantine, 2009.

——. "Root Shock: The Consequences of African American Dispossession." *Journal of Urban Health* 78, no. 1 (2001): 72–80.

Gates, Henry Louis, and Gene Andrew Jarrett, eds. *The New Negro: Readings on Race, Representation, and African American Culture, 1892–1938.* Princeton, N.J.: Princeton University Press, 2007.

Geschiere, Peter. *The Perils of Belonging: Autochthony, Citizenship, and Exclusion in Africa and Europe.* Chicago: University of Chicago Press, 2009.

Giddens, Anthony. *The Constitution of Society: Outline of the Theory of Structuration.* Berkeley: University of California Press, 1984.

Gilbert, William T. "The Administration and Organization of Secondary Schools for Negro Pupils in Eastern Kentucky." Master's thesis, Indiana University, 1948.

Gitelman, Howard M. *Legacy of the Ludlow Massacre: A Chapter in American Industrial Relations.* Philadelphia: University of Pennsylvania Press, 1988.

Glazer, Nathan. "Is Assimilation Dead?" *Annals of the American Academy of Political and Social Science* 530, no. 1 (1993): 122–36.

Glenn, Evelyn Nakano. *Shades of Difference: Why Skin Color Matters.* Palo Alto, Calif.: Stanford University Press, 2009.

Goffman, Alice. *On the Run: Fugitive Life in an American City.* New York: Picador, 2015.

——. "On the Run: Wanted Men in a Philadelphia Ghetto." *American Sociological Review* 74, no. 3 (2009): 339–57.

Gordillo, Gastón R. "Landscapes of Devils: Tensions of Place and Memory in the Argentinean Chaco." *Journal of Latin American and Caribbean Anthropology* 10, no. 2 (2005): 455–57.

Gordon, Avery F. *Ghostly Matters: Haunting and the Sociological Imagination.* Minneapolis: University of Minnesota Press, 2008.

Gottlieb, Peter. *Making Their Own Way: Southern Blacks' Migration to Pittsburgh, 1916–30.* Urbana: University of Illinois Press, 1996.

Green, Hardy. *The Company Town: The Industrial Edens and Satanic Mills That Shaped the American Economy.* New York: Basic Books, 2012.

Gregory, James N. *The Southern Diaspora: How the Great Migrations of Black and White Southerners Transformed America.* Chapel Hill: University of North Carolina Press, 2006.

Grossman, James R. *Land of Hope: Chicago, Black Southerners, and the Great Migration.* Chicago: University of Chicago Press, 1991.

Halbwachs, Maurice, and Lewis A. Coser. *On Collective Memory.* Chicago: University of Chicago Press, 1992.

Haley, Sarah. *No Mercy Here: Gender, Punishment, and the Making of Jim Crow Modernity.* Chapel Hill: University of North Carolina Press, 2016.

Hall, Stuart. "Cultural Identity and Diaspora." In *Identity: Community, Culture, and Difference*, edited by Jonathan Rutherford, 222–37. London: Lawrence & Wishart, 1990.

Hamlin, Françoise N. *Crossroads at Clarksdale: The Black Freedom Struggle in the Mississippi Delta after World War II*. Chapel Hill: University of North Carolina Press, 2012.

Harkins, Anthony. *Hillbilly: A Cultural History of an American Icon*. New York: Oxford University Press, 2003.

Harrison, Alferdteen. *Black Exodus: The Great Migration of from the American South*. Jackson: University Press of Mississippi, 2012.

Hernández-León, Rubén. "Conceptualizing the Migration Industry." In *The Migration Industry and the Commercialization of International Migration*, edited by Thomas Gammeltoft-Hansen and Ninna Nyberg Sørensen, 24–44. London: Routledge, 2013.

Hirsch, James S. *Riot and Remembrance: The Tulsa Race War and Its Legacy*. Boston: Houghton Mifflin Harcourt, 2003.

Hirsch, Marianne. *Family Frames: Photography, Narrative, and Postmemory*. Cambridge, Mass.: Harvard University Press, 1997.

———. "The Generation of Postmemory." *Poetics Today* 29, no. 1 (2008): 103–28.

Hirschman, Albert O. *Exit, Voice, and Loyalty: Responses to Decline in Firms, Organizations, and States*. Vol. 25. Cambridge, Mass.: Harvard University Press, 1970.

Hirschman, Daniel, and Isaac Ariail Reed. "Formation Stories and Causality in Sociology." *Sociological Theory* 32, no. 4 (2014): 259–82.

Hobsbawm, Eric, and Terence Ranger. *The Invention of Tradition*. Cambridge: Cambridge University Press, 2012.

Hughes, Langston. *I Dream a World*. Clearwater, Fla.: Paradise Press, 2000.

Hunt, Darnell, and Ana-Christina Ramón. *Black Los Angeles: American Dreams and Racial Realities*. New York: New York University Press, 2010.

Hunter, Marcus Anthony. *Black Citymakers: How the Philadelphia Negro Changed Urban America*. Oxford: Oxford University Press, 2013.

———. "W. E. B. Du Bois and Black Heterogeneity: How the Philadelphia Negro Shaped American Sociology." *American Sociologist* 46, no. 2 (2015): 219–33.

Hunter, Marcus Anthony, and Zandria Robinson. *Chocolate Cities: The Black Map of American Life*. Oakland: University of California Press, 2018.

Hunter, Margaret. "The Persistent Problem of Colorism: Skin Tone, Status, and Inequality." *Sociology Compass* 1, no. 1 (2007): 237–254.

Hurston, Zora Neale. "'Court Order Can't Make the Races Mix.'" *LewRockwell.com* (blog), August 1955. https://www.lewrockwell.com/1970/01/zora-neale-hurston/court-order-cant-make-the-racesmix/.

Itzigsohn, Jose, and Karida Brown. *Racialized Modernity: Articulating a Du Boisian Sociology*. New York: New York University Press, forthcoming.

———. "Sociology and the Theory of Double Consciousness." *Du Bois Review: Social Science Research on Race* 12, no. 2 (2015): 231–48.

Jacobson, Matthew Frye. *Whiteness of a Different Color.* Cambridge, Mass.: Harvard University Press, 1999.

Jones, Maxine D. "The Rosewood Massacre and the Women Who Survived It." *Florida Historical Quarterly* 76, no. 2 (1997): 193–208.

Kelley, Robin D. G. *Hammer and Hoe: Alabama Communists during the Great Depression.* Chapel Hill: University of North Carolina Press, 2015.

Kim, Sandra So Hee Chi. "Redefining Diaspora through a Phenomenology of Postmemory." *Diaspora: A Journal of Transnational Studies* 16, no. 3 (2007): 337–52.

King, Martin Luther, Jr. "'I Have a Dream' Speech," 1963. Accessed February 6, 2018. http://www.accesstothecourts.org/uploads/JLC_MLK_Speech_re_Dream .pdf.

Lacy, Karyn R. *Blue-Chip Black: Race, Class, and Status in the New Black Middle Class.* Berkeley: University of California Press, 2007.

Lamont, Michèle, and Ann Swidler. "Methodological Pluralism and the Possibilities and Limits of Interviewing." *Qualitative Sociology* 37, no. 2 (2014): 153–71.

Lavelle, Kristen M. *Whitewashing the South: White Memories of Segregation and Civil Rights.* Lanham, Md.: Rowman & Littlefield, 2014.

Lazarus, Emma. *Emma Lazarus: Selections from Her Poetry and Prose.* New York: Emma Lazarus Federation of Jewish Women's Clubs, 1944.

Leavell, R. H., J. H. Dillard, and T. R. Snavely. *Negro Migration in 1916–1917.* Washington, D.C.: U.S. Government Printing Office, 1919.

Lemann, Nicholas. *The Promised Land: The Great Black Migration and How It Changed America.* New York: Vintage, 2011.

"Letter from Ezekiel Archey and Ambrose Haskins, Convict Laborers at Pratt Mines in Jefferson County, Alabama, to Reginald Dawson, President of the Alabama Board of Inspectors of Convicts," May 26, 1884. Alabama Board of Inspectors and Convicts. Alabama Department of Archives and History. http://archives-alabama-primo.hosted.exlibrisgroup.com/01ALABAMA:default _scope:01ALABAMA_ALMA216264210002743.

Levinas, Emmanuel, and Nidra Poller. *Humanism of the Other.* Urbana: University of Illinois Press, 2003.

Lewis, Ronald L. *Black Coal Miners in America: Race, Class, and Community Conflict, 1780–1980.* Lexington: University Press of Kentucky, 1987.

———. "From Peasant to Proletarian: The Migration of Southern Blacks to the Central Appalachian Coalfields." *Journal of Southern History* 55, no. 1 (1989): 77–102.

———. *Transforming the Appalachian Countryside: Railroads, Deforestation, and Social Change in West Virginia, 1880–1920.* Chapel Hill: University of North Carolina Press, 1998.

Lichtenstein, Alex. *Twice the Work of Free Labor: The Political Economy of Convict Labor in the New South.* London: Verso, 1996.

Loewen, James W. *Sundown Towns: A Hidden Dimension of American Racism.* New York: New Press, 2005.

Mah, Alice. *Industrial Ruination, Community, and Place: Landscapes and Legacies of Urban Decline*. Toronto: University of Toronto Press, 2012.

Mancini, Matthew J. *One Dies, Get Another: Convict Leasing in the American South, 1866–1928*. Columbia: University of South Carolina Press, 1996.

Mandle, Jay R. *Not Slave, Not Free*. Durham, N.C.: Duke University Press, 1992.

Marks, Carole. *Farewell—We're Good and Gone: The Great Black Migration*. Bloomington: Indiana University Press, 1989.

Marshall, Thurgood, and Mark V. Tushnet. *Thurgood Marshall: His Speeches, Writings, Arguments, Opinions, and Reminiscences*. Chicago: Chicago Review Press, 2001.

Martin, Elizabeth Anne. *Detroit and the Great Migration, 1916–1929*. Ann Arbor: Bentley Historical Library, University of Michigan, 1993.

Massey, Douglas S., and René Zenteno. "A Validation of the Ethnosurvey: The Case of Mexico-US Migration." *International Migration Review* 34 (2000): 766–93.

Mead, George Herbert. *Mind, Self and Society*. Vol. 111. Chicago: University of Chicago Press, 1934.

Michaeli, Ethan. *"The Defender": How the Legendary Black Newspaper Changed America*. Boston: Houghton Mifflin Harcourt, 2016.

Miller, Perry. *Errand into the Wilderness*. Cambridge, Mass.: Harvard University Press, 1957.

Mills, C. Wright. *The Sociological Imagination*. New York: Oxford University Press, 2000.

Mills, Charles Wade. *The Racial Contract*. New York: Cornell University Press, 1997.

"MMP—Home." Accessed December 1, 2017. http://mmp.opr.princeton.edu/.

Monk, Ellis P., Jr. "The Consequences of 'Race and Color' in Brazil." *Social Problems* 63, no. 3 (2016): 413–30.

———. "The Cost of Color: Skin Color, Discrimination, and Health among African-Americans." *American Journal of Sociology* 121, no. 2 (2015): 396–444.

———. "Skin Tone Stratification among Black Americans, 2001–2003." *Social Forces* 92, no. 4 (2014): 1313–37.

Morris, Aldon. *The Origins of the Civil Rights Movement*. New York: Simon and Schuster, 1986.

———. "A Retrospective on the Civil Rights Movement: Political and Intellectual Landmarks." *Annual Review of Sociology* 25, no. 1 (1999): 517–39.

———. *The Scholar Denied: W. E. B. Du Bois and the Birth of Modern Sociology*. Oakland: University of California Press, 2015.

———. "Sociology of Race and W. E. B. Du Bois: The Path Not Taken." In *Sociology in America: A History*, edited by Craig Calhoun, 503–34. Chicago: University of Chicago Press, 2007.

Morris, Vivian Gunn, and Curtis L. Morris. *The Price They Paid: Desegregation in an African American Community*. New York: Teachers College Press, 2002.

Moten, Fred. *In the Break: The Aesthetics of the Black Radical Tradition*. Minneapolis: University of Minnesota Press, 2003.

Mungo, Sequoya. "Our Own Communities, Our Own Schools: Educational Counter-Narratives of African American Civil Rights Generation Students." *Journal of Negro Education* 82, no. 2 (2013): 111–22.

Nora, Pierre. "Between Memory and History: Les Lieux de Mémoire." *Representations* 26 (1989): 7–24.

Office of the Governor of the State of Alabama. "Governors Announcement to State Convict Board," 1902. Birmingham Public Library.

Ogletree, Charles J., Jr. *All Deliberate Speed: Reflections on the First Half Century of Brown v. Board of Education.* New York: W. W. Norton, 2004.

Omi, Michael, and Howard Winant. *Racial Formation in the United States.* New York: Routledge, 2014.

Ortner, Sherry B. "Subjectivity and Cultural Critique." *Anthropological Theory* 5, no. 1 (2005): 31–52.

Pagden, Anthony. *European Encounters with the New World: From Renaissance to Romanticism.* New Haven, Conn.: Yale University Press, 1993.

Painter, Nell Irvin. *Exodusters: Black Migration to Kansas after Reconstruction.* New York: W. W. Norton, 1992.

Pattillo-McCoy, Mary. *Black Picket Fences: Privilege and Peril among the Black Middle Class.* Chicago: University of Chicago Press, 2013.

———. "Church Culture as a Strategy of Action in the Black Community." *American Sociological Review* 63, no. 6 (1998): 767–84.

Peck, Gunther. "Padrones and Protest: 'Old' Radicals and 'New' Immigrants in Bingham, Utah, 1905–1912." *Western Historical Quarterly* 24, no. 2 (1993): 157–78.

———. *Reinventing Free Labor: Padrones and Immigrant Workers in the North American West, 1880–1930.* Cambridge: Cambridge University Press, 2000.

Penrod, Janice, Deborah Bray Preston, Richard E. Cain, and Michael T. Starks. "A Discussion of Chain Referral as a Method of Sampling Hard-to-Reach Populations." *Journal of Transcultural Nursing* 14, no. 2 (2003): 100–107.

Perkins, H. F. "Response to 'Labor Matters,'" August 6, 1917. Southeast Community and Technical College. Wisconsin Steel Corporation Correspondence.

———. "Response to Mr. Dunbar Re: Colored School House," November 23, 1917. Wisconsin Steel Corporation Correspondence. Southeast Community and Technical College.

Piore, Michael J. *Birds of Passage: Migrant Labor and Industrial Societies.* Cambridge: Cambridge University Press, 1979.

Pitts, Winfred E. *A Victory of Sorts: Desegregation in a Southern Community.* Lanham, Md.: University Press of America, 2003.

Polletta, Francesca. *It Was Like a Fever: Storytelling in Protest and Politics.* Chicago: University of Chicago Press, 2009.

Polletta, Francesca, Pang Ching Bobby Chen, Beth Gharrity Gardner, and Alice Motes. "The Sociology of Storytelling." *Annual Review of Sociology* 37 (2011): 109–30.

Portelli, Alessandro. "History-Telling and Time: An Example from Kentucky." *Oral History Review* 20, no. 1/2 (1992): 51–66.

———. "Patterns of Paternalism in Harlan County." *Appalachian Journal* 17, no. 2 (1990): 140–55.

———. *They Say in Harlan County: An Oral History*. New York: Oxford University Press, 2010.

———. "What Makes Oral History Different." In *Oral History, Oral Culture, and Italian Americans*, edited by L. D. Giudice, 21–30. New York: Palgrave Macmillan, 2009.

Portes, Alejandro, and József Böröcz. "Contemporary Immigration: Theoretical Perspectives on Its Determinants and Modes of Incorporation." *International Migration Review* 23, no. 3 (1989): 606–30.

Pratt, Robert A. *We Shall Not Be Moved: The Desegregation of the University of Georgia*. Athens: University of Georgia Press, 2002.

Rabaka, Reiland. *Against Epistemic Apartheid: WEB Du Bois and the Disciplinary Decadence of Sociology*. Lanham, Md.: Lexington Books, 2010.

Ravenstein, Ernest George. "The Laws of Migration." *Journal of the Royal Statistical Society* 52, no. 2 (1889): 241–305.

Reed, Isaac Ariail. *Interpretation and Social Knowledge: On the Use of Theory in the Human Sciences*. Chicago: University of Chicago Press, 2011.

"Report of the United States Coal Commission." U.S. Senate, 1930. Margaret I. King Library. University of Kentucky.

Robinson, Zandria F. *This Ain't Chicago: Race, Class, and Regional Identity in the Post-Soul South*. Chapel Hill: University of North Carolina Press, 2014.

Sala-Molins, Louis. *Dark Side of the Light: Slavery and the French Enlightenment*. Minneapolis: University of Minnesota Press, 2006.

Sarup, Madan. "Home and Identity." *Travellers' Tales: Narratives of Home and Displacement* 4, no. 5 (1994): 93–94.

Saxton, Alexander. *The Indispensable Enemy: Labor and the Anti-Chinese Movement in California*. Berkeley: University of California Press, 1975.

Schomburg, Arthur A. *The Negro Digs Up His Past*. Vol. 1975. New York: Atheneum, 1925.

Scott, James. *Domination and the Arts of Resistance: Hidden Transcripts*. New Haven, Conn.: Yale University Press, 1990.

Sennett, Richard, and Jonathan Cobb. *The Hidden Injuries of Class*. Cambridge: Cambridge University Press, 1972.

Seuss, Dr. *Oh, the Places You'll Go!* London: HarperCollins, 2003.

Sewell, William H., Jr. *Logics of History: Social Theory and Social Transformation*. Chicago: University of Chicago Press, 2005.

Shifflett, Crandall A. *Coal Towns: Life, Work, and Culture in Company Towns of Southern Appalachia, 1880–1960*. Knoxville: University of Tennessee Press, 1995.

Shircliffe, Barbara. "'We Got the Best of That World': A Case for the Study of Nostalgia in the Oral History of School Segregation." *Oral History Review* 28, no. 2 (2001): 59–84.

Simien, Evelyn M. "Race, Gender, and Linked Fate." *Journal of Black Studies* 35, no. 5 (2005): 529–50.

Somers, Margaret R. "Where Is Sociology after the Historic Turn? Knowledge Cultures, Narrativity, and Historical Epistemologies." In *The Historic Turn in the Human Sciences*, edited by Terrence J. McDonald, 53–89. Ann Arbor: University of Michigan Press, 1996.

Stewart, Alison. *First Class: The Legacy of Dunbar, America's First Black Public High School*. Chicago: Chicago Review Press, 2013.

Stoler, Ann Laura. *Imperial Debris: On Ruins and Ruination*. Durham, N.C.: Duke University Press, 2013.

Taylor, Ronald L. "Black Ethnicity and the Persistence of Ethnogenesis." *American Journal of Sociology* 84, no. 6 (1979): 1401–23.

Telles, Edward E. *Race in Another America: The Significance of Skin Color in Brazil*. Princeton, N.J.: Princeton University Press, 2014.

Thompson-Miller, Ruth, Joe R. Feagin, and Leslie H. Picca. *Jim Crow's Legacy: The Lasting Impact of Segregation*. Lanham, Md.: Rowman & Littlefield, 2014.

Tieken, Mara Casey. *Why Rural Schools Matter*. Chapel Hill: University of North Carolina Press, 2014.

Tilly, Charles. *Stories, Identities, and Political Change*. Lanham, Md.: Rowman & Littlefield, 2002.

Tolnay, Stewart E. "The African American 'Great Migration' and Beyond." *Annual Review of Sociology* 29 (2003): 209–32.

———. *The Bottom Rung: African American Family Life on Southern Farms*. Urbana: University of Illinois Press, 1999.

Tolnay, Stewart E., and Elwood M. Beck. *A Festival of Violence: An Analysis of Southern Lynchings, 1882–1930*. Urbana: University of Illinois Press, 1995.

———. "Racial Violence and Black Migration in the American South, 1910 to 1930." *American Sociological Review* 57 (1992): 103–16.

Tölölyan, Khachig. "The Contemporary Discourse of Diaspora Studies." *Comparative Studies of South Asia, Africa and the Middle East* 27, no. 3 (2007): 647–55.

———. "Rethinking Diaspora(s): Stateless Power in the Transnational Moment." *Diaspora: A Journal of Transnational Studies* 5, no. 1 (1996): 3–36.

Trondman, Mats, Rehan Taha, and Anna Lund. "For Aïsha: On Identity as Potentiality." *Identities* 19, no. 4 (2012): 533–43.

Trotter, Joe William. *Coal, Class, and Color: Blacks in Southern West Virginia, 1915–32*. Urbana: University of Illinois Press, 1990.

———. *The Great Migration in Historical Perspective: New Dimensions of Race, Class, and Gender*. Vol. 669. Bloomington: Indiana University Press, 1991.

Trouillot, Michel-Rolph. *Silencing the Past: Power and the Production of History*. Boston: Beacon Press, 1995.

Turner, William Hobart, and Edward J. Cabbell. *Blacks in Appalachia*. Lexington: University Press of Kentucky, 1985.

"Brown v. Board of Education Online Archive." University of Michigan Library. Accessed April 20, 2018. https://www.lib.umich.edu/brown-versus-board-education/.

Venkatesh, Sudhir Alladi. *Gang Leader for a Day: A Rogue Sociologist Takes to the Streets*. New York: Penguin, 2008.

Veracini, Lorenzo. *Settler Colonialism: A Theoretical Overview*. London: Palgrave Macmillan, 2010.

——. *The Settler Colonial Present*. London: Palgrave Macmillan, 2015.

Wagner, Thomas E. *African American Miners and Migrants: The Eastern Kentucky Social Club*. Urbana: University of Illinois Press, 2004.

Wagner-Pacifici, Robin. "Theorizing the Restlessness of Events." *American Journal of Sociology* 115, no. 5 (2010): 1351–86.

Walker, Corey D. B. *A Noble Fight: African American Freemasonry and the Struggle for Democracy in America*. Urbana: University of Illinois Press, 2008.

Walker, Vanessa Siddle. *Hello Professor: A Black Principal and Professional Leadership in the Segregated South*. Chapel Hill: University of North Carolina Press, 2009.

——. *Their Highest Potential: An African American School Community in the Segregated South*. Chapel Hill: University of North Carolina Press, 1996.

——. "Valued Segregated Schools for African American Children in the South, 1935–1969: A Review of Common Themes and Characteristics." *Review of Educational Research* 70, no. 3 (2000): 253–85.

Walker, Vanessa Siddle, and Ulysses Byas. "The Architects of Black Schooling in the Segregated South: The Case of One Principal Leader." *Journal of Curriculum and Supervision* 19, no. 1 (2003): 54–72.

Walker, Vanessa Siddle, and Renarta H. Tompkins. "Caring in the Past: The Case of a Southern Segregated African American School." In *Race-ing Moral Formation: African American Perspectives on Care and Justice*, edited by Vanessa Siddle Walker and John R. Snarey, 77–92. New York: Teachers College Press, 2004.

Watkins, William Henry. *The White Architects of Black Education: Ideology and Power in America, 1865–1954*. New York: Teachers College Press, 2001.

Wells, Amy Stuart. *Both Sides Now: The Story of School Desegregation's Graduates*. Berkeley: University of California Press, 2009.

Wells, Ida B. "The Convict Lease System." In *The Reason Why the Colored American Is Not in the World's Columbian Exposition*, edited by Robert W. Rydell, 23–28. Urbana: University of Illinois Press, 1893.

Wells-Barnett, Ida B. *On Lynchings*. Mineola, N.Y.: Dover, 2014.

——. *The Red Record: Tabulated Statistics and Alleged Causes of Lynching in the United States*. Hamburg, Germany: Tredition, 2012.

Wiener, Jonathan M. *Social Origins of the New South: Alabama, 1860–1885*. Baton Rouge: Louisiana State University Press, 1978.

Wilder, Craig Steven. *A Covenant with Color: Race and Social Power in Brooklyn, 1636–1990*. New York: Columbia University Press, 2013.

Wilkerson, Isabel. *The Warmth of Other Suns: The Epic Story of America's Great Migration*. New York: Vintage, 2010.

Wilkins, Amy C. "Becoming Black Women Intimate Stories and Intersectional Identities." *Social Psychology Quarterly* 75, no. 2 (2012): 173–96.

Williams, Marco. *Banished: How Whites Drove Blacks Out of Town in America*. 2006. http://www.imdb.com/title/tt0912574/.

Williams, Raymond. "The Analysis of Culture." In *Cultural Theory and Popular Culture: A Reader,* 3rd ed., edited by John Storey, 32–41. Edinburgh Gate: Pearson Education, 2013.

Wilson, Theodore Brantner. *The Black Codes of the South.* University: University of Alabama Press, 1965.

Wolfe, Patrick. "Land, Labor, and Difference: Elementary Structures of Race." *American Historical Review* 106, no. 3 (2001): 866–905.

——. *Settler Colonialism.* London: A&C Black, 1999.

Wolff, Max. "Segregation in the Schools of Gary, Indiana." *Journal of Educational Sociology* 36, no. 6 (1963): 251–61.

Woodson, Carter Godwin. *A Century of Negro Migration.* Mineola, N.Y.: Dover, 2003.

——. "Freedom and Slavery in Appalachian America." *Journal of Negro History* 1, no. 2 (1916): 132–50.

Woodward, C. Vann. *Origins of the New South, 1877–1913: A History of the South.* Vol. 9. Baton Rouge: Louisiana State University Press, 1981.

——. *The Strange Career of Jim Crow.* New York: Oxford University Press, 1955.

Wright, Earl, II. *The First American School of Sociology: W. E. B. Du Bois and the Atlanta Sociological Laboratory.* New York: Routledge, 2016.

Wright, George C. *Racial Violence in Kentucky, 1865–1940: Lynchings, Mob Rule, and "Legal Lynchings."* Baton Rouge: Louisiana State University Press, 1996.

Wynter, Sylvia. "1492: A New World View." In *Race, Discourse, and the Origin of the Americas: A New World View,* edited by Vera Lawrence Hyatt and Rex Nettleford, 5–57. Washington, D.C.: Smithsonian Institution Press, 1995.

Yẹmisi, A., and Francoise Hamlin, eds. *These Truly Are the Brave: An Anthology of African American Writings on War and Citizenship.* Gainesville: University Press of Florida, 2015.

Young, Alford A. *The Minds of Marginalized Black Men: Making Sense of Mobility, Opportunity, and Future Life Chances.* Princeton, N.J.: Princeton University Press, 2006.

Index

African American, use of term, 3, 104, 131, 133, 137, 156, 194, 201

African American Great Migration, 1, 3–5, 23, 25, 29–52, 157–58, 161–86, 193–94, 196, 199, 202. *See also* migration

African Americans: citizenship of, 1, 2, 3, 34, 133–35, 137, 169, 194–95; education and schools for (*see* education and schools); freedom of, 1, 2; home for (*see* home); labels or terms applied to, 3, 90, 104, 131, 133, 137, 156, 194, 201; migration of (*see* migration); race considerations for (*see* race; racial prejudice and discrimination; racial violence); subjectivity of (*see* subjectivity, African American)

Akal, Katina, 61, 62

Alabama: coal miners from, 13, 23, 29–31, 38–41, 43–45, 219n23; conditions of exit from, 33–39; convict leasing system in, 34, 35–37, 42, 219n23; lynchings in, 34, 37–38; migration from, 4, 7, 13, 23, 29–52, 162–64, 194; migration to, 5; post-Reconstruction era in, 33–39; racial prejudice and violence in, 30–39, 82; Reconstruction era in, 33–34; sharecropping in, 30, 34–35

Alcoff, Linda, 202

alcohol consumption, 32, 60–61

Andrews, Arletta, 66

Appalachia: coal mining in (*see* coal mining); home in, 5, 52, 55–73, 158, 159, 161–86; migration from, 2, 5, 157–58, 161–86; migration to, 2, 4–5, 12–13, 22–25, 29–32; race and roots in, 183–86; racial changes/composition in population of, 22–23, 24, 46–47, 55–57, 163

Archey, Ezekiel, 36–37

assimilation, 90

Austin, Gean, 41, 169

Austin-Mimes, Teresa, 29, 52

Baker, Roselyn, 185

banishment, 6, 68, 215n9

Baskin, Dwayne, 29, 70, 174, 184

Baskin, Sanford, 29, 75, 84, 85, 98, 119–20

Baskin-Brack, Cheryl, 40, 117, 143, 148, 150, 151–52

bathrooms: bathhouses for bathing, 69–70, 94; for coal town homes, 21, 67; segregation of, 81

Benham, Kentucky: coal industry changes and decline affecting, 129, 156–58, 161–63, 173–75; coal town creation in, 14, 15, 19–22; coal town ruination in, 173–79; desegregation and integration in, 130, 131, 142–57, 176; education and schools in, 20–21, 56–57, 105–30, 142–57, 176; home in, 56–57, 67–68, 158, 161–86; migration from, 157–58, 161–86; migration to, 23, 29–52; race and roots in, 183–86; segregation in, 80, 93–94, 105–30

Billips, L. A., 15, 19, 44

biopolitics, 23, 218n35

Birmingham, Alabama: migration from, 23, 41; migration to, 5

result of, 103–4; infrastructure for, 163; law and legal changes in, 2, 104

Clark, Kenneth, 88, 89, 135, 138, 153

Clark, Lorene, 40

Clark, Mamie, 88, 89, 135, 138, 153

Clements, Clara, 113, 152, 156

Cleveland, Ohio: cosmopolitan exposure to, 164–65; Eastern Kentucky Social Club in, 182–83; migration to, 162, 163, 170, 172, 182

clothing, 48–49, 50, 164

coal mining: coal towns for (*see* coal towns); convict leasing system for labor in, 35–37, 219n23; employment in, 12–13, 14–19, 22–23, 29–32, 38–41, 43–52, 156–57, 161–62, 173–75; fraternity of coal miners, 86, 92–95; in Harlan County, 5, 8, 11–25, 29–32, 38–41, 43–52, 69–72, 86, 92–95, 156–58, 161–63, 173–79; health issues and hazards in, 17, 36–37, 51, 70–71, 178, 219n23; history of, 11–25; industry changes and decline of, 129, 156–58, 161–63, 173–75; mechanization of, 156–57, 161–62; migration for, 2, 4–5, 7, 11, 12–13, 22–25, 29–32, 38–41, 43–52; mineral rights for, 11–12; origin stories related to, 57–73; paternalistic capitalism in, 19, 72; recruitment strategies and techniques for, 12–13, 40–41, 43–45, 56; research archives on, 8; segregation supported in, 94–95; unionization efforts in, 17–22, 43, 68, 71–72; working conditions in, 16–17, 36–37, 51, 70–71, 178, 219n23

coal towns: alcohol consumption in, 32, 60–61; bathing and bathrooms in, 21, 67, 69–70, 81, 94; boarding houses in, 56; children's recollections of, 58–72; coal industry changes and decline affecting, 129, 156–58, 161–63, 173–75; company control of, 14, 68, 72, 173; education and schools in, 14, 20–21, 55, 56–57, 62–63, 103–30, 133–57, 176, 223n15; entertainment and amenities in, 14, 20, 56, 58–59, 94–95; ethnic groups in, 43–44, 45, 55–56, 90–92, 93, 161, 221n27; fathers in, 60–63, 68, 69–72, 86, 92–95, 178; food in, 59–60, 61–62, 65; gardens in, 61–62; home in, 6, 52, 55–73, 158, 159, 161–86; living conditions in, 12, 14–15, 19–22, 58–73; making of, 12, 14–22, 44–46; migration and ruination of, 173–79; model or utopian, 19–22, 106; mothers in, 63–65; origin stories of life in, 58–72; privacy lack in, 67–68; racial composition of population in, 46–47, 55–57; segregation in, 20–21, 46–51, 55–57, 79–99, 105–30; stores in, 14, 17, 20, 57, 69, 72, 86; village as family in, 66–67

Coleman, John V. (Professor), 106, 107, 113, 122, 142, 155

Coleman, Samuel, 29

colleges and universities: historically black, 108, 110, 142; migration to, 168, 170–72. *See also specific schools*

Colorado: coal mining unionization efforts in, 17–18; Ludlow Massacre of 1914 in, 17–18

colored, use of term, 3, 104, 131, 156, 194, 201

colored schools: black pedagogy in, 119–23; black teacher ideals for, 108–10; characteristics of, meta-description of, 118; children's recollections of, 115–17; closure of, 145, 154, 156–57, 176; desegregation of, 128, 130, 131, 133–57, 176, 223n15; interiority of, 114–19; as *lieu de mémoire* or site of memory, 154–56; Negro discourses on, 139–40; normalization of segregation in, 123–27; overview of, 103–4; parental support for and involvement in, 110, 113, 114, 117, 118, 121, 147–48; principals or professors in, 106,

Du Bois, W. E. B.: *Black Reconstruction,* 196; on desegregation and integration, 139; as founder of sociology, 216n16; on home, 67; on migration goals, 34, 51; misquoting of, in segregation arguments, 137; *The Philadelphia Negro,* 196; research inspired by, 195, 196–97, 202; on second-sight, 78, 95–96, 97, 150; on segregation and effects of segregation, 77, 78–79, 88, 95–96, 97, 123, 125, 149; on sharecropping and convict lease system, 34; on sociological interpretation, 191, 195; *The Souls of Black Folk,* 4, 7, 75, 77, 78–79, 95–96, 108–9, 150, 195, 196; on subjectivity, 2, 4, 75, 202; on teaching, 108–9; veil of the color line theorized by, 195, 196

Duff, Betty Parker, 42

Dunbar, F. B., 19–20, 21, 44–45

Duncan, Melvin, 166

Eastern Kentucky African American Migration Project (EKAAMP), 8, 203–5

Eastern Kentucky Social Club (EKSC), 7, 154–56, 180, 182–83

Eastern Kentucky University, 168

Eastern Stars, 163

education and schools: coal industry changes and need for, 141, 157, 162; coal towns providing, 14, 20–21, 55, 56–57, 62–63, 103–30, 133–57, 176, 223n15; colored schools, 103–30, 139–57, 176, 222n7, 223n15; desegregation and integration of, 128, 130, 131, 133–57, 176, 223n15; fathers encouraging attendance at, 62–63; higher, 108, 110, 142, 168, 170–72; history of, in eastern Kentucky, 104–5; microaggressions in, 125; Negro discourses on, 139–40; normalization of segregation in, 123–27; racial consciousness in, 103,

122–23, 125; segregation in, 20–21, 55, 56–57, 84–85, 101, 103–30; social class reflected in, 110–13, 121–22; veil of the color line encounters in, 103, 109, 123–25

EKAAMP (Eastern Kentucky African American Migration Project), 8, 203–5

EKSC (Eastern Kentucky Social Club), 7, 154–56, 180, 182–83

eminent domain, 6, 197

environmental issues: coal mining impacts on, 12; environmental racism, 56

Errand into the Wilderness (Miller), 43

ethnicity: in coal towns, 43–44, 45, 55–56, 90–92, 93, 161, 221n27

Eyerman, Ron, 200

Fairclough, Adam, 110

Fair Housing Act (1968), 2

families: chain migration via, 167–68, 169–70; children in (*see* children); colored school support and involvement of, 110, 113, 114, 117, 118, 121, 147–48; cosmopolitan exposure through extended, 163–65; family feuds among, 11; fathers in, 60–63, 68, 69–72, 86, 92–95, 178; home lost with migration of, 178–79 (*see also* migration); mothers in, 63–65; village or community as, 66–67, 121, 127, 145–47, 156, 176–79

fathers: children's recollections of, 60–63, 69–72; as coal miners, 68, 69–72, 86, 92–95, 178

Ferguson, Mother, 30

Fielder, Nathaniel, 30

Fifteenth Amendment, 2

Fisk University, 108–9

Florida: education and schools in, 118; migration from, 4

food, 59–60, 61–62, 65

Fourteenth Amendment, 2, 136, 138

freedom, 1, 2

French, Jack, 63, 143, 148, 203

marriage: migration for, 168, 169

Marshall, Thurgood, 88, 135–36, 137

Mason, Curtis, 175, 184

Mason, Delores, 117

Mason, Mike, 63

Mason, Terry, 60

Mason, Vergie, 107, 109, 110–11, 152–53

Masonic Freemasonry, 33, 163

Massey, Bennie, 71

Massey, George, 58–59, 115

Matthews, Jay (Professor), 106, 107, 111, 124

McLaurin v. Oklahoma State Regents for Higher Education (1950), 134

Mead, George Herbert, 78–79

Memorial Day weekends, 7, 155, 179–82, 183, 195–96

men: athletic black male body of, 151, 169; children of (*see* children); coal mining by (*see* coal mining); fathers' role of, 60–63, 68, 69–72, 86, 92–95, 178; gendered migration pathways for, 169–70 (*see also* migration)

migration: African American Great Migration, 1, 3–5, 23, 25, 29–52, 157–58, 161–86, 193–94, 196, 199, 202; from Appalachia, 2, 5, 157–58, 161–86; to Appalachia, 2, 4–5, 12–13, 22–25, 29–32; assumption and expectation of need for, 166–67; biopolitics of, 23, 218n35; chain migration, 167–68, 169–70; citizenship advanced via, 194; coal industry changes and decline prompting, 157–58, 161–63, 173–75; for coal mining, 2, 4–5, 7, 11, 12–13, 22–25, 29–32, 38–41, 43–52; coal town ruination and, 173–79; conditions of exit for, 33–39; cosmopolitan exposure in preparation for, 163–65; devolution of community with, 176–79; as diaspora, 6, 172, 178, 186; dispersion with, 172–73; EKSC reconnections after, 7, 154–56, 180, 182–83; as escape, 25, 29–52;

ethnosurvey on, 197–98 (*see also* research); first generation, 2, 25, 29–52, 163–64, 194; gendered pathways for, 169–70; for higher education, 168, 170–72; home loss and displacement with, 6, 158, 161–86, 195; institutional pathways for, 168–72; intergenerational step-wise, 4–5; for marriage, 168, 169; Memorial Day weekend returns from, 7, 155, 179–82, 183, 195–96; migration industry, 23 (*see also* labor agents); migration network facilitating, 162–65, 167–68; to military, 163, 168–69, 170, 172; "move it on down the line" mentality toward, 159, 165, 166–67; origin stories of, 29–32; pathways to, 40–45, 164, 167–72; racial prejudice and violence prompting, 31–39; second generation, 2–3, 5, 157–58, 161–86; suddenness of, 174–75

military: integration of, 168–69; migration to, 163, 168–69, 170, 172

Miller, Perry, 43

Mills, C. Wright, 191, 195

Milwaukee, Wisconsin: migration to, 163

miscegenation: fear of, with desegregation, 151–52

Mississippi: migration from, 4, 162; racial prejudice and violence in, 82

Morehouse College, 109

Morrow, William H., 41

Moss, Edgar James, 56, 63, 121, 124, 125

Moss, Odell, 29, 59, 115, 169, 184, 185

mothers: children's recollections of, 63–65

Motley, Roland, 71

Mullins siblings, 60, 63, 71

music, 42–43, 202

Myrick, Leona, 7

NAACP, 134, 163

Napier, Belinda, 61, 148

Negro, use of term, 3, 104, 131, 156, 194, 201

Newington, Connecticut: migration to, 172

New York City, New York: coal mining industrialists in, 14; cosmopolitan exposure to, 164; Eastern Kentucky Social Club in, 183; migration to, 5, 162, 163; segregation in, 93

Night Comes to the Cumberlands (Caudill), 9, 12

Nolan, Brenda, 80, 89

Nora, Pierre, 154, 155

North Carolina: education and schools in, 118, 119; migration to and from, 4, 5, 23

Oden-Williams, Debra, 64

Odum, Howard W., 136

Ogletree, Charles, Jr., 135, 137, 138

oil industry: coal mining relation to, 14, 17

Omi, Michael, 104

origin stories: of home, 58–72; of migration, 29–32

Ortner, Sherry, 78, 201

padrones, 43–44, 56

Parks, Gordon, 202

Parks, Katie Sue Reynolds, 159

paternalistic capitalism, 19, 72

Payne, Elkin, 144

Peeples, Porter G., 60, 115, 143, 164–65, 171–72, 184

Peeples, Vera, 120

Perkins, H. F., 16, 19–20, 21, 44

Perkins, William H., 101

Perry, Humes, 56, 184

Pettygrue, Ernest, 29, 61, 69, 80, 98

Pettygrue, Rose Ivery, 105, 106, 153

Philadelphia, Pennsylvania: cosmopolitan exposure to, 165; migration to, 162

Philadelphia Negro, The (Du Bois), 196

Piore, Michael, 157

Pittsburgh, Pennsylvania: coal mining industrialists in, 14; migration to, 3

Plessy v. Ferguson (1896), 133, 134–35, 138

Poland, coal miners from, 12, 22, 44, 47, 92

Pollenitz, Robert, 71–72, 80

population of Appalachia, racial changes and composition of, 22–23, 24, 46–47, 55–57, 163

Portelli, Alessandro, 21–22, 72

postmemory, 25, 218n38

post-Reconstruction era, 25, 33–39, 139, 194

poverty, 11, 109, 195, 216n4

Powell, Betty, 29

prejudice. *See* racial prejudice and discrimination

Price, Charles, 107, 113–14, 153

Prinkleton, Victor, 97–98, 141, 157

privacy, lack of, 67–68

race: labels or terms applied to, 3, 90, 104, 131, 133, 137, 156, 194, 201; population changes and composition by, 22–23, 24, 46–47, 55–57, 163; racial consciousness, 95–98, 103, 122–23, 125, 150–51; racial epistemologies, transformation of, 149–51; racial identity, 77–80, 133, 135–36, 144, 201; recruitment strategies based on, 43; research on, 193–94 (*see also* research); skin color and, 88, 89, 122; spectrums of, 90–92, 220n45, 223n16; subjectivity shaped by (*see* subjectivity, African American)*See also* African Americans; ethnicity

racial prejudice and discrimination: citizenship and freedom limited by, 2; colorism as, 89, 122; consciousness of, 95–98, 103, 122–23, 125, 150–51; convict leasing system as, 34, 35–37, 42, 219n23; environmental racism, 56; inferiority experiences with, 88–90, 125, 136–37, 138, 140, 147,

racial prejudice (*continued*)
149–51, 153; microaggressions as, 125; migration in face of, 31–39; research on, 193–94 (*see also* research); segregation as (*see* segregation); sharecropping system as, 30, 34–35; whiteness spectrum and, 90–92, 221n27

racial violence: banishment as, 6, 68, 215n9; children's experiences with, 77–78, 85–88; citizenship and freedom limited by, 2, 34; communicative aspects of, 87–88; era of racial terror, 6, 31, 34; Harlan County history of, 11; lynchings as, 6, 34, 37–39; migration in face of, 31–33, 34, 37–39; ordinariness of everyday, 77–78; segregation as, 77 (*see also* segregation)

railroad industry: coal mining relation to, 13–14, 17, 70; migration for work in, 3, 30, 42; migration via, 41–42

Ratchford, Jacquelyn, 64

Ratchford, Jeffrey, 58, 181–82

Ratchford, Jerome, 30, 62, 68, 82–83, 84, 85, 117, 123–24, 125, 127–30, 147–48, 164, 170–72, 178–79

Redemption era, 34, 79, 218n8

Reed, Isaac, 22

research: archives of, 8, 203–5; colored schools, 118–19; consent and deed of gifts form for, 211–13; doll experiments, 88, 89, 135, 138, 153; ethnosurvey in, 197–98; impetus and inspiration for, 195–97; interviews and oral histories for, 7–8, 57, 197–201, 205, 207–10; methodology for, 200–201; sample for, 198–200; sociological foundations for, 193–95; theory, interpretation, and form of, 201–3

Robinson, Vera Garner, 29, 60, 61

Rockefeller, John D., Jr., 18

Rodgers, Chuck, 62, 63, 66, 115, 117, 120, 148, 184

Rogers, Betty Jewell Watts, 29

Roosevelt, Franklin Delano, 13

St. Louis, Missouri: Eastern Kentucky Social Club in, 183

San Jose, California: migration to, 172

Schaffer, William "Bo," Jr., 31, 72, 81, 82

schools. *See* education and schools

Scotch-Irish mountaineers, 11, 92, 161, 216n1, 217n8. *See also* hillbillies

scrip system of payment, 72

second-sight, 78, 95–98, 150

segregation: children's experiences of, 20–21, 55, 56–57, 77–99, 103–30, 135–36, 138; citizenship and freedom limited by, 2; civility and, 83–84; civil rights era changes to, 103–4, 133–35 (*see also* desegregation and integration); in coal towns, 20–21, 46–51, 55–57, 79–99, 105–30; desegregation ending (*see* desegregation and integration); desire and envy accompanying, 89–90, 124, 125; doll experiments and, 88, 89, 135, 138, 153; fraternity of coal miners beyond, 86, 92–95; friendship, mutual recognition, and, 84–85, 92; inferiority experiences with, 88–90, 125, 138; Jim Crow and Black Codes on, 3, 6, 20, 34–35, 48, 57, 77–80, 88, 99, 125; legal challenges to, 134–38 (*see also Brown v. Board of Education*); microaggressions of, 125; normalization of, 80–84, 123–27; during physical examinations, 47–51; of schools and education, 20–21, 55, 56–57, 84–85, 101, 103–30; social class and, 91–92, 93, 110–13, 121–22; spectrum of whiteness distinctions in, 90–92, 220n45

Self, racial, 78–80, 201. *See also* subjectivity, African American

Sewell, William, 130

sharecropping, 30, 34–35

Shobe, Professor, 106
Simmons, Arthur, 30, 81, 82
Simone, Nina, 202
skin color, 88, 89, 122
Sloss-Sheffield Company, 36, 37
Smith, Clara, 58, 60, 67, 69, 81, 82, 122, 145
social class: in black communities, 134; coal mining as equalizer of, 93, 121; colored schools reflecting students', 121–22; colored school teachers in separate, 110–13; home reflecting, 67; spectrum of whiteness and, 91–92, 223n16
Souls of Black Folk, The (Du Bois), 4, 7, 75, 77, 78–79, 95–96, 108–9, 150, 195, 196
South Carolina: migration from, 4, 30
Southeast Community College, 130, 144, 170, 171–72
Southern Historical Collection, UNC Chapel Hill, 8, 203–5
Spelman College, 109
sports: in coal towns, 20; desegregation and integration of, 143–44, 151–52; higher education scholarships for, 172; home including, 58, 68; military migration for, 169; segregation of, 80, 146
State of Missouri v. Gaines (1938), 134
steel industry: coal mining for, 7, 12, 13–14, 16–17, 70; migration for work in, 3
Stevens, James, 40
Stevens, Roy, 64
Steward, John, 29, 91, 92, 101, 126, 147, 166–67, 176–77
subjectivity, African American: coal town as home shaping, 73; definition of, 1, 78, 201; desegregation and integration transforming, 130, 155–56; diaspora as condition of, 178, 186; freedom and citizenship transforming, 1, 2, 194–95; home defining, 179, 186; labels or terms

influencing, 3, 90, 104, 131, 133, 137, 156, 194, 201; migration transforming, 1, 4, 51–52, 178; origin stories reflecting, 29–32, 57–72; racial consciousness and, 95–98, 103, 122–23, 125, 150–51; racial identities and, 77–80, 133, 135–36, 144, 201; racial Self and, 78–80, 201; research on, 193–95, 196–97, 201–3 (*see also* research)
Sweatt v. Painter (1950), 134

Taylor, George, 87, 89, 92
Taylor-Ward, Virginia, 29, 61, 79–80, 83, 89–90, 92, 113, 135, 171
Tennessee: coal mining in, 4; migration from, 22; racial prejudice and violence in, 82
Tennessee Coal, Iron and Railroad Corporation, 35, 36, 37, 39
Tennessee State College, 108
Texas: lynchings in, 38, 39; migration to, 163
Their Eyes Were Watching God (Hurston), 7
Thirteenth Amendment, 2, 35
Thomas, Ron, 29, 80
Thompson, Norman, 55
Thornton, Brenda, 30, 60, 84–85, 86, 174–75, 177, 183
Tolnay, Stewart, 199
Truman, Harry, 168–69
Tuan, Yi-Fu, 53
Turner, Earl, 161
Turner, Jeff, 53, 64–65, 80, 94, 121, 161–62, 164, 171, 179
Turner, Tina, 202
Tuskegee University, 108

unionization: coal miner efforts toward, 17–19, 22, 68, 71–72; coal town utopias as alternative to, 19–22; paternalistic capitalism in response to, 19; recruitment strategies to thwart, 43

United Mine Workers of America (UMWA), 17–18, 22, 68, 71–72

United States Coal & Coke Corporation, 15–16, 44

United States Steel Corporation (U.S. Steel): Alabama connections of, 35, 39, 41; author's family history with, 7; coal industry changes for/by, 129, 156–57, 161, 173, 175; coal town control by, 68, 72, 173; coal town razing by, 176; coal towns made by, 15, 17, 18–22, 44–45; convict leasing system use by, 35; scrip system of, 72; segregation by, 20–21, 55–56, 90, 94

universities. *See* colleges and universities; *specific schools*

University of Kentucky: migration to, 170, 171–72; South East Center, 128, 129

urban areas: "Chocolate Cities," 4; cosmopolitan exposure to, 163–65; gentrification of, 6; migration to, 1, 3–5, 129, 158, 162–68. *See also specific cities*

U.S. Supply Company, 20

veil of the color line: education and encounters with, 103, 109, 123–25; research on/within, 195, 196, 203; segregation and, 77, 78–79, 82, 84, 85–87, 95–99, 103, 109, 123; subjectivity within, 6, 77, 78–79, 95–98, 103, 123

village as family: children's recollection of, 66–67; devolution of, 176–79; loss of, with desegregation, 103–4, 145–47, 156; school reflecting, 121, 127

Vinson, Fred M. (Chief Justice), 135, 223n6

Virginia: migration from, 4, 22, 23

voting rights, 2, 34, 51

Voting Rights Act (1965), 2

Wagner-Pacifici, Robin, 127

Walker, Vanessa Siddle, 118

Warmth of Other Suns, The (Wilkerson), 7

Warren, Earl (Chief Justice), 88, 131, 137–38

Washington, D.C.: education and schools in, 118, 119

Watts, Willie, Jr., 29

Wentz Corporation, 15–16

West Virginia: coal mining in, 4, 22; migration from, 30; migration to, 22–23, 174–75; racial changes in population of, 22–23

Whitt, Raven, 61–62, 63, 65, 71, 115, 149, 150–51

Whiteness: consolidated, 90; segregation based on (*see* segregation); spectrum of, 90–92, 220n45, 223n16

Wilberforce University, 107, 108, 109

Wilkerson, Isabel, 7

Williams, Betty, 71, 80, 85, 164

Williams, Vyreda Davis, 29

Willis, Jessie, 40

Wilson, August, 27

Wilson, Woodrow, 18

Winant, Howard, 104

Wisconsin Steel Corporation, 14, 16, 19, 44–45

women: children of, 7, 52, 63–65 (*see also* children); coal mining and conditions for, 7, 51–52; gendered migration pathways for, 169 (*see also* migration); mothers' role of, 63–65

Woodward, C. Vann, 34

Wright, Richard, 202

Yugoslavia, coal miners from, 12, 22, 43, 47, 90–92